SOMETHING IN THE AIR

An Oral History of Popular Music in York Vol. 2. The Beat Goes On

Van Wilson

York Oral History Society
2002

Published 2002 by York Oral History Society
c/o 15 Priory Street, York. YO1 6ET.

ISBN No. 0 9513652 2 3

Printed by J. W. Bullivant and Son, York. Tel: 01904 623241

Cover designed by Mike Oakenfull

Front cover, main picture: The Smoke July 1967. L to R - Geoff Gill, Mick Rowley,
Mal Luker, Zeke Lund.

CONTENTS

ACKNOWLEDGEMENTS 1

INTRODUCTION 3

CHAPTER 1. The Times They Are A-Changin': The 1950s 8

CHAPTER 2. My Generation: The Skiffle Bug 19

CHAPTER 3. Because They're Young: Clubs for young people 41

CHAPTER 4. Listen To The Music: The Rialto 52

CHAPTER 5. Whole Lotta Shakin' Goin' On: The Early 1960s 67

CHAPTER 6. Good Vibrations: The Beat Explosion 101

CHAPTER 7. A Song For The Asking: The Folk Music Revival 123

CHAPTER 8. Flowers In The Rain: Psychedelia 144

CHAPTER 9. The Jumpin' Jive: Jazz 1950s to 1970s 169

CHAPTER 10. The Music Man: Sound Effect Records 193

CHAPTER 11. All The Young Dudes: The Early 1970s 201

CHAPTER 12. Both Sides Now: We Can Swing And Rock 214

ACKNOWLEDGEMENTS

The Oral History of Popular Music in York project, which was funded by the Heritage Lottery Fund, has resulted in this publication (in two volumes), the accompanying exhibition and the collection of interviews, photographs and memorabilia housed in our archives. The following people have generously added their story to our collection, and in most cases have also allowed us to copy photographs:

Charlie Abel, Paul Acton, Tony Adams, Murray and Avril Addison, Carol and John Addy, Gerry Allen, Robert Atkinson, Colin Baines, Sue Baker and Liz Calpin, Nick Banks, Wilf Bannister, John Barry, Johnny Bell, Hilda Bennett, Colin Berriman, Brian Bousfield, Trevor Bousfield, Ray and Tony Broadhead, Dave Brough, Bob and Elsie Brown, Mick Brown, Arthur Burcombe, Ron Burnett, Dave and Sue Byworth, Liz Calpin, Phil Calvert, Colin Carr, Joan Carr, John Cartwright, Steve Cassidy, James Cave, Frank and Lyn Chelin, Rosemary Clegg, John Coleman, Olive Connell, Ray Cooper, Gordon Cottom, Mike Dann, Doreen Davis, Walter Davy, Percy Dinsdale, Charlie Druggitt, Glyn Edwards, Neville England, Steve Flint, Gil Fox, Gill Fox, Dave Garlick, Joan Gaunt, Arnie Gomersall, Ron Goodall, Gerald Goodwin, Mary Goss, Freddie Graysmark, John Greenwell, Neal Guppy, Audrey Halder, Dave Halford, Jean Halford, Bettine Hall-Jackson, Graham Harris, Prue and Neil Hartley, Norman Henderson, Christine Hepton, Terry Herbert, Adrian Holmes, David Horner, Nore Hull, Charles Hutchinson, Steve Jackson, Dave Johnson, Eddie Johnson, Arthur Jones, Dave Kendall, Graham and Val Kennedy, Gloria King, Trevor King, Eddie Lamb, Keith Laycock, June Lloyd-Jones, Malcolm Luker, Trudy Luker, Godfrey Machen, Adrian Macintosh, Brenda and Derek Mackfall, Tiddy Mead, Wilfrid Mellers, Graham Metcalfe, Mick Miller, Pete Morgan, Valerie Mountain, Brian Murphy, Father John Murphy, Harry Murray, Ken Newbould, Johnny Newcombe, John Olive, Brian Parker, May Passmore, Barrie Pawson, Ken Pickering, David Plues, Chris Poole, Noel Porter, Mike Race, Molly Robinson, Ricky Royle, Graham Sanderson, Bob Scott, Phil Scott, Alfie Shepherd, Lew Skords, Peter Stanhope, Barry Starkey, Brian Sutcliffe, Alan Sutton, Violet Taylor, John Terry, Clarice and Dawn Tudor, Pete Varley, Wal Walsh, Sheila White, Joan Whitehead, John Whittle, Pete Williams, Pete Willow, Alwyn Wilson, Brian Wilson, Linda Wood, Denis Wright, Sheila Yeates. Since speaking to us we are sorry to say that James Cave, Doreen Davis, May Passmore, Trudy Luker and Clarice Tudor have died.

I would like to thank the following who helped with research and conducted interviews: David Armstrong, Glyn and Ruth Edwards, Richard Foster, Caroline Stockdale, James Wigby; and the following who helped with transcribing interviews: Joyce Pinder, Philippa Wilson and especially Gill Fox.

For their financial support for this project, we are indebted to:

Supported by the
Heritage Lottery Fund

R M Burton Trust, City of York Council, Joseph Rowntree Foundation, Sheldon Memorial Trust, Patricia and Donald Shepherd Charitable Trust, York Branch of Musicians' Union, York Common Good Trust. We would like to thank Frank Johnson of TDK for the generous donation of tapes, and Jessops for support with the cost of copying photographs.

We would like to thank the following, who have provided information and allowed us to copy photographs: Tim Addyman, Martin Boyd, Mary Cundall, Sheila Barrie, Judith Carr, Catherine Cole, Michael Cole, Frank and Muriel Day, Angela Dunning, Angela Hill, Ben Jowett, Christine Lancaster, Mike May, John McClay, Fred Mills, Richard Monfort, Bryan Pearson, Janet Pigott, Terry Pritchard, Bill Serby, Stuart Thomson, Ken Turner, Greg Wadman, Margaret Weston, Gill Wignall of the Evening Press, Staff of York City Archives, Sue Rigby and Staff of City of York Library.

I wish to thank Mike Oakenfull for designing the covers of the two volumes, Richard Foster for kindly proof-reading the manuscript and making useful suggestions, York Oral History management committee over the last two years, in particular our treasurer Nigel Taggart who managed the funds so brilliantly.

Most of all, I am greatly indebted to Mike Race, Chair of York Oral History Society, who generously devoted so much time to all aspects of the project: interviewing, transcribing, copying photographs, and much of the research (particularly for the first volume), as well as reading and commenting on the final manuscript.

If you are interested in accessing the collection or in becoming involved in oral history, please contact committee member Philip Johnson at York City Archives or on 01904-644381.

INTRODUCTION

At the beginning of the year 2000, York Oral History Society embarked on a three–year project investigating the history of popular music in York from 1930 to 1970 and I was appointed as co-ordinator.

Our remit was to find people who had been involved in popular music in York and to look at the relationship between music and social life in the city. The definition of 'popular' means 'whatever the people like', but in the case of music it tends to mean music which is not classical, (though much classical music was the popular music of its day)! Some types of music are in a class of their own, such as choral and church music, light opera and brass bands, and have been subjects of other publications, so we have not included them in our project. Some music defies categorisation and we may have used labels which are open to question, (one man's swing is another man's jazz), but we decided to keep fairly rigid boundaries to make for easier reading.

In two and a half years, we have conducted more than 130 interviews. Extracts from these, together with background research from the local press and other primary sources, form an oral history collection which will soon be available at the York City Archives for public access. A selection of the material will also be deposited with the city library. The interview tapes, together with more than 1,500 photographs and some memorabilia, provide a resource which is a crucial part of York's social history of the 20th century.

It became clear, as the project got under way, that there were two very different periods within our 1930-1970 time scale, and that both played a significant part in York's culture. Instead of writing one book embracing music from four decades, I decided to split it into two volumes which cover the two separate areas of music in this period. There is obviously some overlap in terms of the time-span, but most musicians fit into one or the other of the volumes. The period of 1930 to 1970 is obviously artificial because music did not start in 1930 and did not end in 1970, but two quite distinct types of music do fit comfortably into these 40 years. The first period, that of dance band music, began in earnest in the 1920s with the arrival of jazz from America. The difficult years of the 1930s meant that ordinary people were in need of escape from their drab and sometimes depressing lives and 'going dancing' to a live band or small orchestra became the most popular form of entertainment in the city, and probably in the country as a whole. It might have 'had its day' in the 1940s, were it not for the Second World War breaking out, and the need for dance band music becoming even greater, as a means of linking people together and lifting their spirits through dark days. It was clear that after the war, the new generation coming up would no longer have those same needs, and the young people born in the late 1930s and 1940s were ready for a change. They were born into a country battling with rationing, blackouts, hardships and little money and they longed for something better. The new music of the 1950s was a reflection of this need and it came fast and furious. The dance band musicians and their older audiences were horrified when rock and roll entered the picture, but they believed it was only a passing fad and their own tastes would prevail as time went on. What they didn't realise was that the change was permanent, and that rock 'n' roll opened the door to ever new forms of music which gave the younger generation ownership of music for the first time. The 1950s and 1960s heralded a social revolution in all aspects of life, and music was a large part of it. Songs about nostalgia and lovers who had to part until war was over, were gone. The new music was upbeat and lively, and it made its presence felt!

I was born in the 1950s and brought up on a diet of Glenn Miller, Tommy Dorsey, Frank Sinatra, Vaughn Monroe and all the 78s my parents played regularly. Even now when I hear Moonlight Serenade and In The Mood, I am taken back to childhood days. There was an enchantment and a romance about that music which still exists but when I saw the first appearance on television of the Beatles, I knew this was something new and exciting, and although I was only a child, it was the beginning of a love of 1960s music for me. At school we talked constantly about pop music. We went to WH Smiths on Saturdays to listen in their record booths to the latest releases and soon knew the lyrics of almost every song that came out. I had a giant poster of the Beatles on my bedroom ceiling and soon came to adore the Small Faces, the Rolling Stones, Simon And Garfunkel, and Bob Dylan. Yet, and this was the unusual thing, I still loved big bands and the songs of Cole Porter, George Gershwin, Jerome Kern and Irving Berlin, but I could not admit this to most of my contemporaries! I only had one friend at the time, whose name was Jan, who shared my love of dance bands, 1960s pop, and classical music.

I recall my mother taking me to see Tommy Steele at the Rialto on my birthday and how the event stood out in my life as being quite mind-blowing, (though I would not have used that phrase at the time!) I couldn't remember the year but assumed I must have been nine or ten. When I recently looked at some old Rialto programmes, I discovered that we actually saw Tommy on my sixth birthday! The Evening Press review of this concert described it as a 'screaming success' when 'nearly everybody from Tommy down to the just-more-than-toddlers (and there were a few) joined in the fun'!

Volume one of this publication covers the music of the dance band era and jazz in the 1940s and 1950s, whereas volume two covers the beat explosion, and the minority interests of folk music and jazz in the later period. The two volumes explore what music was available and where, and try to show why people decided to become musicians and what music meant to them. Many people cannot explain exactly what it is about music that speaks to our emotions like nothing else can, that has such power to transform our mood. What is it about a few notes played in a certain order and at a certain tempo, which can communicate with us somewhere deep inside? It was William Congreve who wrote, 'Music has charms to soothe the savage breast'. I saw evidence of this when walking through York city centre recently. A pair of musicians were playing a selection of Irish ballads in St Helen's Square, a sweet and gentle sound. Beside them sat a man who can often be seen fighting and shouting abuse at the public from a park bench near the City Art Gallery, but his face was that of an angel as he listened in raptures to the music. He was positively beaming.

Music is the only universal language which people of all nations and races have in common. Our tastes in music may vary but we must agree that music in itself stands out as a prime feature of our lives, and that all people, from babies in the womb, to teenagers and adults in all walks of life, are affected and touched by music. There are instances of people who have been in a coma, and when their favourite music is played to them again and again, they are restored and come back to life.

Although bigger cities like London, Liverpool, Manchester and Leeds are known for their popular music, York does not always spring to mind as a centre for music. But throughout the 20th century it has had a strong and vibrant music scene, with countless musicians living and performing in the city, entertaining audiences large and small. In fact York is still a vibrant and busy place and, even in the present days of discos and karaoke, live music has not died. In the last year I have joined with many others in seeing and enjoying musicians at the Barbican, Grand Opera House, Theatre Royal, City Screen, Black Swan Folk Club, Olde White Swan, National Centre For Early Music, Three Legged Mare and other places in the city.

The aim of this book is to give a taste of the popular music scene from the 1920s to the 1970s, letting the musicians tell their own stories. The subject is such a large one that it is impossible to cover everything and everyone, and though we spoke to more than 130 people, there were many others who also have their story. The time limit for the project has meant that we have had to omit some of the people we wanted to interview, but the publications and exhibition will give the reader a flavour of what it was like to play and listen to popular music through those decades, and for those who want to look at our collection, it will be available in the city archives when it has been fully catalogued in 2003.

Throughout York's history, things have progressed because of the belief and determination of individuals with a vision. This is certainly the case with music. John Xaviour (Jack) Prendergast, who ran the Rialto cinema and ballroom from 1927 to 1961, was an entrepreneur and a pioneer with numerous friends in the world of showbusiness. He was instrumental in bringing many famous national and international artists to the city and encouraged his own son, York's most famous musician John Barry, to make music his career. In the 1940s Bert Keech had the concession at the De Grey Rooms and provided music for dancing night after night through the war years, not only for locals but also the many airmen and women stationed in the area. From 1950, Johnny Sutton ran his big band there, and was known for giving young budding musicians the opportunity to play and to learn their craft in his band. In the 1960s Neal Guppy with his Enterprise club took a lot of young beat groups under his wing and opened a club which was a live music venue specifically aimed at young people.

Mention music to anyone who has lived in York during the last 50 years and these names crop up again and again, along with the Bousfield Twins, Len Cundall, Derek Dunning, Neville England, Bob Halford, Bobby Hirst, Hugh Robertson, and later Steve Cassidy, Johnny Newcombe and the Goodall Brothers. But there are many more well-known and well-loved musicians who have spent years entertaining the people of York, who provided music as a boost to morale in wartime, who lifted the spirits in the grey austerity of post-war Britain, and who took advantage of the new music of the 1960s and made music less elitist and more open to everyone.

Nearly everyone we spoke to in this project, testified to the importance of music in their lives, some even said that their lives centred around it and others that it was their way of expressing what they wanted to say. They would probably echo the rock musician Sting, who recently said, 'If I had my way I'd never speak to anyone, I'd just sing. To sing is to soar, to be like a bird with total freedom to go where you want'. The American writer Robin Meyers put it like this, 'The best way to listen to music is to go where human beings are making it, to see the faces attached to its creation for the ear is close to the heart'. Arthur Mason, in an article in 1931, wrote that music has the power to 'soothe and restore the sick and suffering', giving the Biblical example of King Saul being healed of his nervous sickness by David's skill on the harp. He quoted Shakespeare's description of music, 'a medicine, a sweet and oblivious antidote', explained that even Pythagoras played the harp night and morning to keep his mind active and went on to say that, 'Our pleasure in music's beauty, the sense of restfulness, or of exhilaration, we get, our consciousness that there is that in music which inspires thoughts outside the pressing thoughts of every day, these things prove music to be a mental and emotional restorative'.

Music can also, perhaps more than anything else, evoke memories of an important time, place or person. Just to hear a few bars of a particular song can take you back to those special moments when you first fell in love, when you first discovered the joy of living, when, in the face of despair, you found hope. And music, as well as speaking to our emotions, can help develop the senses. Educationalists have acknowledged that calm classical music in the background can help children concentrate more on their studies. Perhaps loud hip-hop music has the opposite effect? In a recent speech, Neil Hoyle, of the Incorporated Society of Musicians, said that the society wanted music to be 'a spiritual focus, a mutual bond of real meaning, a shared medium for daily hopes and fears and a means of giving people their identity in a world of globalised pap', for, 'we believe music and the arts exist to nourish the soul'.

This book is dedicated to all York musicians past and present,
who have given so much pleasure to their audiences

May your heart always be joyful
May your song always be sung
May you stay forever young

Bob Dylan

CHAPTER ONE. THE TIMES THEY ARE A-CHANGIN': The 1950s

In 1955, ten years after the Second World War had ended, dance bands were still entertaining large crowds and the top 20 charts were filled with bland fun songs from artists like Rosemary Clooney, Doris Day, Jim Dale, Joan Regan and Dickie Valentine. But by December of that year, Bill Haley had reached number one with Rock Around The Clock and a new, powerful and exciting sound came in on a tidal wave. A few months later, in 1956, with the advent of the king of rock 'n' roll, Elvis Presley, songs like How Much Is That Doggie In The Window? gave way to Hound Dog, and popular music changed forever.

Countless publications, films, television documentaries have discussed what happened on a global scale at this time, and this is not the place for further analysis except to say that when skiffle and rock 'n' roll arrived on the scene, for the first time young people had ownership of their music. Parents had never seen anything like it, some were shocked and disgusted and wanted it to be banned, but others were delighted to support their children and eagerly bought guitars and other instruments for them. The economy was gradually improving and some of the older generation who had been subject to the rationing and austerity of wartime wanted their children to have the things they themselves had to do without.

This was a time when the whole country relaxed and began to enjoy life again, following the dark days of war. Many families had two incomes for the first time, holidays with pay, and there was an urge to live it up. Probably for the first time, it was understood that an important part of growing up was to reject parents' culture and values at least for a time, and that it was possible to take what you wanted from the previous generation and leave the rest. The 'age of the teenager' had arrived, and young people were no longer mini-adults, behaving and dressing like their parents. They wanted their own identity, and this came through in both fashion and music. The boom in industry meant higher employment, decent salaries and young people with spending power. They knew what they liked and what they didn't! Suddenly music was being dictated by the younger generation, which was a huge change from the pre-war days when older people were leading the bands and enforcing discipline in the playing.

The older generation of musicians thought that rock 'n' roll was a temporary aberration, an anarchic force that could not last. They were wrong. But rock 'n' roll did not come out of a vacuum. Elvis Presley's main influences were country and gospel music. He was the first white man to sound as if he performed with his whole being. But the effect of seeing a man who exuded sexuality through his act, led to a sanitised version of the raw and earthy rock 'n' roll, in the form of clean-cut singers like Pat Boone. Although the music was new, many pop singers realised they owed a debt to the big bands of their parents' generation. A few years later, Ray Davis, of The Kinks, would write a song about the local palais, where his sister danced to the big bands. He sang, 'The day they knocked down the palais, part of my childhood died'.

There are several examples of prominent rock stars whose introduction to music came through their parents. Paul McCartney's (of the Beatles) father played in dance bands. Pete Townsend's (of the Who) father Cliff was one of the saxophone players in the RAF dance band the Squadronaires. York drummer Mike Dann recalls playing in a jazz band in Nottingham with a guitarist called Fred Baker, whose son is the flamboyant drummer Ginger Baker.

Television producers quickly got in on the act and launched the television programmes Oh Boy and 6.5 Special which began in February 1957, and radio programmes such as Saturday Skiffle Club. Young people were swept up in the excitement. Many did not have musical talent but still wanted a piece of the action. They enjoyed themselves for a while but did not pursue it. Of those who had real talent, many went further. The new music was upbeat, cheerful and happy, in contrast to the songs of nostalgia and loss that filled the 1940s. It was simple, much of it forgettable, but it lifted the spirits, it made people whistle on their way to work.

Young people also wanted their own space. No longer content to sit at home with mum doing her knitting and dad reading the paper, they wanted to be out with their peers, enjoying themselves. Youth clubs opened up all over the country, including York. In September 1954, Melbourne Street Youth Club was open four nights a week until 9.30pm, offering not only keep fit, films, discussion groups and indoor games, but plenty of music and dancing. Carr Lane Youth Club opened to cater for some of the 800 young people living on the new estates in the area. Subscriptions from members were used to buy pop records. Rowntree's Youth Club, which met in the ballroom in Rowntree's Dining Block, started a Tuesday night Bop For A Bob in 1957 as an experiment. Three years later it had moved to the Folk Hall in New Earswick due to the increase in numbers when '500 jivers would get lost in a world of their own'. Dancing continued from eight to 11pm without a break and some dancers could keep going for three hours!

Fulford Youth Club found that its room at the social hall in School Lane was becoming inadequate as membership grew. In February 1961 the Minister of Education described young people in England as 'about the best human material you could get anywhere in the world' when defending the government's plan to put money into youth clubs. The leaders of Fulford Youth Club said that their club had 'an inner vitality' which would be of lasting influence on young people's lives. St George's Garrison Church Youth Club opened in 1960 and soon started to hold 'bops' on Saturday nights which they thought would help to 'keep young people off the streets'. The Catacombs Christian Youth Club opened in 1968 in the old St Sampson's Church Hall, and was open to anyone, even youngsters out of Borstal and the leader, Mervyn Moorhead, got involved in helping young people in trouble, even going to court on their behalf and visiting them in detention centres. He said that 'it is a fact that at least some young people have been kept out of prison and Borstals through the work of the club' so it fulfilled a need that no other club could meet. In February 1962 York's first purpose-built youth centre opened in Moor Lane. The club was so popular that in 1983 a society was formed to organise reunions and to maintain social links. Some years later, in February 1970, the Old Priory Youth Club became the first one in the city to offer free guitar classes, with a professional teacher.

The most popular activity for young people in York was music, whether listening to it or playing it. And opportunities to play it were opening up. Ray Broadhead recalls joining a harmonica band in the mid 1950s:

Ted Levitt Show Band. Ted Levitt standing in the centre. Ray Broadhead far right at front.
(Courtesy Ray Broadhead)

We lived in Acomb and we'd sit in the local park and strum and play music together. One of the lads was already in a harmonica band. We played at Rowntree's Theatre in Dick Whittington the pantomime. There was two harmonica players dressed as cats and I was a minstrel.

The band was the Ted Levitt Show Band. Ted had started it in 1937 when he was 15, and it was called the Silver Star Harmonica Band, though it later included mandolins, accordions and drums as well as harmonicas. He ran it for 50 years (apart from six years in the navy during the war) up to his death in 1987. The band raised more than £100,000 for charity.

After a while, Ray became more interested in playing guitar:

I think the first place I ever played was Holgate Working Men's Club talent night. We had an old tea-chest bass and we were only 15. Then came Elvis Presley, and it all changed. We had one of those old wind-up gramophones, and we'd sit out in the street, wind it up and listen all day long. Don't Be Cruel was my favourite. Then we got together and started our first band, Ray Charles And The Beat Boys. A local pub heard of us and wanted us to play there. But then it started in the Burns [in Market Street, now the Hansom Cab] nearly every night. At this time there were very few groups appearing. We just loved the music, Cliff Richard And The Shadows, I think it was the tremolo on the guitar, and the echo, which was different to anybody else's music. A while after that we started doing working men's clubs, and we'd see the old bands from the 1940s, to us it was really old-fashioned. Their music was old, ours was modern and 'with it'.

Ray's brother, Tony, who became the drummer with Ray's group recalls:

When you're 17, 18, you feel wanted up in front of people. The music was brilliant and it was just good to be up there, something we enjoyed doing, a way of releasing energy.

In 1960 the group performed during a play at York Theatre Royal, A Taste Of Honey, and Ray remembers:

There was another group playing at that time, but one night they couldn't make it, so we had to come in and it turned out we could do it better than they could, so we got the job, for two weeks. They wanted us to do a summer season in Scarborough, but we were all apprentices, it was too far to go. But it was a lovely experience. We played background music for the play, like Apache for the crying and sad bits, and Shazam for the loud and noisy bits when people came on. We did a cabaret act one night at the City Arms. We asked at the Burns if we could have the night off, but the landlady said, 'No', so we ended up doing

Ray Charles And The Beatboys C1960. L to R - Ray Broadhead, vocals, Tony Broadhead, drums, Rodney Glaholm, bass guitar, Geoff Wilson, lead.
(Courtesy Ray Broadhead)

12

Ray Charles And The Beatboys. L to R - Linda Russell, seated, Rodney Glaholm, Tony Broadhead, Geoff Oakland, Ray Broadhead. Burns Hotel. c1961.

(Courtesy Ray Broadhead)

half an hour at the Burns, and running through the street, with our drums, amplifiers, and guitars, to play for half an hour at the City Arms, then back through the town. We did it twice to the City Arms, and three sets at The Burns, but the gentleman at the City Arms didn't think we were very good that night, because we weren't as smooth as we could have been!

Of course in them days when we played anywhere, we'd take our equipment on the bus. We put the drums under the luggage rack and the amplifiers and guitars, and off we went to town. Sometimes we couldn't play, because when we got there, it was so foggy in them days, nobody had come out, so we had to go all the way back again. I think one of the first places that had music on was the White Horse in Coppergate. They had their own group, more like the King Brothers' style, and that was still old to us. You got skiffle, 1950s stuff, but I think they were the first with amplified music. We did Diana and The Story Of My Life, Michael Holliday. Later we liked Billy Fury and Marty Wilde. I'd buy records on a Saturday, you went to Hugh Robertson's in Pavement. 'Have you got any new records out?' And on Saturday night you were singing it.

Ray's group now consisted of himself and Tony, with bass guitarist Rodney Glaholm. The lead guitarist changed a few times. The first one was Geoff Wilson who now lives in Australia and Murray Addison played with them for a while. The group started to wear colourful clothes, copying Cliff Richard and Marty Wilde by having pink and mauve jackets with a black shirt and white tie. They had the jackets made at Piccadilly Menswear. Ray recalls one unusual booking they had in 1961:

We had some gypsies in and they asked if we'd play at a wedding down Leeman Road. They had these big marquees and mobile caravans , and there really was thousands there. They wanted us just playing every now and again, and would give us a shout when they wanted us. We were at the wedding meal, the only bit we couldn't see was the wedding ceremony, we had to go out then. We saw all the presents. There was one of those long bread loaves and it was hollowed out, and absolutely stuffed full of money.

Tony also enjoyed it:

During the meal you each got a whole chicken on your plate, a bottle of whisky and a bottle of wine between every two of you. It was massive, like a big circus, all lined up with rows and rows of tables with white cloths on. We were there until early in the morning. We didn't play a great deal, and were sat amongst ourselves round the camp fires. We were like a juke box. It was one of the best experiences I've ever had. A bit frightening really, because towards the end of the night, you're sat there round the fire, and just wondering whether they were going to let us go.

We once went for an audition to Butlin's at Filey. I'll never forget this as long as I live. We got it through a manager, Godfrey Machen. The following day I was on the bus leaving work coming through Exhibition Square. You know the newspaper's placards, it said, 'York group for the tops'. So I had to buy a paper to see who the group were and there's a big piece about how we passed this audition with flying colours, were set to go to the top, but we'd all had to turn it down because we were apprentices at the time. This was all unknown to us. We wasn't told we'd passed with flying colours, we wasn't told we were set for the top but somebody had told the Press that we'd had to turn it down.

Ray chose his stage name because his first two names were Ray and Charles, but there were occasions when he was confused with the American soul singer of the same name:

We were in Blackpool once and we had the name on the back of our car, a Zephyr Zodiac. We were Ray Charles And The Gaylords then, and this gentleman wound his window down and says, 'Do you know Ray Charles?'

Anne Monahan and Iris Lewington, members of the York Branch of the Johnnie Ray Fan Club dance in ecstasy to their idol's music. Yorkshire Evening Press April 1955.

(Courtesy of City of York Library)

We says, 'Yes, he's sat in t'back of the car', but he was very disappointed, 'cos it was me!

Rock 'n' roll, like much music in Britain, was exported from the USA. One of the biggest stars at this time was singer Johnnie Ray who was the first rock n' roll pin-up, having made his debut before Elvis Presley. The York Gramophone Society was formed in September 1955 to 'present programmes of works by certain composers or of certain types of serious music'. They stressed the word 'serious' as, 'after all, some people take Johnnie Ray seriously!'

One person who definitely did so was Beryl Bradley. A large picture appeared in the Yorkshire Evening Press in November 1955 showing fans of Johnnie Ray dancing in the bedroom of the president of the York Branch of the Johnnie Ray Fan Club, 18-year-old Beryl. The walls were covered with large glossy photographs and even her earrings had miniature pictures of Johnnie. Soon after opening the club she had 100 members, including a boy ill in hospital with tuberculosis in Manchester. Beryl had travelled over to show him her cuttings and photos. In pride of place in her house was the personally autographed photograph given to her when she met Johnnie in his dressing-room after a show in London. The writer of the article, Yorkshire Evening Press reporter, Stacey Brewer, asked his readers not to 'confuse these boys and girls with the Teddy Boy toughs or the street corner louts, these are decent youngsters with a sincerity of purpose'.

The other major export from America at this time was the jukebox. In March 1957, the Golden Fleece in Pavement and the Old White Swan in Goodramgate applied to install jukeboxes in their premises but were refused by magistrates. York's Chief Constable Mr C Carter described them as 'unsuitable and undesirable instruments to have in a public house bar or lounge'. He thought that as the licensee had no control over what was played, the music might annoy other customers. Five other pubs were granted permission to have record players or radiograms. Two years later in 1959, the owners of York Empire told York Licensing Justices that if they banned jukeboxes from the Empire and other places, it would drive youngsters out on to the streets and into pubs and would cause hooliganism. The Bench was eventually persuaded to allow a jukebox in this 'special case'. In April 1959, the Justices also insisted on fixing the attendance limits at dance halls. The Empire was restricted to 600 for dances, Christie's Ballroom in Clarence Street to 650, the Assembly Rooms to 500 for its dances, but the Railway Institute Gymnasium could admit 1400 for dances and 2000 for seated events.

During the 1950s, dancing was as popular as it had been before the war. The Central School of Dancing in High Ousegate achieved success in the International Dancing Masters' Association tests. The principal Kenneth Parkes led the highly successful formation tango and waltz teams. The Saturday practice classes danced to Derek Dunning And His Strict Tempo Band. The same premises housed the new Court School of Dancing which opened in November 1955. Dancers were invited to 'be there on the first night, and meet Courtenay Castle, the man who brings dancing to millions', and could become members for an annual fee of only sixpence.

By 1959 there were several record shops in York. Mackenzie's in Bridge Street had become the Record Browserie for 'pops, jazz and classical records, players and grams'. In the early 1950s it had advertised as the first self-service music shop outside London, and 'York's only record browserie', offering self-service, and soundproof listening hoods with 'any record and any artist'. Hugh Robertson opened a new branch of his record shop in Acomb in 1955 selling classical and popular records, portable record players, gramophones and sheet music.

In 1956 the Regency School of Dancing, which adjoined St George's Cinema in Castlegate, offered classes every night of the week except Sunday, for beginners or improvers. The principals, Eric and Dorothy Smith, said their object was 'to raise the standard of dancing in York' and decided to present an open novice waltz and quickstep competition. Another popular school of dance was Mary Macpherson's Dance School in the church hall on Bishophill. She was known affectionately as Mary Mac. She had started teaching dance during the Second World War and trained many leading dance partnerships. After her death in 1966, the school was taken over by Rita and Dennis Cole.

By the early 1960s, the Court School held classes every night but Sunday, with a Friday teatime teenage class and a Saturday afternoon children's class. The school was run by Stanley Flood and his wife Elsie, who had worked for the Court organisation in London previously. Up to 300 children turned up for the Saturday classes. In March 1964 the Regency Dance Studio held its Dance Of The Season in the Assembly Rooms to the music of Johnny Sutton And His Orchestra.

The Assembly Rooms, which had been closed during the war to be used as a food office, was newly restored and opened for dancing in 1951 and this was the heyday of dancing in the city, with the hall being booked for dances for two years ahead.

In January 1962 the twist was the hot new dance, but some of York's dance schools refused to teach it, calling it vulgar and tribal. One teacher said that if the school taught it, 'it would encourage the sort of students we do not want. If people really want to learn, my advice is to drop a cigarette end and then move about trying to stub it out. They will find they are doing the twist'. But another dancing school decided to start twist sessions once a week and when the BBC band leader Victor Sylvester began to include it in his concerts, this gave it the stamp of approval. He said that even the waltz had once been regarded with disgust until Queen Victoria made it respectable. Couples at the New Earswick Bop For A Bob still preferred to jive, but the Empire was finding a growing number of twisters amongst its dancers.

Godfrey Machen got involved with music in the late 1950s. He became chairman of an Entertainments Committee in Acomb which put on a concert running for two nights at Acomb Church Hall called Ace High with Johnny Acey as the star. Amongst the other acts were the Gambling Men, Ace Skifflers, a boy trumpeter, the Ace High Lovelies dancing, Jenny Jones 'sweet singer of songs you love', and music in the intermission from Jimmie Hourigan And The Variety Orchestra. Godfrey recalls:

It was a small group of people who got together to try to present live entertainment, because you didn't have videos in those days. There was a wealth of people wanted to go to my shows and some of the artistes there were really top class. My father was concert secretary at various working men's clubs, so that enabled me to see artistes and the ones who were very good were keen on doing other shows as well. And in the 1950s it was possible to put on a full show, with an orchestra, for about £25. We had a very successful dance using a pop group and a dance band at the Acomb Church Hall and it was one of the most successful nights there had ever been in York. People were travelling from all over and what we tried to do was give the proceeds to charity.

There was something about the 1950s. I don't think there's been a period like it. A lot of people say it's the 1960s, but I think recovering from the war could have had a lot to do with it, people were so much happier, they wanted to be entertained. From 1955 onwards when you have Bill Haley And The Comets, rock 'n' roll came in and that blew your mind. Nobody had ever got up in a cinema and started to dance and cavort about, it was just not the done thing. In the 1920s and 1930s, you had a lot of very sedate music. When you came to rock 'n' roll, you didn't stick close to your partner, and you could dance on your own. You had a lot of styles coming out, and brightly coloured clothing.

Music hall lasted until 1955. You had twice nightly Variety, in which you had a top of the bill artiste, and speciality artists. You went to the Empire on a Monday evening, the theatre on a Tuesday evening, and you went dancing, and we had ten cinemas. So you had plenty of things to go to.

CHAPTER TWO. MY GENERATION:
The Skiffle Bug

At the same time as rock 'n' roll arrived from the USA, the British had their own home-grown version, skiffle. It was simple and basic, and dance band musicians labelled it 'piffle', but it gave many young people an opportunity to get involved in music. The Beatles, of course, started out as the Quarrymen skiffle group.

Ray Cooper, who played in dance bands during the 1950s, found skiffle an important learning curve in his musical career:

I heard this unique sound, and it just struck a chord. The thing about skiffle is, it put into the hands of young people the ability to make their own music. Up to that point music had been almost in the sole domain of the professional, or part-time professional band players. Young people weren't thought of as being able to go out and play. It was a very important milestone, evolving almost by accident. It was a combination of many things coming together at the right time, and it inspired so many young people at that critical point, about 1956, when skiffle groups were springing up all over the place, and we were encouraged to take up different instruments. Because of pure circumstance I was given the task of playing the tea-chest bass, because, unlike the guitar where you're just playing chords, to play a bass line you've got to have a reasonable musical ear, and so I found I took to it quite readily.

It was the first time you were playing on your own, without playing along with adults. Because skiffle is closely related to early forms, traditional jazz, folk and blues, as the skiffle craze veered towards more rock 'n' roll and away from its folk roots, I lost a little interest. It became too commercialised. I occasionally played banjo, so as the skiffle craze waned a little, it opened out into traditional jazz. A skiffle group was fairly easy to form, but when you've got to start playing instruments like clarinets, trombones, trumpets and the like, you need a bit more musical ability. The key year is 1956, the happening year for music, when the top ten chart was founded and Bill Haley came from America to this country. He landed at Southampton and took the train to Victoria Station, and was mobbed, and that's the same year Lonnie Donegan made top of the pops with his famous Rock Island Line, which, strangely enough, was recorded 18 months earlier and had lain almost dormant. The Chris Barber Jazz Band had Donegan as banjo player, and he'd been making experiments, adapting folk music, and blues style music and giving it a bit of an extra flavour, and this is how skiffle evolved.

In November 1956 the Rialto Cinema and Ballroom in York presented Lonnie Donegan and his skiffle group with the Merseysippi Jazz Band. (Lonnie did not play again in York until 2000 when he joined with Van Morrison to perform a few numbers at Van's concert at the Barbican). In October 1957, the Rialto advertised a 'Sensational Teenage Music Show for all ages', entitled The Big Beat. As well as 'the queen of skiffle', Nancy Whiskey, and guest star Michael Holliday, there were several others on the bill including the John Barry Seven, a new group who had good reviews and closed the show with a 'spectacular finale spotlighting drummer Ken Golder'.

In December 1959, several types of music could be found in York. For lovers of dance bands, Billy Davies And His Orchestra were playing at Rowntree's Ballroom for modern and old time dancing, Johnny Sutton And His Music were playing at the De Grey Rooms on Wednesdays and Saturdays. And Johnny Newcombe And His Band were appearing at the Empire, with their skiffle music.

Johnny Newcombe was the first skiffle player in York:

My father had a guitar so he taught me a few chords when I was about 14. I qualified to go to Leeds College of Art and while I was there the arty types got a bit of music going. I dragged me father's guitar out and started playing old American blues stuff. Then some of the lads in the class got together, a few guitars and the old string bass and we played the odd thing round Leeds. Then we took it to York, and the first place we played was Joseph Rowntree's School dances, and that was the Wabash Four. [These fellow students were Tony Hodgson and Norman Ackroyd on guitars and vocals, John Hawley on washboard and David Richardson who played tea-chest bass] *They were all from Leeds and it was just a short thing and that fell through so I thought I'd form my own group in York. I went to Carr Lane Youth Club and met Dave Garlick, Dave Johnson, and a guy called George Clipperton, who was a youth leader, and we got together and played at the youth club. That lasted a short while then we got Norman Goodall, who was a good bass player. We started off with a slap bass, and we were going to a gig one night, and this bloke put the string bass on top of the car, and it blew off and smashed to pieces. So then he got an electric bass. Everything just changed after that, no more string basses, except for jazz groups.*

That was early 1957. We started rolling then. It all happened in one big quick burst over 18 months and then everybody joined the wagon, and went along with the wave. We were resident at the Buckles, on Tadcaster Road, and that started it off for all the pubs around York.

The second group to start were the Gambling Men. Johnny helped them to get started:

Wabash Four at Rialto c1958. L to R - Dave Garlick, Dave Johnson, Johnny Newcombe, Norman Goodall.
(Courtesy Dave Johnson)

They were going to the Catholic school in Leeds [St Michael's] and I was going to the Art School and we would catch the same trains every morning and night. I'd take me guitar and play in the compartment, and I taught them how to form a group. I don't know whether they had any bookings before it, but the first one I got them was at the Odeon, because I knew the manager. We played at the American air base at Elvington. It was terrific, the Americans were fairly rich and where you got £4 or £5 for a gig in York, there you'd get £20 and all free beer and meals.

We played at the Empire a few times and I got myself on 6.5 Special and worked with a guy called Jim Dale. Stanley Dale was his agent, and he wanted me to go professional and work with Jim but I had the group, and I was still at art school. We worked with Chas McDevitt, Nancy Whiskey, (Freight Train), Marty Wilde, John Barry, the Everley Brothers, the Crickets. We played holiday camps and entered skiffle competitons. I was on holiday in Skegness and there was this resident group Rory Storm And The Hurricanes. They lent me a guitar and I just sat in with them, and played a bit. The drummer later left to join another group, and that drummer's name was Richard Starkey [who became Ringo Starr of the Beatles]. So I got to play with him for a short while.

L to R - Johnny Newcombe, Dave Johnson, Dave Garlick. RAF Leconfield
(Courtesy Dave Johnson)

The Wabash Four played at the Rialto quite a lot. One night I was in the dressing room watching 6.5 Special, with this guy sat on a chair, playing banjo. I said, 'Can I borrow your guitar?' and he said 'Yeah, go on, if you like'. So we sat playing together for a while, and he was at the bottom of the bill then, more-or-less doing his first show, he'd only made one record, Move It. That guy was Cliff Richard.

I was taught piano when I was younger so I knew all the basic music. I didn't want to learn music on the guitar. From my memories of the piano teacher, it was too stiff and I'd get rapped over the knuckles for improvising. You weren't allowed to do that in those days! And I always liked to improvise. So I didn't get tuition because I thought it was too tight, it won't make you expand, to do what you wanted to do. I had the basics, so when I said I could play an E flat, or B flat, or go on to the diminished, they weren't just words I'd pulled out of the air. I knew exactly what I was talking about.

At the Odeon, they would put a film on and in the middle while they were changing reels, we'd play. At the Rialto, they put Barry on [John Barry] and he'd be top of the bill, and we'd go on with Barry, and then he used to put us around different places. Me and Barry used to travel all over doing gigs. When Barry was starting to climb, we went to see him in the Odeon in Leeds. We sat in the audience, me and Dave [Garlick], and I said, 'Let everybody file

The Wabash Five 1950s outside the Wild Man. L to R - Johnny Newcombe, Norman Goodall, Dave Johnson, Dave Garlick, Ted Rutter.   *(Courtesy Dave Garlick)*

out and we'll go down and see if he's still in the dressing room'. We waited a bit and then got up and he was walking up the aisle and he goes, 'Hey, Johnny', and this other guy's walking along with him, and he says, 'This is my new singer, Adam Faith. We're just going down the pub for a beer, are you coming?' We had a train to catch but he said he'd give us a lift home. He used to call my mother Auntie Lou, and he was dropping us off and I said, 'She'll be disappointed if you don't go in and see her'. We lived in Dringhouses then so he trails this young guy in, and me mother's usual thing, 'Oh, we'll have something to eat', and she gets all this bacon and eggs. She says to Adam Faith, 'Are you gonna have something to eat?' 'Oh I can't, the doctor says I can't have this, that and the other'. So she just said, 'Oh get it eaten'!

I'd just made my first guitar then, and I had it leaning up against the wall and I showed him it and he thought that was fantastic. I made a guitar when I was 16, first solid one. I've made basses for people, sound good as well. And treble boosters. This guy lived next door to us and he was a radio fiend, so he made this old radio with a grand total output of about two to five watts! It weighed a ton, 'cos it was all valves, and it had a great big transformer in it, and with a real heavy stroke on your guitar, this sound would probably almost fill a room. Then we'd get Linear amplifiers, 15 watts, then 30 watts.

I'm not saying I was terrific, or really smart, or better than anybody else, I was just first in. The first kid on the block. And that does help. They always remember the guy that finished the race first, or the guy that first stepped on the moon, but the second or third one is a little bit hazy. There's guys far, far better than me. I'll never be as good as them, but I was at the front of the queue. The influences, first of all it was American blues, traditional jazz, a big mixture. We were just coming out from a post-war depression. Everybody started to struggle, and they wanted something, an excuse to have a go, and I think that's what did it. Even if they couldn't be musicians, they wanted to feel as though they were part of it. We got no resentment from anybody. All the musos then were, and as far as I know, still are, the best guys in the world. There is no friction between musicians, in fact it's about the only breed in the world that go around sharing everything they've got.

Once the flood gates opened, it happened. You didn't have to wear yourself in, it suddenly happened like a bomb going off, no fuse. After that first initial thing, we did a few pub residencies, and then working men's clubs started up, and that's where your money was. And they'd take you on for a Sunday morning, Sunday afternoon, Sunday evening. You'd play all day, triple your money.

First dress we had was checked shirts. I had a red one, and from there we upgraded to pullovers and black trousers. I had a red pullover with a

'J' printed on it. Then I went on to light grey suits, light grey bow tie which I made myself, and the others had charcoal suits, with black ties. We were quite dressy. When things started to blossom, we changed from the more sombre colours to purple jackets, and red jackets, but still with bow ties. All the suits were made by Jack Leeming, made up for myself and the group, and all the other groups found out about it and he became the regular supplier for all the groups around York. He was a brilliant tailor.

In March 1957 an article in the Yorkshire Evening Press called Johnny Newcombe the 'skiffle chief' after the Wabash Four had passed an audition to appear at the Leeds Empire. In May 1957 when Johnny was only 16, the Wabash Four first appeared at the Rialto and in June, they were voted number one in the first round of a big skiffle competition at the Palace Theatre, Hull. Their number Worried Man Blues got a huge reception. In the finals, 23 skiffle groups took part and the group came fourth. The guest stars were the national skiffle group the Vipers who told Johnny that they thought his group were the best in the contest.

Later that year, he wrote to the BBC asking for an audition. The reply made it clear that the profession was becoming overcrowded and that there was a policy of giving work to those musicians who relied upon it for a living. They invited Johnny's group to 'write to us again when you have gained some professional experience, and we shall certainly reconsider your application'. That summer, Johnny went to Butlin's in Filey and entered the National Skiffle Competition with four other lads, two of them from York and the others from Sutton-in-Ash. They won first prize, which was £25, having played three numbers, Diggin' My Potatoes, No Other Baby and Cumberland Gap.

In November the group made a 45-minute tape recording in a York club for relay over the broadcasting system at RAF Leconfield. In early 1958, they auditioned for ABC Television at the Guildford Hotel in Leeds. They were invited for a second one in February, auditioning for the programme Bid For Fame. Soon after, the group travelled to Bury to enter a charity Carnival Skiffle Competition with the judges Chris Barber, his wife, jazz singer Ottilie Patterson, and jazz enthusiast the Earl of Wharncliffe. The first prize was a recording test. Johnny's group came second. In February 1958 the Rialto had a sensational all-star show headed by Johnny Duncan And His Bluegrass Boys and including Marty Wilde And His Wildcats, Colin Hick, (brother of Tommy Steele), and The Cabin Boys and local group Johnny Newcombe And The Wabash Four, who started off with their signature tune Wabash Cannon Ball and performed nine other numbers.

In July, the council wrote to Johnny to ask the Wabash Four to play for two sessions at the Assembly Rooms on Christmas Eve for a fee of £5. 5s. and on New

The Wabash Four setting out for the carnival at Bury. Back L to R - George Clipperton and Dave Johnson. Front L to R - Johnny Newcombe and Dave Garlick. 1958.
(Courtesy Dave Garlick)

Year's Eve for a fee of £8. 8s. This was when skiffle and rock 'n' roll were becoming acceptable and dance bands no longer reigned supreme. The Regency School of Dancing advertised its Saturday Dancer's Nights, with ballroom dancing and 'jiving to the music of Johnny Newcombe and his Skiffle Group'.

After Dave Johnson left the group, they became Joni And The Newcomers. Johnny believes that:

It's possible that we weren't just the first group in York [perhaps first in England], when we started it was before Tommy Steele and there wasn't any groups before he started. The Liverpool scene didn't get into the market 'till after the York music scene had been established for about five years.

Dave Garlick was the singer with the Wabash Four:

A lot of those skiffle tunes were easy to play for amateurs, for up and comin' youngsters with big ideas. You could buy a guitar quite cheap and a tea-chest bass didn't cost anything, you made it yourself and you could get away with a lot of songs that were three chords. I remember, out of the blue, we called in the Buckles Inn on Tadcaster Road one night and asked them could they do with a group playing every week. We did a quick audition, and they agreed, and we played there every Sunday night for at least a year. They had this advert, 'Don't stay at home among the snifflers, come to the Buckles and watch the skifflers'. So you kicked off being quite chuffed because you could get through a tune without any major expense, no electronics, no microphones and speakers. We had some good nights. No one had cars then. It was always a queue a mile long for the bus in Rougier Street, then we moved on to the Wild Man and played there regular, and a lot of times at the New Central Club, bottom of Tanner Row, and we got quite well known locally. Eventually you get a bit more with it and think, 'We've gotta move on'. Some of the personnel changed over time, and we eventually got a proper bass and microphones.

Johnny's mother, she knew Prendergast. I don't know quite how it came about but we finished up going for an audition to the Rialto. A lot of the shows we did, there'd be a well known act topping the bill. We did one with Johnny Duncan And The Bluegrass Boys, Last Train To San Fernando, a smashing fella. He'd even have a session with us after the show. They weren't snooty. If you liked the same music as them they thought it was great. I remember once we were rehearsing for this show during the afternoon and Russ Conway was top of t'bill. This chap came in on his own, little suitcase, and, 'Is there anywhere you can go to get something to eat?' 'Well Mr Conway, we're going across to the Edinburgh Arms for a pint and a couple of sandwiches'. He says, 'Do you mind if I come with you?' And he went with us to the pub!

I went to Butlin's at Skegness and won a skiffle competition there. I was on me own when I went there, playing-wise, and came across these lads from London practising. So we got together and finished up winning it. I says to these lads, 'Just keep everything straightforward.' I always had the theory that doing the simple things great was better than trying to do it more complicated and not getting it right. As long as we held a good beat, a good rhythm that people can tap to, we got away with it. The prize was presented by Blighty Magazine, that was the only magazine where you got any kind of pin-ups, and whoever was pin-up of the month presented the cheque, which was £25, the cost of your holiday.

Then we got into more rock 'n' roll type stuff. Jerry Lee Lewis. We were all mates even though we were in different groups. In the army, I was stationed at Newbury and I'd be able to get home for weekends sometimes and always called in the Wild Man or Buckles. Most clubs in York we played at one time or another. I have to say the worst thing that could happen would be a busload of middle-aged women. They were devils. We'd get a lot of that at the Wild Man because they'd be stopping on the way home from t'coast. But we had a good following of regulars who were all mates. Johnny was the leader as far as the name was concerned but we did everything more as a team. It was a case of, 'That's a good one just come out, we'll have a go at that'.

Suddenly guitars were on the market. When you first started you didn't need too much amplification. Johnny played lead guitar and we eventually got plugged in with speakers, and we got mikes. Not as sophisticated as what you get now. Everything's electrical. That's why I like live music. That's when you know how good people are, instead of being disguised behind all the electronics.

I think the odd time that we played at the Rialto we might have got a fiver. A pint of Sam Smith's brown was 1/-. We did have the chance to go full-time in them days but most of us would be apprentices learning a trade. You just daren't take the risk. What do you do at the end of the season if you haven't got anywhere else? Plus you knew you had to do National Service. That was always a bugbear. I finished up having to do two and a half years 'cos we got six months added on. But the guitar went to Germany with me and made up me wages a bit. When I was in Newbury we had a group. National Service was people from all walks of life so we got Emile Ford's drummer doing his National Service.

I think what also helped a lot was being in youth clubs. I was in the YPF for a lot of years at the Friends' Meeting House in Clifford Street. Used to go camping, play table tennis, plus they'd play records for dancing. Even at school, in our last year, we could take records to school for music lessons. The world was just beginning to open up again after wartime. It was a different world, the start of spreading your wings, expressing yourself.

It's been enjoyable and I've got some good memories. I wouldn't swap those times, whatever I've done, I'd do it all again. I can get very emotional about it, if particular songs have meanings. I don't mind with country music, the sadder it is, the better I like it. And if we've been playing and seen somebody sniffling in the audience, then, 'I've cracked it'.

Although Johnny's group was the first skiffle group, Norman Fowler's was the youngest. The Gambling Men, all aged 14, were formed in mid 1957 and consisted of Norman Fowler on vocals and guitar, Terry Herbert on washboard (who later moved on to drums), Ian Early on guitar, and Patrick Byrne on home-made tea-chest bass. Ian was the only member of the group to take guitar lessons and also adapted folk songs for the group to work on.

They performed at many church halls in York as well as working men's clubs and reached the semi-final of the New Central Working Men's Club talent competition in early 1958. They came second and after their performance, had to dash by taxi to Christie's Ballroom to appear as support for the Ken Mackintosh Orchestra. For the competition Norman sang a duet with new group member Michael Mallen, The Rose I Always Wear, a skiffle song that had been sung by Lonnie Donegan and Johnny Duncan on a recent television programme. (By 1964, Michael Mallen had adopted the stage name of Toni Ross and became a musical director in London for shows starring Danny La Rue and Diana Dors, as well as doing the musical score for a jazz ballet in Liverpool. Before this he had spent two years running dance bands in the Royal Corps of Signals and playing classical music at concert engagements. He had also been offered a contract to play in Las Vegas).

In April Norman's group competed in the All-Yorkshire Skiffle Championships at the Baths Ballroom in Goole. In a short time they were asked to appear at the Rialto in a variety show topped by Michael Holliday and in August, they supported Doug Green And His Band at a Grand Ebor Ball at the SS Empire. By January 1959 the group were being written about in the national record weekly Disc. When they supported Marty Wilde at a concert at the Rialto, the Press reviewer said that he had 'rarely heard an act opening a show receive such attention and appreciation from the audience. The boys showed talent and stage presence'.

In March the Gambling Men appeared at the Folk Hall for the New Earswick Camera Club's annual Camera Queen Dance. (Dancing to Jack Mann And His Music, with Norman Fowler And His Skiffle Group as support).

A big concert at the Rialto in May 1959 saw Norman Fowler And The Gambling Men support Cliff Richard who was top of the bill. The review stated that the group 'gave a magnificent performance'. The audience shouted for more but there was not time for them to give encores. In just a year they had moved from skiffle to include 'anything that rocks with a beat'. They had become more polished and wore smart outfits and had better equipment.

Norman remembers this period and how the group started out meeting up on Friday nights in 1957:

One of us was a pianist, the only one with any musical knowledge. The rest of us just strummed along and made a lot of noise. Eventually we got things kind of in tune, learned two or three songs, and then inflicted ourselves on people who ran dances. 'Would you like us to play at the interval at your

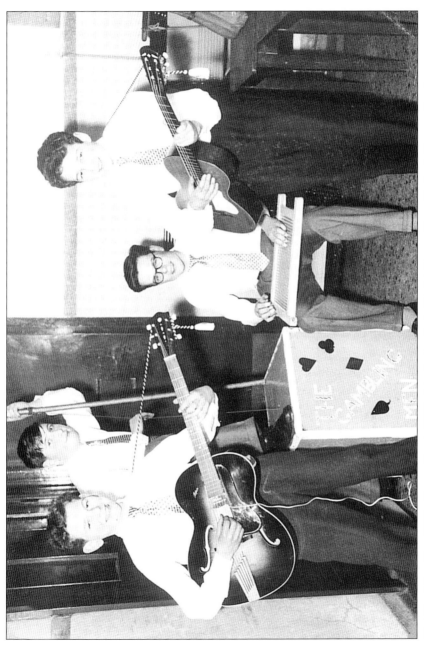

The Gambling Men Skiffle Group March 1958. L to R - Ian Early, Patrick Byrne, Terry Herbert, Norman Fowler.
(Courtesy Norman Fowler)

dance, for nothing?' So they would say, 'Okay' and we'd go in front of an audience and we got the bug. People said nice things about us and that goes to your head, and eventually we auditioned for Jack Prendergast at the Rialto, and he put us on a show with Michael Holliday, who had big hits at that time. I was completely stage struck then. It was magical to be on a wonderful stage, under lovely lighting, and singing through good microphones, because mostly, if you played anywhere, you didn't have a microphone system of your own, you relied on what was in the place you played and usually it was awful. The Rialto had wonderful theatre sound, so that was what hooked us. Eventually we got paid bookings, and signed up for an agent, who got us work at dances all over Yorkshire. Jack Prendergast was managing us, and we were on with Cliff Richard and Marty Wilde, which was a great experience 'cos they were our heroes then.

Music seemed to take off in York. There were bands in pubs everywhere and some good players. We worked for a chap called Jim Blyth who had a dance hall in York called Christie's, and a ballroom at Selby, so he'd book us to play at these two places. They would be packed with people dancing.

The Gambling Men (looking rather smoother) in 1960. L to R - Norman Fowler, Patrick Byrne, Terry Herbert, Mike Mallen and Ian Early.   *(Courtesy Norman Fowler)*

31

The Escorts And Sylvia. L to R - Sylvia Leon, Mick Goodrick, Michael McNeill, Colin Berriman and Derek Boyes touring American bases in France 1965.

(Courtesy Colin Berriman)

Norman had grown up in a house filled with music:

My parents always had records on, and my mother played the piano, and could knock a tune out of anything, guitar or mouth organ. I remember the first thing my father did on a morning was put on the radio downstairs, and it had a terrific bass note. I think that must have had a big influence on me. We had a lot of Fats Waller records, Bing Crosby and all sorts.

I was called a few different names, first of all it was Norman Fowler And The Gambling Men, then Jack Prendergast decided that Norman Fowler wasn't a good enough stage name, and it ought to be Sammy Browne. It was at the time when there were all sorts of names like Steele and Wilde. A Sam Brown was a belt as well. I didn't mind what they called me as long as I could sing in any show, so for a while I was Sammy Browne.

Norman remembers the new music came from jukeboxes in coffee bars:

And Radio Luxembourg was the thing that you could tune into on a night and hear this crackly rock 'n' roll music, Gene Vincent and Buddy Holly, it was really exciting, and thousands of young people were listening all over the country. We were fed up of Workers' Playtime and Music While You Work, and

the only time you got to hear records would be on Saturday morning,
Saturday Club, which had live music or on television, Oh Boy. What
happened, what shoved Alma Cogan off her pedestal, was that younger people
were coming along that had a different sound, and the older ones didn't like
it. It's really ludicrous now, people saying about Elvis, that you couldn't hear
what he was saying, because his diction was really good. And even Gene
Vincent, you could hear what he was saying, but the older people couldn't
hear it because they didn't have their ears tuned in to that kind of music and
they said it was a racket. Just as now when I watch Top Of The Pops, I think,
'This is absolute garbage', but it's their [today's young people] music now. I
saw Jerry Lee Lewis when he was at the Rialto and he was stamping on that
Bechstein piano that they had there, that Count Basie had played on, this
wonderful concert grand, and he was playing with his feet and I don't think
Jack liked that much.

In May 1958 another young York skiffle group called the Planets started meeting
every Friday night at the Columba Club in Sir Thomas Herbert's house on
Pavement, for a skiffle session. They comprised of 13-year-old Michael McNeill
and four 14-year-olds, Malcolm Addison, Malcolm Fletcher, Ronnie Allpress and
Peter Watt. The boys, all members of St Michael's College in Leeds, played at a
few gigs, including a York City Supporters' Club Dance in the Assembly Rooms
as well as a regular booking at St Joseph's Social Club in Burton Stone Lane.
Stacey Brewer wrote in the Yorkshire Evening Press, 'If there are any ghosts in
the house which was once the home of St Thomas Herbert, I hope they like
skiffle. If not, they must be walking around with their puzzled heads
underneath their arms every Friday night when the rafters of their ancient home
resound to the enthusiastic music of a young York skiffle group'.

When the Gambling Men broke up, Norman became Steve Cassidy and formed
a new band, the Escorts, who were very popular:

Jack Prendergast took us down to London to record with Joe Meek, who had
[produced] by then some really big hits, a world-wide hit with Telstar. He had
his own studio in a bathroom, we recorded with him, and he wanted to call
me Johnny April. Again if he was going to release the record I didn't mind.
But we didn't get our record released, which was sad because we were good.
All of us were good players, and enthusiastic, we could write stuff, we had a
really good band and we were young. If there was a chance that was missed,
that was it. Joe Meek used to record people, then he would sell the tapes to
different record companies. But I think he'd tried something on with our
guitarist, and he tried something on with me, and he quickly realised that
neither of us were going to play that kind of game. We were too interested in

Steve Cassidy And The Escorts. L to R - Ian Early, Colin Berriman, Steve Cassidy and
Norman Goodall. *(Courtesy Steve Cassidy)*

*girls by then, and anything else was just alien to us. We were only kids
anyway, 16, 17, but that was disappointing.*

*You'd get these dance bands and they'd kind of look down their nose at you,
with your little guitars strumming, and it was really only a few years on
when they were basically out of work. The dance bands went out of fashion.
We had a great sax player in Norman Hughes and Michael McNeill, the
guitarist, played with Val Doonican and has been all over the world with a
fellow called Leapy Lee, who had one hit, Little Arrows.* [Another group
member, Ian Early went to Leeds College of Music and went on to be a top
session guitarist in Manchester for Syd Lawrence].

*It's not really about somebody being a better player than you, or a better
singer than you, though there are some outstandingly wonderful singers, that
are in another realm. There's plenty of people who are pretty good singers
who have made an absolute fortune who aren't in that realm, they just kept
going, kept doing it and it paid off, they had hit after hit. I think it's also
having somebody, I mean if the Beatles didn't have Brian Epstein, they might
have been just another Liverpool band, but he actually got behind them and*

Johnny De Little, Frankie Vaughan, Steve Cassidy and Jack Prendergast at the Rialto 1963.
(Courtesy June Lloyd-Jones)

promoted them in a big way. People might argue that such talent would have found its way to the top, but I'm not so sure about that. Good writers need an outlet. If you're going to write songs and all you do is record 'em on your tape recorder, or on albums that you're going to tote round yourself, there's not the same kind of drive to improve your talent.

Jack Prendergast was great for building up your self esteem and self belief, which is a very important part of anybody who wants to be in showbusiness. He was a great guy, a real character, always looking for the next opportunity. He would invest in young people, and he was straight as a dye. There was no hidden agenda with him. I could go along and listen to him for hours, talking about people that he'd helped in showbusiness and he just liked to talk, and I was fascinated by listening to him.

And Neal Guppy. He had a club in Walmgate, and we played there. It was a tiny place but he promoted all kinds of music, and he was good for music in York and for young people. It was a place where people could go, different to a pub. He had special music nights for classical music, and he had really good quality hi-fi stuff, electrostatic quad speakers that nobody else had. John Barry was the only other person to have them, in his flat in Cadogan Square.

We would play round Doncaster and at RAF stations and dance halls like Goole Baths. In winter they covered the bath with a dance floor. On the same circuit was Screamin' Lord Sutch and Alvin Stardust who was then Shane Fenton And The Fentones. Sometimes they would advertise some band, say from Liverpool, and they'd fill the dance hall, and then would announce over the microphone that the band had had an accident, or couldn't turn up. The people had paid their money then, and there was plenty of other bands playing. And we fell for a really incredible scam once when there was about 12 bands on, apparently auditioning for some programme like Saturday Club and we all struggled to get our stuff on and off really quickly, and we all played, and then nobody got on that programme, and I don't think there was anybody listening from there. It was just a great idea to get all these bands working all night, fill the place with people that had all paid and somebody got a lot of money out of it. But you fall for those things when you're young.

I think bands are wiser now, many of these younger bands have been carved up and somebody's made millions, but they haven't, out of their music, and there was a lot of that happening. And in a way, young people probably don't mind that 'cos they want the fame. But somebody else is making the fortune. What do you do, if you're a young band and somebody says, 'Sign this contract and we're going to promote you, and you get five per cent of your work'? If you don't do it, you're still singing around the same places you did before. You might be tempted 'cos you might think, 'I can get out of that eventually'.

It was exciting. I've never really been too nervous, 'cos it's like an ego trip, you want to show off really. It was a good time to be young then, it was absolutely amazing. I had a fan club, and somebody organised it. Only a small-time thing, but ever so nice that somebody wanted to do that. With the Escorts, we would probably try and learn four or five new songs a week, and we'd finish up doing three of them and then build up a huge repertoire of songs, because you used to have to play for a long time. You would play from eight to 12 and there was a half hour interval.

I was disappointed when Norman Hughes went to work with the Swingalongs, 'cos he was a good player and I didn't like to lose him. We tried auditioning for another saxophone player and we couldn't find anybody with his quality. Then the Escorts decided they would join a girl singer called

Sylvia [Leon] who was from Harrogate. She was very good and was on television and made a lot of records. She married Michael McNeill, the guitarist in the band. They went to work in Germany on American bases and I stayed. They came back and said, 'You must buy this, everybody in America is talking about Bob Dylan, he's gonna be a great star, you could sing his kind of stuff'. And he looked a bit like me when I was that age. So I bought a Bob Dylan album, and I listened to it and thought, 'It sounds terrible, I don't like this'. But I listened again, and then I just got hooked, and I loved Bob Dylan's music. I started playing in folk clubs and singing Dylan songs. There would be other people on the folk scene who would show different finger picks, and other bits of stuff on the guitar, so I got to be a better player because of the folk scene. The Escorts came back and then we kept picking up and working again with each other, and then later on we changed the name to Britannia and worked in Europe quite a lot, Belgium, France, Spain, and Italy and that was great. To travel and be paid, instead of paying to be there.

We were still getting plenty of work around Yorkshire, and getting a good name, and we were auditioning whenever we could, for the BBC or anything that looked promising. Then Jack Prendergast told me that John Barry had got a song for me, and would I like to go and record it with his orchestra in London. So you don't pass up a chance like that. I made the record with John Barry and that was a great experience. Living in Cadogan Square, where he lived, and rubbing shoulders with all his famous film star friends, I thought, 'This is wonderful, this is it'. The record was released, and there was a big launching 'cos he'd joined the Ember record label at that time, and it was at the Grosvenor House Hotel, a huge party, with a photograph of me about 20 foot tall, and all the other people signed up, all their photographs around.

The record was called Ecstasy and in 1964 it was getting a lot of airplay on Radio Luxembourg. Sandra Storey from Acomb started a fan club for Steve.

You needed an agent who believed in you, and got you work, and important work like television. I was on Ready Steady Go and my record was due to be the next one on Juke Box Jury, but Jack Prendergast was told that it didn't get played 'cos they talked too long on the other records. It was played a lot on Radio Luxembourg, but it wasn't a hit. I had a contract to make two more records with Ember, but John Barry quit the label then, it didn't happen as he would have liked and so I didn't bother taking up the contract. Eventually we got an agent from Hull and I was doing a lot of work, seven nights a week singing at different clubs and on shows. Then I went to Newcastle to audition for New Faces and I was on that show. Terry Wogan was on the panel, and Mickey Most, and they were quite influential and they said wonderful things.

The Slickerjacks skiffle group 1957. L to R - Fred Davy, Dave Sharpe, Bert Thompson, Barrie Pawson, Wilf Hall. Front - Maurice Green. *(Courtesy Barrie Pawson)*

If I'd written the script I couldn't have said anything better. Having had all sorts of other kind of breaks, I thought this was a really good one, because I got a hundred marks, which meant you got on another programme. I was on another programme, out on New Year's Eve, and Danny La Rue was on the panel, it was a good ego trip. It could be the opposite though because you didn't know what they were going to say about you. You did the show in the afternoon, they watched you, then it was videoed and they said stuff about you, and if you didn't like it, it was tough luck.

Pete Willow recalls being taken to the Clifton Cinema Ballroom when he was seven in 1957 to see his uncle's skiffle group play. He was lifted up to sing a few lines into the microphone. His parents bought him his first guitar for his tenth birthday along with a small washboard from Stubbs:

You got a Bert Weedon Play In A Day book, and most people learnt the chord shapes and would buy sheet music which had the chords. When I was 16 I got an electric guitar, a Broadway with one pickup from Bulmers and I had a job as a delivery boy then, with a carrier bike. I remember coming down Lord Mayor's Walk with the guitar in the basket, sticking up out of a Stork margarine box, feeling really proud and thinking, 'I'm gonna make it now, there's no stopping me'. Then I bought a small 15 watt Selmer Truevoice amp with a 12 inch speaker and a tremolo, from a York musician, Don Hattee, who played steel guitar. I worked with Don, he was a really nice man. I bought it for £5, he let me pay for it at a pound a week. It was big enough to play in your front room at home. You see the Beatles using them in the early days and whatever the Beatles used is now collectable.

Another York skiffle player was Barrie Pawson. He first played for a parents' night at Acomb Youth Club:

You could learn three basic chords - C, A7 and F, or G, D7 and C and you could play anything. We were 17. I just sang Lonnie Donegan and Chas McDevitt stuff. Lads found they could get together with a couple of guitars, and could make a bass out of a tea-chest. You turn one upside down, drill a hole in the middle, put a piece of cord through it with a knot in the end so it doesn't come out, fasten a broom handle to it, and then just use one string. You know how kids play musical saw, there are some clever people can play tea-chest bass and actually pick the notes out.

Barrie started out with Fred Davy, Wilf Hall, Dave Sharpe, Maurice Green and Bert Thompson. Bert Thompson left soon after, Pat Hunter joined for a spell in 1958 and Dave Sharpe was replaced by Brian Hattersley. Barrie recalls:

We named ourselves the Slickerjacks, a style of jacket popular at that time, a very thin overjacket with piping down the front and the sleeves. We all bought one. We'd been to see this Wabash Four and we decided it was on for us to have a go.

We looked round for somewhere to practise. We had a room in the Golden Lion, [St Sampson's Square] but we only lasted a couple of weeks. Then we went to Phoenix Club but finished up eventually at the Naval Club down St Mary's every Tuesday night and it was only half a crown a night. We played at Severus Working Men's Club. We were paid one pound between five of us, plus all the beer we wanted. We set up with cheap guitars and we went round the different clubs in York touting for business. If you were a new act wanting to get around, they'd say, 'We're doing a charity do at so-and-so for the old aged pensioners, will you come and do a turn?' No money in it, but you got your name known gradually. I'd bought meself a G banjo because I felt a bit strange not having performed before, the two lads behind had got a prop to hold. We played at the Knavesmire Hotel, Tang Hall Club, York Anglers' Club, and New Earswick Bop For A Bob. It seemed to command a following amongst the young ladies.

In October we went for an ITV audition but we never heard anymore. We had a repertoire of 20 or 30 songs including My Old Man's A Dustman, Putting On The Style and Worried Man Blues but they were skiffle and some of the groups, like Johnny Newcombe's, carried on and introduced other numbers. We argued about whether we should introduce some new material as skiffle was waning but we folded in February 1959 so we didn't actually go a full year.

The Wabash Four, the Saints, the Starliners and the Gambling Men. They were the prominent groups in York. We had a good time but were eventually restricted by our lack of repertoire and our naïve belief that it could always be like it was. We had no pretensions of either greatness or stardom, just to earn a few beers and to entertain a few people.

Skiffle was a bit of fresh air really when I look back at it. There hadn't been anything else on the social scene other than dance bands from the 1930s and 1940s. It was a new convention, that people could get together and entertain in a little group.

CHAPTER THREE. BECAUSE THEY'RE YOUNG:
Clubs for Young People

Some people say that skiffle was dead by 1959 but it was a milestone in popular music and many young people, who gained confidence by playing skiffle, progressed on to other things.

In a series in the Yorkshire Evening Press in January 1960 about York teenagers, it became clear that older teenagers wanted more leisure provision. Youth clubs were fine for the younger adolescents but nothing really catered for those over 16, except for the pub scene. In the article, a probation officer commented that young people were in the main well-behaved and that too much publicity was given to the rowdy gangs who were really just the minority. Young people needed an outlet for their energy and many were 'bored', an attitude which affects every generation. The writer suggested that more coffee bars be opened to young people who could meet their friends and be left alone by adults.

Although there were many youth clubs in York, they closed at 9.30pm and were not open at weekends. There were no dance halls specifically for young people. But in the early 1960s two clubs opened in the city which became hugely popular. Both were run by men with a concern for young people and an insight into their needs. The first was Father John Murphy who came to Our Lady's Church in Acomb as a curate in 1963 and stayed for eight years. He started Sunday night beat dances in the church hall, and encouraged local bands to play there, as well as booking well-known groups from elsewhere.

Father Murphy remembers:

Putting on the dances was my idea because I had already done a similar thing in Leeds. I did everything because my committee helpers, though very responsible, were only teenagers. We had over 300 every Sunday evening from all over York. I enjoyed the company of teenagers and I'm sure thousands must have gone there in the five years that I had the youth club. We booked groups from different agencies, it was live entertainment, and we had a very good disco in between. A group of the teenagers would pick the records, we bought about two a week from the top 20 so that we kept au fait.

Music has been very much part of my relaxation in life, although one couldn't say there was much relaxation when you have 300 teenagers, but it was really marvellous. The young adults had a great social meeting place, they felt they were safe, which I think is important. It would be hard to guarantee for that number today. I was very strict with any misbehaviour, whether it was a boy or girl I would catch them by the backside of their pants and collar of their coat and right through the swing door, so therefore we hadn't much bother. I hope they respected me for it. We never ever had anything by way of vandalism or real trouble. Arguments over a girl but nothing terribly serious. The music brought people together from all sorts of districts. The place was full but it wasn't uncomfortably full, we had nice corridors where you could sit and talk. There was the real rock 'n' roll, the real fast stuff and then slower, smoochy type of songs. At that time music was the bait that brought people together, it was important to them and they got rid of a lot of energy. Music has played a big part in my life, I would always go where there is music and seek out where I could hear and enjoy it.

The other and more significant person in the development of facilities for young people was Neal Guppy, who started running a music club in 1961, with jive parties at Clifton Cinema Ballroom on Friday nights and at the Woolpack on Peasholme Green on Wednesdays and Saturdays, with dances at Acomb Church Hall and Betty's Ballroom. Neal had to take his hi-fi equioment by taxi each time but eventually:

By 1963 I'd got my settled premises in Walmgate. It really started off as a very large flat and to save moving the equipment about I took over the ground

Enterprise Club jive party at The Clifton Cinema Ballroom in 1962. Neal Guppy facing the camera in centre. *(Courtesy Neal Guppy)*

York Group Four Shades of Black. Keith Bellman on keyboards, Ray Morris, bass, Mel on drums, John on guitar. 1967. The Enterprise Club members went on Sunday rambles. On one occasion in 1963, they stopped for lunch at the Lastingham Arms and Keith Bellman began to play the piano there, with the rest of the members jiving outside the pub.

(Courtesy Neal Guppy)

floor from Mr. Chalk who owned the premises. Then I hacked my way through the concrete to the cellar, did some alterations, and that became a sort of cavern which was becoming popular because of the Beatles. So I ended up with a large lounge for concerts and meetings, a coffee bar on the ground floor and this cellar which was only a tiny place but catering for a lot of people. That's the time my club was best known because every Friday, Saturday and then Sunday nights I had live groups on, from 1964 onwards. I had folk nights on Tuesday nights, classical music on a Monday night and live jazz in the cellar on occasions.

From the inception of the club, the groups were only too pleased to be able to play. There were schoolboys, people in the fifth or sixth year or at the Tech College and they were forming groups. Many imitated the Shadows and then at a later stage were moving over to greater musicianship and taking off the Beatles. In fact I remember one of the last of my most successful dances at the Clifton before I lost it to bingo, Twist And Shout was played and it was the shake that they did rather than jive at this stage. For the first time I ever experienced, every single person in the whole place stood up and danced. Lads that would never dance suddenly started to jump around. All to Beatles numbers, a hell of a night that was.

In the rock 'n' roll era quite a few groups formed to play in pubs but they were generally mainly in their 20s. There was a Teddy Boy culture and that's when live rock 'n' roll bands started. Then the advent of the Beatles, who were followed by the younger people. One of the very popular groups of the 1960s was Tony Adams And The Viceroys. The noisiest band was the Cheavours, and they were remarkable in that you could hear them halfway across York. The Scorpions who later became the Shades Of Black, they were the first group to play in my cellar in 1964. I thought it was too small but it turned out to be better than a ballroom 'cos it was that closed-in atmosphere that people wanted.

At that time young people were wanting to search for new outlets for entertainment, and complaining bitterly of nowhere to go and my intention was to say, 'Let's do it for ourselves'. There are always practical limitations which young people often wouldn't see themselves but my idea was to try something and then if it didn't work, chuck it, and if it did work, do it, because obviously that was a way of succeeding and so that's how we carried on. I just considered myself as an agent or a catalyst for youthful ideas, but what I did do was, I was always very careful and I wouldn't let people into the club on a Saturday night after nine o'clock unless they were members. You didn't know whether they'd been out drinking and whether they'd had too many. If they were prepared to walk away then I suspected they were civilised enough to be able to come into a place and be trusted. It was a marvellous way of sorting them out because those that were belligerent, it was that element that needed to keep out and was the reason for which parents by and large were very happy for their sons and daughters to come to my club because they knew that there was never trouble inside. I think in all the years I've run the place I doubt if there were half a dozen minor battles within the club caused by members themselves. Any battles were people trying to get in late at night after they'd had too much to drink and being forcibly stopped. What used to happen is if I started to get trouble then it would soon feed back to my members and I would have reinforcements. I could usually provide 20 people, often lads that were good rugby players, standing behind me saying, 'No, sorry but try again on another night'.

I carried on until 1969 and then extended the premises 'cos Mr. Chalk had closed the shop in front and I took over part of that to produce another big lounge. By then there were two pop cultures, what I called the Tamla Soul Group, who used to dance and who we called the boppers, and then there were the people who liked what we called blues or progressive music in those days and they were the freaks. They tended to be the ones that were going to move on and go to university, whereas the middle-of-the-roaders were Tamla Motown and soul followers. So I had two little cultures in the club at once. In the cellar I had the boppers for most of the time and then in this new lounge I had the freaks and then we had a no-man's-land in the coffee bar between the two where they could argue against each other's culture. They were always arguing about whose music was best but it was on a friendly basis, and to me that's what young people are about, each defending their own particular corner. I felt it was a lot better to have that kind of vying within the club in a positive way than it was to have two separate cultures that never met.

The main group that played for me were Steve Cassidy And The Escorts who were particularly good musicians. They were the resident group that played in the Boulevard on Tadcaster Road. They played that kind of music but Steve's first night as a folk singer was in my cellar on my first folk night. In fact the first night we ran jazz for part of the time with the rest of his group and then he sang folk for the other half of the evening. But they didn't reside together too well so I put jazz on one night and folk on the other and then started to get different folk groups coming.

I never worked on the large scale, I was tempted to when I first had my successes at the Clifton Cinema, getting 200 people into a dance for example, but I felt that overall I wanted to keep this atmosphere of people helping themselves rather than me promoting it on a large scale. It wasn't trying to

Enterprise Club jive party at the Woolpack, Peasholme Green. 1962.
(Courtesy Neal Guppy)

cater for a mass, rather was it trying to draw people who were going to be positive of nature and largely do their own thing.

I called my dances jive parties and they remained as jive parties till about 1968. The first discotheques came to this country about 1963 in London, places like the Marquee and the Tiles on Oxford Street. From then the name discotheque started to be currency but it didn't move to York until about four years later. Funnily enough the first people to use the word discotheque in York were the Tang Hall Hotel, they set a room aside with flashing lights, dark painting and fluorescent paint and that became a discotheque. Very different from the original ones in London and quite different from the night clubs in Paris.

It declined because the bands got so good that they were starting to play stuff that was not commercial. Bands themselves enjoyed performing and whilst they could strum a few chords they played dancing music, which the girls particularly would enjoy dancing to, and so the lads would follow. By the late 1960s you were getting really good performances from people and they

46

couldn't be bothered to play simple stuff. They weren't therefore as popular, I used to have to try and persuade them. 'Look play some straightforward pop, get them dancing and then play your stuff. If you've got a rhythm then they'll follow you, but play the pop stuff first'. At that time Tamla Motown was coming in, there was still room for a cellar atmosphere provided it was recorded music and that was when we got boppers coming in and dancing to soul. At the same time there was a quickening of interest amongst those people who liked listening to the Cream, Jimi Hendrix and groups of that nature. They had some strong instrumentalists who, in a previous era, would have been called jazz musicians. Moody Blues were coming out and Fairport Convention but they were a different kettle of fish and weren't necessarily bands that you would dance to, but you'd certainly sit and listen to them. It developed into two pop cultures in one place and there was a healthy antagonism between the groups, there was always people in the middle, not sure which way to go but there was always enough to argue about. With people that's the very essence of their life finding something to argue about. The wider the mixture of people you get around you, the more colourful for your own life, the more enhancing it is. So I set out with that in mind, and some of the healthiest nights we ever had at my club were, because as well as pop music being on, I was always involved in arguments about religion, philosophy and politics.

By 1966, when Neal was 27, he had 1,500 members, and had to give up his teaching job to run the club full-time. In the late 1970s the club moved to Nunnery Lane. Although it is now a different kind of club, it remains the longest running club in the city.

Neal also found himself acting as an agent. He began to get enquiries for beat groups and as he had a telephone, he was quite happy to be the intermediary:

I said to the group, 'If you pay me ten per cent I will write out simple contracts and book you in in different places'. I knew one or two people, there was a lady who had the Red Lion pub in Selby, she used to have groups every Friday and Saturday. There was me keeping groups going three nights a week, I'd be booking groups and one or two other places and bigger dances every so often in the university for example. The Circle B Combo were a favourite group of mine and they were my resident group in the cellar in the early stages when I started on Saturdays. They played about every fortnight, they were a grand crowd of lads, largely from St. Peter's School, basically motivated by groups such as the Rolling Stones and wanted very earthy, simplistic music.

The 1960s was marvellous. You didn't realise that at the time, you just took part in it. I've always loved and been very sensitive to the large scale great

Neal Guppy aged 27 at the Enterprise Club, Walmgate, April 1966.
(Courtesy Yorkshire Evening Press)

music and I've always wanted other people to hear what I hear. I remember one particular occasion, when we had the lads listening to the blues progressive music and there was a band that was popular at the time, the Nice, and it produced Five Bridges Suite which is from Sibelius's Karelia. I said to one of the lads who was a pure straightforward pop man, 'I'm glad to see you like some classical music then'. 'What do you mean?' 'Well, the Five Bridges Suite, it was the Alla Marcia from the Karelia Suite, that's Sibelius'. 'Who the ... is Sibelius?''He's a classical composer'. 'It can't be, it's the Nice'. 'Of course it is, where do you think the themes come from?' All pop music is based really on harmonies that have existed earlier. The great composers, people like Stravinsky, are researchers, they come up with new harmonies that people don't like at the time but another 50 years on, people are loving their kind of harmony. Mahler's another example.

Generation gaps usually occur simply because of the prejudices of older people to try and formulate their sons and daughters' lives around their own ideas, rather than letting their sons and daughters come up with some new ideas and perhaps taking the better ones on board themselves. I've learned

48

far more from younger people than they've probably learnt from me, and I hope I will continue to do.

Glyn Edwards started going to Guppy's Enterprise Club when he was 16:

It was an ideal venue. Neal introduced a scheme for senior members of 18 plus and he built a bar in the front room of the club. You could go down into the cellar for dancing, they had one type of music in there, another in the upstairs lounge and in the bar another type of music. He had a DJ upstairs, it was Chris Lister for quite a while.

Eventually it was possible to go to a different venue almost every night of the week for music and dancing. The Beat Hive at English Martyr's Church on Dalton Terrace and Our Lady's in Acomb, Father Murphy's place. He was certainly a legend, a real maverick of a Catholic priest. Then you could go to the Boulevard on Tadcaster Road, La Bamba, Vickers Social Club in Cromwell Road, the Assembly Rooms at weekends, and the cellars at King's Manor. I don't know how on earth they got round the fire regulations but there used to be some good do's down there. Later the Cat's Whiskers, the Old World in Stonegate, and most of the groups in that time would go socialising at the Hypnotique down Lady Peckitt's Yard.

We spent an awful lot of time at Guppy's but we started going to bona fide concerts. York University had some really good groups on at Central Hall but there was no dancing. If you did stand up and dance, a steward would tell you to sit down again which was a bit strange when you've got rock groups belting out stuff. Guppy's was an absolute godsend because he welcomed parents with open arms to go down anytime they wanted to see what was happening. He was very strict on drugs. If there was a hint of it, or even if he got to hear about anything off the premises, that was it. It was that popular that you were much more frightened of losing your Guppy's card and not being allowed to go there, than anything that would happen legally. If you weren't allowed to go to Guppy's anymore you were like a social outcast. But it was an ideal atmosphere because you had your independence, there was all types of music, you could meet your friends, yet you were still under some form of control even though you didn't realise it.

York probably was a microcosm of what was happening in the rest of society. It was an exciting time and it was hip to be youth and everything was moving quickly. There was always a feel of something happening. When the youngsters now say, 'I'm bored', initially you discredit that statement but then in retrospect when you realise what we could do every night of the week, you

The Enterprise Club

Proprietor: NEAL GUPPY

Telephone No. YORK 22879

MEMBERSHIP CARD

1963/64

(Not Transferable)

This card should be produced at the door for attendance at each function.

Membership Card for The Enterprise Club 1963.　　　*(Courtesy Neal Guppy)*

can understand some of their frustrations. But music was much more important then than it appears to be now. Your social life revolved around music, either listening to live groups or records. I was a 'mod' type with a Lambretta, one of 'the out crowd' that would meet in Exhibition Square on our scooters. That was probably about 1968, 'cos we weren't allowed in some of the Greek coffee bars because they didn't like crowds of young people. But there was never the stuff that went on in Brighton or London or Manchester. York was quite a parochial place, there was mods and rockers but never any trouble between them. They often mixed at the same do's like English Martyrs' and Our Lady's and just got on together, there was never any gang violence.

It usually just ended up us congregating in town. The bikes weren't that reliable to go very far, but we might go to the coast now and again. As time went on that just fizzled out and I got more into the folk and rock scene with people of my age at Guppy's. Occasionally when we were 17, we'd try and get in pubs and try and get a pint of bitter, but there wasn't a great deal of drinking as such. You didn't want to go out and get tanked up, the most important part was just to be there, be seen, listen to the music and maybe meet a few girls.

When you analyse it, of course, although you were different from the establishment, you were all uniform in your difference but that's something you don't realise at the time. Whether it was in actuality or whether it was all perception, it seemed to be youth driven, it wasn't something that was being given to you. Now you feel quite privileged to have been around at the time when it was so ground breaking. And it's certainly a vindication of how good the music was in those days, the fact that they do repeat them again. You only have to look at a chart anytime from 1964 right through to the early 1970s, and out of the top 20 there'd probably be 15 that you would class as a supergroup whereas now the charts are made up of one-hit wonders and nonentities. When you think of all the talent about at those times, the Beatles, Rolling Stones, the Kinks, the Hollies, the Who, just innumerable top groups. They all had their individual sound, you instantly knew who it was. There's boy bands now, all the same.

CHAPTER THREE. LISTEN TO THE MUSIC:
The Rialto

Jack Prendergast who owned the Rialto Cinema and Ballroom made a significant contribution to music in York. He organised several seasons of popular concerts at the Rialto from the 1930s to 1961. In the 1950s he advertised a season of concerts with 'artists of national and international repute'. The first to appear was Dickie Valentine, quickly followed by Sidney Bechet, Stan Kenton's Band, Lionel Hampton and the Billy Cotton Band. The Empire had closed down in June 1956 so the Rialto was the only venue to stage such events.

In March 1957 the Platters and Eddie Calvert appeared, and jazz player Gerry Mulligan in the May. Sarah Vaughan appeared in June 1958 but unfortunately the hall was only half full, even though those who were there said the concert was 'wonderful'. In August 1958 there were rivals in the city with the Empire re-opening and presenting Eric Delaney And His Band, and Ronnie Aldrich of the Squadronaires at Christie's Ballroom, but it was the Rialto which sustained entertainment over the next few years. Tommy Steele appeared there in September 1958, with Cyril Stapleton And His Orchestra in October 1958.

As well as providing a wealth of music for the people of York Mr Prendergast also encouraged his own son, Barry Prendergast, now John Barry, to play music. He began playing trumpet with the Johnny Sutton Dance Band in the 1950s, then formed his own group the John Barry Seven, in which he sang and played. Three of his numbers which the group performed were We All Love To Rock, Rock A Billy Boogie and You're Mad. Barry went on to compose and arrange music for other singers like Adam Faith, and then for films. His best known arrangements are for the James Bond movies, but he has won Academy Awards for several other film scores.

The audience at the Rialto on March 10, 1957, got a surprise entertainment bonus, when they saw the first public appearance of the John Barry Seven only three weeks after their first rehearsal. The group intended to play only three numbers but the audience yelled for more and more and they played nine numbers in all, including Rock Around The Clock. John took most of the vocals as well as playing trumpet. Keith Kelly, a York shoe salesman sang a calypso, and the rest of the group were Mike Cox, Derek Myers, Ken Golder, Fred Kirk and Ken Richards, all from Scarborough or Leeds. The group was one of the first in the North of England to use an electric bass. Two months later in May, the group topped the bill in a two hour rock and skiffle session.

The second configuration of the John Barry Seven 1960. L to R - Jimmy Stead, Denis King, Dougie Wright, John Barry, Mike Peters, Vic Flick and Les Reed.

(Courtesy Norman Fowler)

The York Festival took place in the Assembly Rooms in June and July 1957 and the John Barry Seven were to 'demonstrate the art of rock 'n' roll'. The director Hans Hess said that the step had been taken to accommodate young people who wanted something of more popular appeal and less highbrow.

John Barry's sister, June Lloyd-Jones recalls:

It was always exciting at the Rialto. I remember as a tiny child, running down the gangways with my father, and there was the anticipation of something going to happen. I don't know if it's imbued in you, my father was always excited about what he did. He put every bit of his energy into anything he was doing so I think that was imparted to all of us. The live element is what was good in those days. Records were costly, and a lot of people wouldn't even have players. Business was good. When you saw these people, they were stars. Dad had a very good agent in London called Harold Fielding and they worked extremely well together. Dad used to tell me that they never actually had a contract to sign, just a handshake. And that was held right through. Can you imagine that these days? Shake of a hand?

Barry was always interested in music, bought a lot of records, He learnt counterpoint and harmony with Francis Jackson, the Master of Music at the Minster at that point. My father promoted his group and they were a huge success. I remember to this day the first time they played and the applause at the end. You thought, 'It's gonna be happening'.

Peter Stanhope spent three years involved with the Rialto as a photographer:

I remember plucking up the courage to go to the stage door of the Rialto with my camera and Jack Prendergast poking his head out the door, with his jaunty little trilby, double breasted pin stripe suit, and his bow tie, it probably had polka dots, and white carnation in his button hole. I said, 'I've come to ask if I can take some pictures of the stars that come to this theatre? Some people collect autographs, I collect photographs' It was something like, 'Well, lad, you better come in'. And I was through the door, and that's when it started, a wonderful three years. That was about 1957.

At the end of the show I would approach the stars, 'Do you mind if I take a picture of you for my collection?', and by that time I'd got the flash on, and usually I could get a picture behind the curtains before they went off the stage. Gradually I got to know the way the back stage runs, and the way that stars behave. I met all kinds of famous people, from the skiffle days through the last remains of the variety era. One of the first was Lonnie Donegan. I remember two things in my life that made me think, 'There's something beyond Mantovani and Ray Martin', and one was Blue Suede Shoes by Elvis Presley, and the other was something like Rocky Mountain Railroad by Lonnie Donegan. I remember a nice little picture of him, in a casual sweater, with his guitar across his knee. Then I photographed Johnny Duncan, Chas McDevitt, Nancy Whiskey, a few well known skifflers. On the first night I went there it was John Dankworth and Cleo Laine, and from the jazz category there was Count Basie, Duke Ellington, Sarah Vaughan, Ella Fitzgerald and Lionel Hampton, the drummer and vibraphone player who used mellow zylophones. This was really swinging jazz.

Then I struck up a deal with Melody Maker and New Musical Express. I'd take the pictures, 35 mm, 12 pictures to a roll, and would rush home to Fairfax Street, and I had a little dark room under the stairs. I'd develop the films, print them and send them off in the post.

Skiffle gave way to rock 'n' roll with Tommy Steele, Cliff Richard in the early days, and Marty Wilde. I was tall and slim and dark haired and had heavy spectacles, and he said, 'You look just like Buddy Holly'. By this time I'd met Jack Prendergast's son, Barry, because he was always back stage regaling the crowds with his favourite record collection. He had this idea to start his own rock band. The story goes it was originally called the John Barry Prendergast Seven, but Stacey Brewer, the entertainment reporter on the Evening Press in those days, says, 'Oh that name'll never run, there's too many words in that name, just make it John Barry'. So I took pictures of the Seven and the pictures went in the showcase outside the Rialto.

The coffee bar era was about 1956. In Goodramgate there was a Mr Taylor, who was a tailor. He started taking on the young crowd and making up these zoot suits, drainpipe trousers, and high button jackets, that suddenly became fashionable when the young lads decided that they wanted to get away from dad's three-piece suit. One half of his shop he made into a coffee bar, when there was no coffee bars outside Old Compton Street in London, which is where Tommy Steele started. The Two I's coffee bar. Mr. Taylor opened a coffee bar, and that's where we'd go and play records and things started in this town. Wimpy Bars were in the era of skiffle, the very first hamburgers.

Me and a mate, Kip Smith, decided to take lessons at the Court School of Dancing. On a Thursday night you had an hour's tuition, and then dancing afterwards. We could then practise on the girls who came along, and crush some toes. Saturday night was more of a party night with games and food. Stan Flood, the manager, was a wonderful old man, always very careful never to have any alcohol on the premises. It was an L-shaped ballroom, so there was a little corner hidden from the stage, where he played his records. But if he found you snogging round that corner, you were out on your neck. I remember this small slim person in a polka dot dress, and short cuban heels because you'd never dance in stilettos. This little lass could dance, she'd got medals for it, bronze, silver and gold, she was really good. One night, I summoned up the courage to ask her to dance and three years later, we got married.

Pete Varley also knew John Barry. They met in the Green Howards Army Band:

It was in Suez 1952, and I was told there was some lads come to join the band, and there was one from York. We got very friendly over there but he was always studying, every night. [John Barry took a correspondence course with an American arranger, Bill Russo, and was very committed to music even at this time]. *When I came out 18 months later, he said, 'Go and see me dad, at the Rialto'. I finally went in about 1954, and finished up working back stage at the Rialto.*

When Barry came out, he formed the John Barry Seven. They rehearsed in the Clifton Ballroom [also owned by Jack Prendergast]. *After so long they went professional, and I'd go round with them all over. That was the first Seven, 'cos they changed after three or four years. He was arranging music and writing, and then they started backing Adam Faith.*

The Rialto was the spot. Jack got Stan Kenton, the greatest band in the world, and Kenton played a John Barry arrangement that night. And Basie, I sat at the stage when he was on, and he was most interested when I told him I tried to play trombone, he sat and chatted and he was totally wonderful. But it was the start of the decline of the big bands then. He was so enthusiastic was Jack and he always looked after anybody who worked for him, 'cos he was on the boards years ago. Nobody else would have done it. He took risks, and some he'd win on, and others he'd lose on. He was so keen to keep the music live in York, and the Rialto was the only place. He kept going as long as he could and then in the end, bingo came in and he finally sold out to Mecca.

We went down for 6.5 Special in the studios at Twickenham and the recording with Joe Meek. Jack always booked us into the Garrick in Leicester Square and we lived like kings. I worked at the Theatre Royal for 15 years as well, late night bar concerts, groups and folk singers, after the Saturday night shows.

When Johnnie Ray came [to the Rialto] he was absolutely the rage. They were all queuing to see him but he didn't wanna know. They put him out through the back door, straight through the window of a taxi, and he was in the Station Hotel five minutes later. When Gerry Mulligan came, they couldn't find him, he was in the Edinburgh Arms, and he staggered down the side of the Rialto but when they put the saxophone in his hands, he went on and he played like magic.

Cliff Richard and the Drifters came and they decided to go round the fair, Cliff and Jet Harris, before the show. They were wearing white shoes and they'd got all dust off the fair at St. George's Field, and they painted their shoes, and went on with wet paint on their shoes. Jack would sit on a chair at the side of the stage watching what was going on. He was a big outgoing character and he'd tell you straight. He'd say, 'As long as your feet are comfortable, and you've food in your stomach, you're all right'.

One York man who loves John Barry's music is Dave Brough who played in a York group in the 1960s:

I'd gone to the Ri one night and he was stood up at the back, just to sort of say, 'Hello' 'cos we'd done one show there with one of the package shows. I'm a big fan of his now, his music is absolutely fantastic. He's a better arranger and writer than he was an actual musician. He was writing good stuff with the John Barry Seven but when you think of Dances With Wolves, Midnight Cowboy and Out Of Africa, it's beautiful. It amazes me when they write

Steve Cassidy 1964.   *(Courtesy Norman Fowler)*

music for each individual instrument in an orchestra, and make it all come to life. That's really talent.

June Lloyd-Jones recalls staying with her brother when he had just written the score for the film Chaplin:

And he said, 'June, I just want you to listen to this', and he put it on and within two minutes the tears were rolling down my face. I don't know what it is about his music but he just manages to get something that touches you. When David [her late husband] and I went on holiday, we'd hear some of Barry's music, even on the 'plane. And he sees the whole film when it's finished and then he writes. He's obviously getting ideas but he knows what he's writing to exactly. There's one film which he gets the most letters about of anything and that's a film called Somewhere In Time.

I had the privilege of meeting John Barry for the first time this year (2002) and watching him receive the Honorary Freedom of the City. During the press call he was seated at a piano in the foyer of the Assembly Rooms and as the photographers were setting up their equipment, I was able to observe him playing the piano and I saw how he was lost in his own world of music, a world which has brought pleasure to so many people.

Jack Prendergast sold the Rialto Cinema and Ballroom to Mecca in 1961. Bingo was the new craze. Young people would have missed out completely if it had not been for Don McCallion, who became general manager of the Mecca Casino in 1962 and ran a series of pop package shows. According to Stacey Brewer, the concerts were not staged by Mecca but Don personally hired the Rialto and staged the concerts. The first was in April 1962 when young singer Helen Shapiro wowed the audience. She had taken singing lessons from Maurice Burman, drummer with Geraldo's big band. June Lloyd-Jones explains why her father sold the business:

The bottom dropped out of the film business, people weren't cinema-goers anymore. And he was of an age he wanted to retire. It comes to a point, how much longer do you go on? The music wouldn't have sustained it 'cos that was one night a week, unless we had a very big orchestra which ran three nights. He'd worked hard all his life, he was 63 by then, which was young, he was still involved in the business with his other cinemas and with promoting Barry and being involved in the variety club, a whole range of other things until the day he died. He was 80 then and still active, a very clear-thinker. He was one of those people who was born before his time with ideas which are only now coming into being. I remember him saying, 'The way to be going is to have complete family entertainment, where they can take their children, where you've got a cinema, a restaurant, other activities going on'.

Rosemary Clegg (neé Carr) recalls the heady days of seeing groups at the Rialto. She was keen on dancing from a young age:

I joined the Court School of Dancing in High Ousegate and enjoyed ballroom dancing. We were taught to waltz and quickstep but occasionally had an evening with no lessons and just dancing. We learned to rock 'n' roll and jive, dancing to Elvis and Bill Haley. In 1960 I started going to the Garrison Youth Club in Fulford. I was about 13. To us girls, the music was the most important at the time. We could listen to up-to-date records three or four times a week, like Teenager in Love and Rubber Ball. We also had a bop on a Saturday night with local groups live.

I left school at 15, in 1962, and went to work at Nancy Lockwood's Hairdressers in Fishergate. The ladies who worked at the Rialto came to have their hair done at Nancy's and invited any of us to help sell programmes at the live band shows. In exchange we could watch the show for free.

I saw so many groups at that time that I can't remember them all. The Rolling Stones, Roy Orbison, the Bachelors, Joe Brown And The Bruvvers, the Small Faces and, of course, the Beatles. I felt so smug on the morning of a show, walking to work and passing queues of girls sitting on the pavement waiting for tickets, knowing I wouldn't have to queue and I could go in free. I remember being asked to help with crowd control which is very funny looking back. Four or five of us girls aged 15 to 19 to hold back crowds of screaming girls! Boy did they scream! All through the show and afterwards. The younger ones of us, including me, were very aggrieved not to be allowed up into the bar to meet the groups afterwards. You had to be 18 and a few of the older stylists were allowed to go and one even got a date with one of the Bachelors. I doubt if today's teenagers would put up with those rules. They would go anyway.

Up to the early 1960s, popular music was still heavily influenced by America. But in 1962 the emergence of the Beatles and the Mersey Sound meant that Britain was leading the music scene and exporting groups to the rest of the world.

In February 1963 Helen Shapiro was to top the bill at a package show at the Rialto, with the Beatles as second billing. Helen contracted flu and did not appear so singer Danny Williams took her place The Beatles only rated seven lines in a one-page review. The Beatles returned on March 13. Chris Montez topped the bill, followed by the Beatles then Tommy Roe. John Lennon was ill and could not play so the group performed for the only time in their career as a trio. After the show, George Harrison told Stacey Brewer, of the Yorkshire Evening Press, that the Beatles' next single, From Me To You, had been written by them in the coach as they travelled from York to Shrewsbury following the February concert.

On May 29 they came back again with Roy Orbison topping the bill and tickets were sold out two weeks before the concert. This time the Beatles were headline news. In only two months they had shot to fame and From Me To You, their first number one hit, remained in the charts for 21 weeks. (There is still some doubt whether Please Please Me was a British number one. It was top in three of the four published weekly charts, but only made the runner-up spot in the now widely quoted fourth.) Stacey Brewer wrote, 'The Beatles could have sung a Liverpool bus timetable and scored a hit'.

By their fourth and final appearance in York, on November 27, they were topping the bill. Arriving early in York in their Austin Princess limousine, they dropped in at the York Motel on Tadcaster Road for a meal. I lived in that area and remember a friend of my brother's dashing round to our house to tell my elder brother Mike that he'd heard the Beatles were at the motel. They ran down to the main road to try to catch a glimpse. I wanted to go too but was not allowed! Half an hour later he came back gloating because they had seen a car go by the Knavesmire with the Beatles inside. There was no-one else around so they knew that when they waved madly, they got a personal wave in return, which was more than the crowd at the Rialto got, as the Beatles were rushed in through the front door to avoid all the fans at the back door. Before the concert the police had to work out a special 'Beatle plan' and arrange traffic diversions. As well as 100 policemen, another 40 special constables were drafted in on 'Beatle duty' for the occasion. Some young people had started queuing at lunchtime in the hopes of seeing their heroes. The Rialto management had been sent hundreds of requests for autographs, and even a dress which the owner wanted the Beatles to sign so that she could raffle it for charity. There were 1800 fans inside the auditorium and another 400 outside jammed behind crush barriers chanting, 'We want Paul, George, John, Ringo' throughout the concert. In fact they stood for five hours in the cold. Stacey Brewer's review in the Yorkshire Evening Press said that, 'their final, frenzied frantic version of Twist And Shout threatened to lift the roof off the Mecca Casino'.

In January 1964 package shows continued at the Rialto and a special Merseybeat night was advertised with the Fourmost, the Merseybeats, and four other Mersey bands, as well as local group Steve Cassidy And The Escorts. Unfortunately the show ran into difficulties as the Fourmost did not appear and the Merseybeats were only there for one of the two showings. Delays between each act seemed to go on interminably and the audience had really had enough, some of them walking out before the end.

Three weeks later another beat show featured the first appearance of the Rolling Stones, Swinging Blue Jeans, Mike Sarne and John Leyton and this was a great success. The following month the chart-topping Hollies were there, supported by the Bachelors, the Chants and the Matadors. In March Jerry Lee Lewis appeared supported by Gene Vincent, the Animals, the Paramounts, the Nashville Teens and York's own group Tony Adams And The Viceroys.

Around this time my brother, as well as having seen the Beatles by chance, also met the Rolling Stones, by a quirk of fate. Mike was about 16 and I'd be 11 when, one Sunday, the rest of the family went to the coast for the day and Mike stayed home. When we returned he told us that he had found out that the Rolling Stones were staying at the Abbey Park Hotel on the Mount, just passing through after a gig in Scarborough. Mike had rushed there with a copy of one of their EP (extended play) records and they all signed it. He told us that Mick Jagger, Bill Wyman and Charlie Watts were very friendly and chatty, but Brian Jones and Keith Richards were aloof. Another lad who was there had a camera and took a picture of Mike with the group but we never got to see the photo. Mike invited them all to come to our house for tea but they politely refused, saying they had to be on their way. My parents were horrified at the thought that they might have returned home from Scarborough to find 'five long-haired louts sitting at the kitchen table'!

Advertisement for Gerry B And The Rockafellas from Ousebeat magazine 1964.
(Courtesy Adrian Holmes)

On November 11, after a seven-month break, pop package shows started again. The first was to star P J Proby, supported by the Pretty Things and the Barron Knights. But less than a fortnight before the concert, P J Proby had to pull out as there were 'appearance difficulties'. The show was saved when Chuck Berry was secured to take over top billing, but six days before the show, he too pulled out due to contractual problems. Another concert was arranged for December 16 with Herman's Hermits topping the bill, supported by the Honeycombs, the Poets and Hullaballoos. Herman's Hermits had flown in from Los Angeles and had not been to bed for 30 hours when they arrived. The final stage of their 'nightmare' journey was a six-hour drive to York through a pea soup fog. They arrived in York just as the first house was ending and had no time to test or balance their gear. Yet their performance was described as first class. In March 1965 a number of York groups played at the Mecca at a concert in aid of a number of Boys' Clubs. Gerry B And The Rockafellas, the Morvans, the Scorpions, the Shifters, Corvettes, Circle B, the Innominates and the Vampires gave their services. Miss R Cheetham, secretary of the 50-strong York Frankie Vaughan Fan Club, admitted that, 'I don't understand beat. But that's what the teenagers want and it's one way of raising money for charity'.

In December 1964 the assistant manager of Mecca, Eric Morley, announced that the company was going to spend £4 million on an expansion plan in the north, to include the York venue. The new dance hall was to be on waste land behind the Mecca Casino, and would be on stilts, at a cost of £500,000. It was to be called the York Locarno, and would accommodate 2,000 with room for 300 cars parked below. It eventually opened in the autumn of 1966, and was named Tiffany's but in 1967 after only eight months, it was obvious that it had failed and it closed. It re-opened in December 1967, as a club called the Cat's Whiskers for dining, dancing and cabaret.

Part of the building had been a casino, and re-opened on October 29, 1969. It became the Heartbeat Discotheque, open Monday to Saturday from 8pm to 1am, calling itself 'York's most luxurious In Place'. One of the regular attenders was Dave Byworth, who still runs reunions for the members:

It was the Beatles that got me going at first. I'd go to school dances at this little green hut at the bottom of Cornlands Road when we was about 12 [in 1964] and they played all t'chart music there. It was at the bop at New Earswick, the Tinned Chicken Club on a Saturday night, when I first heard soul music proper, when I was about 14. The first big impression was when I went to see Edwin Starr, in the Museum Rooms opposite the Museum Gardens. Once I'd seen him, I was hooked.

The Heartbeat was advertised in the Press months before it was open. We'd go to Guppys before that and it was a natural progression from there to the Heartbeat. It was out of this world for me personally. I think it was the music that they played - Otis Redding, Marvyn Gaye, Supremes, Four Tops, Temptations, Isley Brothers and some good rare records from America. We were on the dance floor all night, sometimes three or four nights a week. It was a hectic frolicsome time. You made friends, girlfriends, boyfriends, soulmates, people met there, they got married. Everyone was good to everybody and it was very close. I think we were all soul brothers and sisters somehow within the music.

Some wore flares but I wore parallel trousers with turnups, high-waisted ones like me grandad had, and long jackets with a big 16 inch vent up the back and lots of buttons on the cuffs. It was smart suits sometimes, the material was mohair and terylene, and the shirts were Ben Sherman button-down collars. We had fancy two-tone shoes, wet-look patent leather in green and red, or cream and chocolate. Hair was long, I remember having mine back-combed with big long sideboards. Big thick kipper ties with massive knots in them were worn. The girls wore mini-dresses of all colours and giant platform shoes or bib and brace hotpants.

The live bands were on at the Assembly Rooms, all-night dances with the Drifters, Johnny Johnson And The Bandwagon, Root And Jenny Jackson, JJ Jackson, the Fantastics. It was one heck of a time, we were just out every night. I met me wife at the Heartbeat. It closed in 1971 and they turned it into an over-21 club. A lot of people were really upset then, there was a lot of heartache and we moved on to the Hypnotique after that. These over-21 people ran what they call a northern soul club. We were not northern soul. It was more popular soul, the ones that got into the charts, but there was a lot of good artists that never got into the charts, rare group records that came over from America, the DJs played 'em in there. You'd be on the dance floor for two or three hours, it was real tail-feather shaking stuff. I think the music

Dave Byworth at the Heartbeat Soul Club reunion 2001. *(Courtesy Van Wilson)*

liberated us. It was a transcending feeling. We loved each other, but we didn't really know it. We know it a bit better now! Without music life would have been boring. It makes you feel absolutely great, you don't need drink or drugs, you just need music and it does summat for you. I mean people might get off on Mozart or somebody might get the same transcendent feeling listening to line dancing or country music if it's their thing. With soul, the words are talking about love all the time, that's what I felt was at the root of the Heartbeat.

The Heartbeat was a place where you could go on your own and there was always someone there you could be friends with. We were totally free in the Heartbeat, we could all do our thing. Johnny Walker appeared from Radio One on June 5, 1971 in the Heartbeat and it closed on October 10, and the last record was I'm Gonna Miss You. There was about ten clubs in York, but that was the one for us. Kids cried their eyes out when the Heartbeat closed because there was a Junior Heartbeat for kids that were of 13 and 14. We've got the Junior Heartbeat who come to our reunion dances now, plus the Senior Heartbeat. The place was something real special. I still miss it. I'd like to buy it now, take it back and promote dancing in York.

Dave's wife, Sue Byworth, recalls:

I'd go twice a week but Dave went every night. I wore hot pants, little tank-top fair-isle jumpers and blouses with big sleeves underneath them or wide trousers and platform shoes. Carmen Gear jeans, with high waistbands and I had a long black leather coat. You could go on your own and you wouldn't feel out of place and you wouldn't be frightened because it was one big happy family. You couldn't do that now.

Sue's friend, Prue Hartley, enjoyed the club and remembers groups of people crying when it closed. It was important to Prue because she met her husband Neil there:

We had what was called a feather cut, short on top and longer at the sides. We used to call it the Tufty Club. The only sad occasion I remember was the night they announced Tammy Turrell had died and everybody was heartbroken. She sang with Marvin Gaye a lot. I can remember sobbing.

I used to listen to pirate radio all the time. That's where I first heard soul music and I thought it was marvellous. It was either that or real heavy, Black Sabbath, Deep Purple and Pink Floyd. We'd all go to Scarborough on bank holidays. Pile on the train, or if you were with a scooter crowd, you'd be on the back. We had portable tape players and we'd put a tape on with Motown stuff and stand around in a big circle on the beach at Scarborough. And

Sunday afternoons we'd go in the Museum Gardens with our tape players. There'd be little groups of people all over and there'd be Motown music wherever you went.

Sue's husband, Neil Hartley, started off in the coffee bar scene:

I started tagging on with me elder brother to the coffee bars in town, the Acropolis and Dinos. Then we started going to nightclubs and the main one was the Heartbeat. That particular club and that crowd were all into Motown and American imports, it was worth your weight in gold was a good American record. We'd frequent the Centre Bar in town, the Hypnotique, Intercom and Old World. There was plenty to do on a night. You started off with mods and rockers and we'd have a good laugh with one another. Then rockers went one way and we moved into this soul. We went from the scooter crowd with parkahs on, into suits. Just called smoothies.

Stephen Flint was a Heartbeat member and he loved dancing:

I came from a musical family. My maternal grandparents had a business in York called York Piano Service and Records opposite Clifford's Tower. I was a chorister at St Paul's on Holgate Road until me voice broke and me father worked for Selecter Northern Records from 1960 so we got all the free records. In 1966 he transferred to Polydor, part of a German company, Deutsche Gramophone Gesellschaft, but they were also distributors of Stax and Atlantic labels, the soul labels with Otis Redding, Carla Thomas, Aretha Franklin and Wilson Pickett. So I got demos before they actually came out. About 1968, I'll have been 15, we could play records at Lowfields School. I remember playing I Spy For The FBI by Jame O'Thomas. It starts with a really haunting sax solo and everybody came flooding into the room asking what it was. That's how I got into soul music and went to the Enterprise Club and Neal Guppy, the owner, banned a certain section of us for popping pills, stimulant pills, which were technically illegal. When the Heartbeat opened, I was there the very first night with a few friends and I just lived and died there for quite a long time. We'd go there first then over to Manchester to a legendary club called the Twisted Wheel which was all night Saturday night and then a coffee bar in Manchester Piccadilly Gardens called the Blue Dolphins on Sunday morning. Then an all-dayer at Oldham called the Top Twenty. Sunday evening we went home and back to work on Monday morning knackered.

The term Northern Soul was coined by a music journalist that used to like the blues and soul, a guy called Dave Godding in about 1970 so the reason for it was that places like the Wheel and the soul all-nighters were still playing 1960s stuff 'cos rare stuff was still being found in America from obscure artists and they came over here. In the south they'd gone on to the more funky music, but northern soul stayed with the 1960s for ages. I suppose the height of its popularity was at the mid-1970s Wigan Casino.

There was a DJ in York called Richard Walker, he'd play chart stuff like Spirit In The Sky, Black Night, Paranoid and another guy from Leeds played soul stuff. A school friend called John Steel took over from him, and he was getting imports that were being played at the Wheel in Manchester, and that started the soul explosion at the Heartbeat.

I love music. I've got very diverse musical tastes, I like sacred music and I sing in choirs off and on. I've gotta sing bass now, I can't manage tenor. I like Brahms' Requiem and Handel, and Callas. I love the blues as well, I'm a blues guitarist but not in a band, just for myself.

In 1970, Coca-Cola had a national dance competition and the heats were held at the Cat's Whiskers. The manager of the Heartbeat dragged a few of us out to go into the dancing contest there, and I won. I went down to the finals in London but I didn't get anywhere. It was held at the Lyceum Ballroom in the Strand and I'd gone to buy a new pair of leather-soled loafers in a King's Road shop. The dance floor was like glass in the Lyceum Ballroom and with these shiny brand new leather soles on, I was just like Bambi, I couldn't move. They played over and over again Edwin Starr's Twenty Five Miles at pedestrian pace, and they played it live, it was pretty uninspiring but a good experience. But it was interesting, the judges were Cathy McGowan from Ready Steady Go and Lionel Blair, the television tapdancer.

CHAPTER FIVE. WHOLE LOTTA SHAKIN' GOING ON: The Early 1960s

As skiffle and early rock 'n' roll waned, beat groups began springing up all over. The format of three guitarists, lead, rhythm and bass, and a drummer, started with the Shadows. Some groups featured a solo singer, and others followed the Beatles format, four musicians who also handled the vocals.

The jazz singer, George Melly, performed at the Cavern in Liverpool and wrote how one lunchtime, he and his band had gone for a break, and returned to find 'amplifiers on the band-stand', something ground-breaking! This may have been the Beatles or another Mersey group but it astounded the older musicians. One of the amplifiers would have been the Vox AC30, which was popularised by the Beatles and which is still considered desirable today. Pete Willow talks about Dick Denny who was the brains behind the Vox AC30, one of the most famous amplifiers in the world:

He's a jazz musician who drew the circuitry for the AC30. At first it was the Vox AC15, but they were not loud enough and so they manufactured the

The Stalkers c1963. L to R - John Olive, Dave Nettleship, Michael McNeill, Terry Herbert, Ron Allpress. *(Courtesy John Olive)*

Mal Dyman And The Tycoons. Boulevard 1964. L to R - unknown, Terry Herbert, Mal Dyman (Mal Addison), Ron Allpress, John Olive. *(Courtesy John Olive)*

AC30. Dick Denny went on stage with the Beatles as technical adviser in the mid 1960s. He was to meet up with the Beatles when they were playing in Scarborough before they went to America, he was there to test the big Vox amplifiers, the Vox AC100s. He passed through York and stopped off to visit Scotts in Petergate to buy some York ham.

He sent me one of the original circuits for the Vox. I asked him why he wired speakers the way he did, with two eight-ohm speakers up to 16. He said that he had wired them two different ways, turned his back and got his technician to play both and his ear told him in the end which way to do it, not the technology.

One familiar complaint heard in York was that the city did not provide a young people's dance hall like the Astoria Ballroom in Leeds and the Spa in Bridlington. Beat groups starting out would play in youth clubs and church halls and then graduate on to pubs. But as the 1960s progressed, there were other options. 'York's answer to the Cavern', the Boulevard on Tadcaster Road, held its grand opening in December 1963 with guest stars Peter Jay And The Jaywalkers supported by Steve Cassidy And The Escorts. There was also the Assembly Rooms for those who could afford it, and it hosted a Christmas Beat Carnival featuring Steve Cassidy And The Escorts and Mal Dyman And The Tycoons.

Mal Dyman And The Tycoons at the White Horse 1964. L to R - Mike Swales, John Olive, Terry Herbert, Mal Dyman, Ron Allpress.   *(Courtesy John Olive)*

The Tycoons had started out in 1962 as the Stalkers Guitar Group and initially supported dance bands like Doug Green And His Band at Ben Johnson's Cricket Club Big Carnival Dance. The Stalkers found they were getting very popular and they had a number of bookings at the Coffee House in Tadcaster where a poster invited people to 'Stomp to the Stalkers'.

By the spring of 1963, the group had become Mal Dymans And The Stalkers, and were playing at an Easter Jive at Acomb Church Hall, and the village hall in Copmanthorpe for a 'Coffee House Dance, twisting and twanging to Mal Dymans and the Stalkers'. Two weeks later a Bonanza Ball invited the audience to 'Hop with Mal Dyman and the Stalkers', and enjoy 'stampin', stompin', stalkin' and smoochin'.

Young people had to be earning a reasonable wage to afford to go to these events. Some had their own way of seeing the groups. Pete Willow remembers the lively music scene in York in the early 1960s when he was only a young teenager:

I remember jumping up and looking through the window of the Burns, the Londesboro' and the White Horse. I was too young to drink then. You could

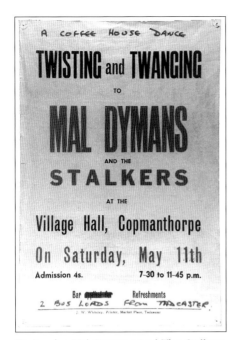

A COFFEE HOUSE DANCE

TWISTING and TWANGING

TO

MAL DYMANS

AND THE

STALKERS

AT THE

Village Hall, Copmanthorpe

On Saturday, May 11th

Admission 4s.   7-30 to 11-45 p.m.

Bar   Refreshments
2 BUS LOADS FROM TADCASTER

J. W. Whiteley, Printer, Market Place, Tadcaster

Poster for Mal Dymans And The Stalkers
1963 at Copmanthorpe Village Hall.
(Courtesy John Olive)

hear the music but you couldn't go in.

We'd go to the Assembly Rooms but we never had any money. I earnt £2 16s, but you spent everything you'd got, you couldn't save anything. So we'd climb over the gates of the Judges Lodgings, up the drainpipe, along a big wall and drop down at the back. One night we got in before anyone else and they couldn't understand it, we were the only ones in there and they hadn't opened the front doors! I saw Pinkertons Assorted Colours, Heinz, the Lovin' Spoonful, Alan Bown, the Foundations. Then we'd go to the Boulevard but we couldn't afford to pay. We'd drop in through the top of the gents' toilets, but it had a slippery slide down and you'd nearly end up going into the toilet if you didn't land right. Heaven knows what people thought when we came in through the roof. They were just stood there and we'd appear, three or four of us descend down from the roof and just walk off!

Colin Carr began playing in 1956 when he was 14. He had started on the trumpet bugle in a cadet band and later the side drum. When some friends got together to play Shadows numbers, he was invited to bring his drum down to the rehearsal:

I wasn't very good, but there was an advert for a drum kit for £15, and I bought that. I began to learn by watching drummers on television, and I'd go round town and watch drummers in groups. I never had a lesson, but having played the military drumming, you knew how to hold your sticks, and how to control them, so it helped although it was a different style.

My first kit was a mixture of bits from different kits, the bass drum probably a John Grey and the snare drum a Premier. I covered them with Fablon, so they were all matching. First of all our group was the Four Aces, and in about a year we had four rhythm guitarists before we got the one that stopped with us for five years. We changed the name to the Clubmen, because the lead

Barry Adams And The Swingalongs 1964. L to R - Norman Hughes, sax, Barry Adams, vocals, Steve Bennett, drums, Ian McLaren, bass, Geoff Oakland, lead guitar.

(Courtesy Tony Adams)

guitarist had a guitar called a Vox Clubman. There was my best pal, Graham Cambridge, who died four years ago, David Bignall and Anton Betteridge. First of all we just played instrumentals, 'cos none of us thought we were good enough to sing. Anton worked at the slaughterhouse, which was on the site of Asda. His boss was very interested in our group and let us practise in one of the sheds amongst all the dead animals. It was awful! There was a pub called the Spittlebeck up Malton Road, now a restaurant, and we approached the landlord and said, 'Could we come and play? I think it was £2 shared by all of us.

A couple of months later, Anton says, 'I'll try singing', so he did about three songs and we went into the White Horse quite a lot, and there was Barry Adams And The Swingalongs playing five nights a week. But they moved on to the club circuit. At first the clubs wouldn't accept groups, they wanted somebody in a black coat singing The Road To Mandalay. They wouldn't have these banging and crashing Teddy Boys, playing drums and guitars. But eventually groups became popular even with older people, and they had to let groups in on the club scene.

71

The Clubmen at York Theatre Royal 1963 in the play Semi-Detached. L to R - actor James Beck, David Bicknall, Graham Cambridge, Colin Carr and Anton Betteridge.
(Courtesy Colin Carr)

THE HORNETS

The Boys with Stings in their Strings

BURNS HOTEL
Tuesday and Wednesday
LONDESBRO' HOTEL
Friday and Saturday

Yorkshire Evening Press advertisement from early 1960s for The Hornets. *(Courtesy Colin Carr)*

We approached the landlord of the White Horse and said, 'Can we stand in?' So occasionally we would. We knew ten instrumentals and three songs but as time went on we improved and got a residency, once a week, at the White Horse, and then our big chance came when a new landlady, Barbara Fletcher, took the Londesboro' in 1962. She put an advert in the paper, 'Group wanted, Friday and Saturday'. We applied and she gave us the job. So it was big time then! We bought ourselves blue jackets, the thing was to look smart, black trousers, silk ties and black and white shirts. After a couple of years, we all got brown suits in a certain material that when you got lights on it, glowed red. We were really proud of these suits and I kept mine for years.

In August 1963 the play Semi-Detached was on at the Theatre Royal produced by Donald Bodley and starring the actor James Beck, who later found fame in the hit TV series Dad's Army. Colin's group, the Clubmen, appeared in the theatre each night to play from one of the boxes during the performance:

The Clubmen played up to Anton getting married in 1964, and we couldn't replace him with a singer-guitarist, so we moved to a five-piece group. We got Col Smith, from Bilbrough, as the singer and a lead guitarist, Bri Smith, from Gerry B And The Hornets and we became the Hornets. Gerry had left to join the Rockafellas. We spotted Col in the Castle, there was a resident group there, the Borderbeats, and he'd get up and sing just one number every Saturday night, Bits And Pieces. He was only 16. We liked his style, he was really confident, so we asked him to join.

73

BEN JOHNSON CRICKET CLUB

CARNIVAL DANCE

CHURCH HALL, ACOMB

FRIDAY, 19th OCTOBER

Non-stop Dancing 9 p.m. to 1 a.m.

DOUG GREEN and his Band

supported by "The Stalkers" Guitar Group

Balloons   Competitions   Excellent Spot Prizes

TICKETS 2/6

OBTAINABLE FROM CLUB MEMBERS

Tea, Coffee and Biscuits on Sale 10 p.m. to midnight

NO ADMISSION WITHOUT TICKET AFTER 11 p.m.

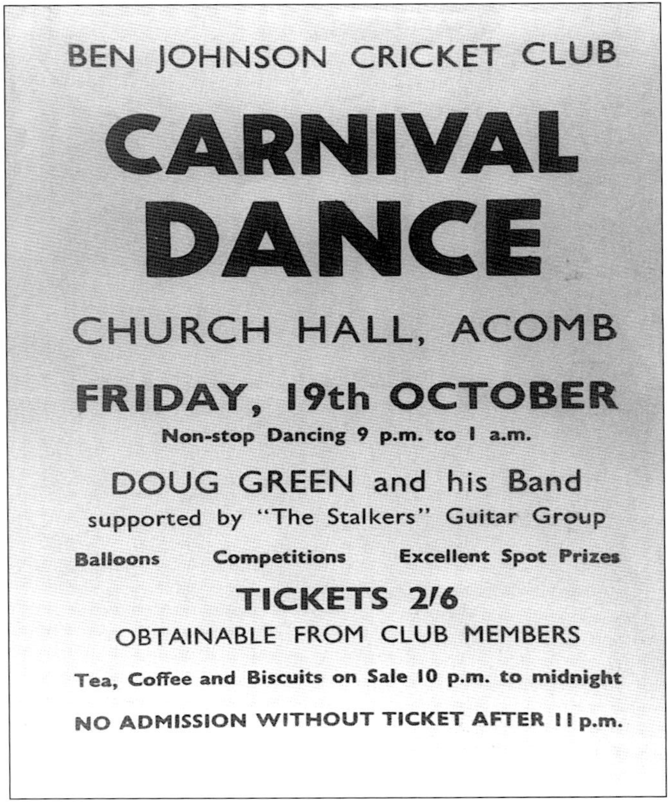

Poster for Carnival Dance at Acomb Church Hall with Doug
Green and his Band, supported by The Stalkers 1963.
(Courtesy John Olive)

ACOMB CHURCH HALL

EASTER MONDAY
APRIL 15th
8.00 - 11.30

EASTER JIVE

featuring

MAL DYMAN

and the

STALKERS

admission
at 3/-
door

by entertainments inc.

Poster for Acomb Church Hall - Mal Dyman and Stalkers c1963.
(Courtesy John Olive)

The music generally in the 1960s was happy music, it wasn't serious, so when you went into a pub, it would be packed out, and everybody that went in would like the music. If you've got music which would give you a lift, obviously the atmosphere was just buzzing. When something came out in the charts, it was a race to see who could get it off the quickest and the best. I got interested in the Shadows, the first drummer was Tony Meehan, and I copied his laid back style. Then later on when the Mersey Sound started, I'd probably play the same style as Ringo, I'd get it beat for beat, as he would play it. We formed a bond in the group, and sometimes we'd practise six nights a week. There were groups that were real popular, in the limelight, Barry Adams And The Swingalongs, they were more rock 'n' roll and Elvis Presley, Gerry B And The Rockafellas, Steve Cassidy And The Escorts, he liked Buddy Holly but his heart was in folk music, then the second rate groups which weren't so well known but equally good. At the other end you got the 16 year olds just starting and like us when we started, weren't very good, and then you got groups who were practising, but never made it to a gig. In the town centre there'd be six main pubs, the Coach and Horses, we called it the Big Coach, on the corner of Nessgate, and the Castle, which was opposite. A singer called Ray Duvall, was there for a few years. [His real name was Raymond Lindley and he was called York's own Sinatra]. The White Horse in Coppergate, the Burns, that's now the Hansom Cab, the Londesboro' in Petergate and the White Swan in Goodramgate.

The early 1960s was the best time for me. The music was new then. The rest of the time couldn't compare with it, it was just scratching the surface. In 1963, you could tell what they were singing about, the lyrics were simple, and the melody was the sort you could whistle. I liked the Beatles, Hollies, Searchers, I was into nice melody. The peak of it was short lived although the legacy has gone on.

I was fortunate enough to see the Beatles. Anton's boss, Malcolm, wasn't short of a bob or two. He booked a block of eight seats, and he took the Clubmen, and his wife and two children, and they were really good seats. It's an experience I'll never forget. They were so famous then, they took the world by storm, and you just couldn't believe you were so near to them, when they came running on to the stage. The way they announced it, the curtains went back, there were just drums on a rostrum, all gleaming and shining, and three guitars, and the compere would be teasing you, waffling on. Then, 'And here they are, the Beatles', and they'd run on, and it was just deafening. The girls were absolutely out of their minds. And you were sat there, so involved in it, you're struck dumb. It just got you. I've never felt like that since, so emotionally involved.

We played in Selby three nights a week, we'd get the train and travel in our brown suits. Four of you dressed the same, you felt so famous walking along the platform. We'd get to the Golden Lion and as we walked through the door, all the heads'd turn. 'The group's here', you were like a big star walking in.

There was a family called Russells, they were the Ousebeats. Mick Russell, the drummer, Jim Russell, and his sister Linda, she sang.

The group were formed in 1962 and as well as the Russells, they also featured Tony Lee on rhythm guitar, Stephen Harkuss on bass and Sheila Dobbin as the other vocalist. They were managed by Mrs Eve Russell and appeared on Opportunity Knocks in August 1965. The Russells' neighbours promised that the whole street would be watching and voting for the group.

Colin goes on to say:

There was a girl in Selby, in a group called Susan And The Spacebeats and she played the organ. But it seemed to be a male domineered scene, the groups.

There's some really good guitarists in York like Geoff Oakland who was with the Swingalongs. They were playing at the White Horse and his living accommodation was a Hillman Minx, parked down the passageway! I remember they were on at a barbecue at Skelton, in this big marquee, and there's a stage but only half the gear. I says, 'Aren't the Swingalongs playing?' 'They were, but two men came along and took the equipment away'!

The Wild Man [on Tadcaster Road] was a popular venue, but difficult to get to. Me and my pal would go on the bus but you had to leave early. The first time I went it was the Rockafellas with Johnny Newcombe, before Gerry B, and they were on a stage in the corner, two of them in scarlet jackets and two in violet jackets, and a light on them. It looked so professional, just like the Palladium. When Gerry joined them, they played all Mersey Sound and it was always my ambition to join them. They split up and reformed a couple of months later, and I was the drummer but Gerry changed the style. He was aiming to go into showbusiness as an impressionist, so instead of being a beat group, which was my music, they were doing comedy and although I achieved my ambition, they'd changed the style, and it wasn't really what I wanted to do. Gerry dressed up as various characters, and did impressions. A bit of music and then it would stop, and then he'd throw a cigarette in the air and catch it!

Gerry B went on to become the comedian Dustin Gee. In 1986 he sadly died at the age of 43, having collapsed on stage with a heart attack. Many York musicians from the 1960s attended his funeral at St Oswald's in York, which was overflowing and afterwards some of the musicians who were there hit on the idea of starting reunions. Colin recalls:

Afterwards we went over to the Gimcrack and we were talking about the old times and one of the lads, Mick Mills, had a pub at Bilbrough. He says, 'Why don't you come to my pub, we'll have a reunion?' So he put it in the paper and we went, not expecting what was going to happen, but lots of people turned up, the pub was absolutely heaving, and the music went on and on. All those lads who hadn't played for years got up and did a bit. We were meeting people you hadn't seen for 30 years.

The next year we had a really good reunion at the Wild Man and people came from all over who weren't even connected with groups. We did another at the Promenade Club and then one in Huntington Club. It holds about 350 people and I think 500 people turned up. It was a charity and everybody played for nothing. Whereas the original reunions were like a jam session, people just getting up, what we tried to do after about three years was to get the original groups together as near as possible.

One of the first groups on the scene in York was Barry Adams And The Swingalongs who were resident at the White Horse in Coppergate in April 1961. In 1963 they made their first broadcast on the BBC. By then, the group consisted of singer Barry, Norman Hughes on sax, Geoff Oakland on guitar, Steve 'Sticks' Bennett on drums, and Ian McLaren on bass. Ian had come to York in 1960 and was the only one of the group to have a GCE in music. Geoff had the reputation of being one of the fastest guitarists in Yorkshire and spent many nights practising until 3am. Norman Hughes had played sax with the National Youth Orchestra at the Royal Festival Hall, and could also play clarinet and harmonica. Steve had played drums on television in Athens while there with the army and had also played with a service band, so there was a lot of experience in the group. In an interview in 1963 Barry Adams said he thought that the reason music hall was dead was because entertainment had gone into the pubs and working men's clubs. He gave an example of being booked at a music hall venue but on arrival, the manager pointed to the group's guitars and told them to, 'Get 'em out'. Barry said that if such places did not welcome beat groups they would soon be left empty.

In May 1964 the group were set to go professional and got a recording contract with Philips, with Barry and Geoff Oakland writing both sides of the first of their six-record deal. Unfortunately their drummer Steve Bennett could not get released from the RAF who refused to let him buy himself out as they were short of air-frame mechanics. The group's manager Tony Stokes (who had been instrumental in making sure the group looked smart and had good equipment) was quoted as saying, 'If Steve is not released it will shatter the chances of all the lads. It might cost £200 to get him out but whatever the cost, and I am ready to sell my house if need be, we want him out'. A month later the group had changed their name to Danny Adams And The Challengers and it looked like great success was on the horizon when their manager signed a contract for four years with the Noel Gay agency, worth £48,000. On July 25 the group appeared on Thank Your Lucky Stars, the first York group to appear on national television apart from the well-known John Barry Seven. In July 1964 their first record Bye Bye Baby came out.

York's MP Charles Longbottom agreed to help with problems over the drummer. He asked in the House of Commons how Steve Bennett could be released from the air force, claiming that because Steve had gone straight into the RAF from school, he had not realised that he had a talent for music. He had another four and a half years to serve but desperately wanted to buy himself out and be professional with the Challengers. The RAF said that they needed him as they were short of men in his particular trade so could not release him unless it were on acute compassionate grounds and that was the end of the story.

For dances in bigger halls, many beat groups started out supporting dance bands, such as the 1963 York Rugby Union Football Club who held a carnival dance at the Merchant Taylors' Hall with dancing to the Cavaliers Dance Orchestra, supported by the Deneagers, a skiffle group. Within only a couple of years, it was the other way round and their dance was held at Bettys Bar without a dance band, only cabaret by the Deneagers Skiffle Group. Advertisements for groups in the early 1960s used phrases like 'twist and shake non-stop to Tony Adams And The Viceroys', 'shake and twist to Roy And The Zeroes', 'Rendezvous for the bright young set, spotlight on the new big beat wave, Gerry B And The Rockafellas, and the Astrals at the Assembly Rooms'.

Dave Brough was a member of the Deneagers. His uncle Stan Brough was well known in York as a band leader in the 1930s, and Dave's father Geoff played drums in the band. Dave recalls how he started singing:

Dad used to take theatricals in from the Empire and one of the acts that stayed with us was a singer. He'd get jobs in clubs round Leeds, Bradford and Wakefield and would take me to see him. I'd be about 13. Unbeknowing to the audience in these working men's clubs, we would have rehearsed a number at home and just after he'd finished part of his act, he would get the club audience to sing a couple of songs with him. Then he'd make out he'd heard me above the rest, get me up as though we were complete strangers and say, 'Right, how would you like to sing?' So he'd sing and I would harmonise

The Deneagers 1955 at St Maurice's Church Hall. L to R - Maurice Bradford, Brian Morrison, Dave Brough, Mick Jennings. *(Courtesy Dave Brough)*

and at that time of night, the audience would think it was pretty good. And then he let me sing a couple of songs on me own and we'd clear off out of there before people sussed us out. Johnny Kenwood. I wish I knew where he was now. It was his old beat-up guitar that he gave me, and I got a book on how to play the guitar and picked it up. I was in St Maurice's choir and we formed this little band.

Maurice Bradford who was in the choir, and older than us, played bass. Two mates from school, Brian Morrison would play drums and Mick Jennings would play his mother's washboard and thimbles. I decided I'd ask at a working men's club if we could play and this was the Anglers' Club. We did that and then a couple of dances as a back-up for ballroom dancing. There'd be a proper band there and we'd get up in the interval and do a few songs.

This guy called Ray Broadhead, he went under the name of Ray Charles and they did all the Cliff Richard. I played with them and I had just got this new guitar and I was too loud for 'em. They gave me a felt plectrum to cut the sound down! I was with them for a while and Johnny Newcombe asked if I would join his group because they were losing their vocalist. In those days it was Elvis, It's Now Or Never and Ready Teddy but also Bobby Darin stuff, like Dream Lover.

We played at the Burns, it was as rough as anything. One night I was playing, just got this new guitar and I was frightened to death it was going to get scratched. In those days they had a waiter service, and these five waiters were heavies, they were gorillas. Some soldiers came in from Strensall and started creating bother, and one of the big lads went over. 'Just cool it, because people wanna listen'. He warned him twice and then a fight broke out. It was like a John Wayne movie. I jumped off the raised area and ran with me guitar to the other side of the room, and turned me back on the fight, holding my guitar against the wall. Can laugh about it now but it made me feel ill.

We were doing shows every night. I was an apprentice and my boss found out that I wasn't going to night school and he give me the ultimatum, either I stopped or I lost my job. So that was it. But it was great to sing with proper musicians, a treat.

Barry Starkey began playing when he was at Nunthorpe Grammar School:

I got blissfully roped in but I got so involved that it was untrue and I really enjoyed it. The 1960s, I still think, is the best period for music. At school they split you into alphabetical order on the desks and in 1961 we had Shepherd, Sims, Starkey and Sutcliffe in order. Alfie Shepherd got a guitar, and then Dave Sutcliffe decided he wanted to play, he used to be right into t'Beatles so he bought a bass, and Mal Sims got a rhythm guitar and they said, 'You'll have to be drummer'. We were the Four S's.

The only entertainment for the night other than a glass of still orange was to try and get Radio Luxembourg tuned in on the old box radio. So we decided, 'We're gonna go for it'. We had Watkins 20 watt amps and practised in the garage at the back of me dad's house in Jute Road. We got a girl called Brenda to sing for us so we became Brenda Church and the Four S's. Then we were the Roosters.

We ended up as the resident band at the Acomb Hotel Saturday nights. I was 16. It was good clean fun, and we'd fill that place, only a small room, but we'd get 200 in. My cousin, John Starkey, got interested and could sing quite well, and we became Johnny Starr And The Jetsons. St James the Deacon, that was another of our main venues. We played with Steve Cassidy, his second backing group.

I had a two-tone Ford Zephyr at 17, it looked good, light blue at the top, fawn at the bottom. We'd all go out Friday night and put in a bob, petrol was 4/11d.

We had some great nights.

The first lighting system that Neal Guppy had at Walmgate, I built it. I was into electronics. I was reading this magazine Practical Electronics and they said you get this lighting system, buy these bits and alter the lights to flash in time with the music. I bought it in a box, ordered trans-formers and transistors. We used to do it in t'group for a bit and I sold it to Guppy. It was intense that period, three to four years and York suddenly went bananas.

The Red Roosters 1964 at Acomb Hotel. L to R - Dave Sutcliffe, Barry Starkey, Brian Burley, Gordon Johnson, singer, and Mal Sims at front. *(Courtesy Barry Starkey)*

Between April 1963 and May 1964, Barry played at the Acomb Youth Club, Westfield Youth Club, Osbaldwick Church Hall, Leeman Road Club, Tang Hall Youth Club, Poppleton Road Club, Huntington Club, St James The Deacon, Wigginton Recreation Hall, Yorkshire Yeomanry Dinner at the Ainsty, Dodsworth Hall at Poppleton for a reception, the Londesboro' Arms, dance at Our Lady's, Fulford Barracks Canteen, St Aelred's Youth Club and a dinner for Shepherds at the Ainsty.

Colin Berriman is widely regarded as one of the best drummers around and he has been very dedicated since teenage years:

I had three uncles, Harry Berriman played drums, Arthur Berriman played trumpet and Oswald Berriman played the organ. On a Sunday afternoon on the bowling green they always had a brass band. I loved standing behind this band, the noise of the drums, and the clashing of the cymbals, that was such an excitement for me. My uncle being a drummer meant he always had a drum kit at home, and I used to tinkle on that. I was about 12 and I pestered my father for a drum kit for Christmas. He says, 'No, it'll be a nine-day wonder'. I says, 'I'm really keen'. Anyway, he bought this drum kit, and it

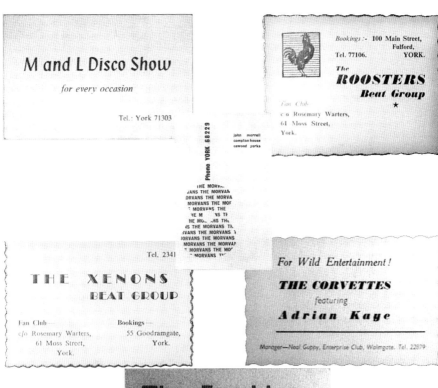

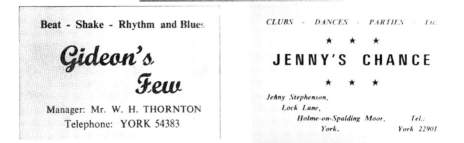

Cards advertising 1960s beat groups, the Xenons, Jenny's Chance, the Roosters, the Everblues, the Cutters, the Corvettes, Gideon's Few, the Morvans, the M & L Disco.

(Courtesy Barry Starkey)

didn't sound like anything I heard on records, so because the sound was terrible it ended up in my bedroom, and my father says, 'There you are, I told you so'. Then my uncle, came down, and tuned 'em up, damped them down, and put cellotape all over them, and they sounded quite respectable.

Soon Colin was playing with the York City Harmonica Band, but quickly moved on to other things:

One Sunday afternoon the concert chairman of this particular working men's club, came up and said to the band leader, 'Would you mind if we borrow your drummer for Saturday night? Our regular drummer's been taken ill'. And he says to me, 'If you help us out this weekend we'll pay you 10/- for Saturday night, and 12/6d for Sunday night'. That was my first public engagement, and I was so nervous, the worst two nights of my life. It was a very good grounding, playing with these two wonderful musicians I worked with in this club, it taught me discipline, it taught me all the old time dances, the ballroom dances, which over the years became invaluable. The more experience you get, you can then apply for different kinds of work. On piano it was Stan Seeds, and saxophone, Ben Ryan. Two lovely people. And that's when I met Johnny Newcombe, he heard me play and offered me a job with his band.

After I'd being playing drums for four or five years, I got to the age of 18 and went to music lessons in Leeds. I was quite dedicated, and I wanted to become a proficient musician. If you're working in a big band, it's quite important the drummer reads, and drum music, you're reading four lines at once. The bottom line as the bass drum line, the second line is the snare drum line, the third line is your high hat cymbal, the top line is your cymbals, or the third line may be your tom tom figures. But you're reading four lines and your four limbs are doing separate rhythms.

I liked watching Rob Illing, he was a very good drummer. I had a lot of respect for some of the drummers in York that worked in the big bands. Ken Kenyon, Ray Phillips, Leo Burrows, I got great pleasure out of sitting at the back of a dance hall, listening to them. I love rock 'n' roll, I loved the 1960s, but my great stuff was always big band music and jazz. Buddy Rich was my favourite drummer. In more recent years, Dennis Chambers, Gene Krupa. After a Buddy Rich concert you were so enthused you used to dash home and get your sticks out and practise.

Music brought a lot of people together. All the groups then played in pubs and I was lucky enough to play in the Escorts with Steve Cassidy. There was a reason for playing to a good standard, because that drummer down the road

Trio at Phoenix Working Men's Club 1959. L to R - Colin Berriman, drums, Stan Seeds, piano, Ben Ryan, sax. *(Courtesy Colin Berriman)*

was a bit better than you, so you practised harder to get as good. It was very healthy, very exciting.

We'd do a lot of venues in the West Riding, in those days quite a lot of swimming baths would board the pool over in the winter months and make them into dance halls. It was either Doncaster or Barnsley Baths and we were on the same show as the Beatles. They were just starting to creep in then. I was tuning up and faffing on, and Ringo Starr said to me, 'That's a real lovely roll that you do, it's so smooth'. And so I showed Ringo Starr how to do a roll!

Colin went to France when the Escorts decided to play over there:

With a girl singer from Harrogate, Sylvia Leon, a cornet player and a guitarist, we went to the American forces bases. It was quite an experience, our piano player was acting as band leader, and our wages were paid to him and collected from a post office wherever you were working. After the first month we'd run up a great big hotel bill and a food bill on the American base. We said to the band leader, 'It's pay day, get yourself to the French post office and get our wages'. He went, but he didn't come back. We were stuck there. No money. Anyway this club we worked at, it was quite good, 'cos our girl singer would sing quite a lot of Tamla Motown, and soul and they loved her to bits and thought she was wonderful. So we explained the problem and

Sylvia Leon with unknown girl singer at Wetherby Town Hall 1962. Steve Cassidy on right at back. *(Courtesy Colin Berriman)*

the sergeant at the club says, 'We'll have a word with your agent and see if we can get you booked back here for another month', and within that month they passed the hat round every night collecting money so we could pay our hotel bill and our food bill, and get enough petrol to get back to England at the end of the month.

In the 1960s I was destined to become a professional musician. But then when you start doing the circuit in France and Germany six nights a week, month after month, it really becomes hard work, and after a while you can get really sick of it. Music's nice when you're doing it when you want to do it, but when it becomes a living then it takes on a whole different meaning, and the magic goes out of it.

After about 18 months I came back to York. I'd had enough of living out of a suitcase, travelling the road, I wanted to settle down. I got married and then I joined the Tycoons then a band called Gerry B And The Rockafellas. After a short while that band went professional and I worked all over England, then I got a job with a band in Germany. But then I'd really made my mind up I'd had enough. We all reach a crossroads in life, and you make a decision whether to keep going, and keep working.

All the big bands in York had gone by this time. I worked at Westfield Club in Hull. That was my best job, the most demanding, the most interesting job. Because every week was totally different. Every cabaret that came through was different. I worked a full week with Ken Dodd, and we, as a band, got paid for playing from half past eight until midnight, but every night you're still on that stage at half past one. We didn't get any more money for it, but it was interesting working with him.

I was in the same band as Pete Williams and a piano player called George Roberts, the best piano player in the whole of England. He really was a fine musician, took his music very seriously. He certainly didn't suffer fools on the music stand. If you couldn't work to a good standard he would make sure you knew about it. I was lucky enough to work with George on the Canberra ship and went to the Caribbean for three weeks with the band. That was an experience, so if you're not rubbing shoulders with good musicians you don't get a chance to do that kind of work. When you have a really good night, if there's a good cabaret, and the band's good, at the end of an evening there's such a lot of elation. Everything's gone right, the audience have loved it, you get feed back off them, and it really is a lovely feeling.

When I'm behind my drum kit I feel comfortable, I feel happy, I'm at peace with the world.

Linda Wood was probably the youngest semi-professional singer in York popular music circles when she began singing in York pubs in the early 1960s, and certainly one of the very few females. She was only 15:

My father, Edward Cook, was concert secretary of the INL [Irish National League] Working Men's Club for quite some years. He used to tape me and when I was first asked to join a group with Tony Agar and Anton Betteridge, they listened to this tape and I was supposed to have sung with absolutely perfect pitch. I'd memorised how the singer sang it, and I sang it exactly the same.

I was very young when I got interested in music. I used to walk down the stairs with a broom handle in me hand at about five or six years old, singing The Train Runs Through The Middle Of The House, as if I was coming down a big grand staircase, like Shirley Bassey with a fabulous dress on. If I wasn't singing I was whistling. There was music in my head all the time.

I can remember one of the group, it could have been Anton, had this great big flash American car. Soft top, the hood was back, and it was all red leathered interior. They came down Etty Avenue where I lived. I'm one of 11 children. And it was really mega this great big car coming to pick me up. They drove me to the White Horse in Coppergate and we did the audition upstairs. I was asked if I'd like to join and I said, 'Yes'. Somebody had to push you from behind. My dad knew I had a voice and so he pushed it.

We performed there twice a week, we were called Linda And The Group. I was treated like a lady, looked after. Nobody would actually come up to me and cause any rumpus and my mother and father were always there. I'd sing Dusty Springfield's songs, I Only Want To Be With You, You Don't Have To Say You Love Me, and I Just Don't Know What To Do With Myself, really good strong powerful songs.

With the first group I had a lovely 'rainbow' dress, shiny cotton, puffed out, with a big net petticoat underneath. If we were in a big club I would wear a long white chiffon dress just past the knee, and Grecian over the front of the breast and then a long sash going down the back that was pleated. All the edging was in a gold thread-key design.

I was in the group about a year and a half. And when I was 16, the lead singer of the Scorpions came round to the house and asked my father if I could sing. I remember singing Where Have All The Flowers Gone? with them and Island Of Dreams, Da Doo Ron Ron, and Bobby's Girl. The Scorpions just listened to me singing and one of them would write it down, then transpose it on sight more-or-less into the key I wanted.

I had a crush on Phil Calvert. I used to think he was gorgeous. I sang at the Zarf club with them and at Guppy's. We also did a lovely gig at the Flask Inn, on the way to Whitby. It was the landlord's daughter's 21st birthday. They had a male singer as well. I would come on and do two three-song spots. We'd go to the Rialto too. I saw the Beatles three times. I got a cigarette off Roy Orbison and kept it under my pillow for months until it dried up and disintegrated! As soon as I got into the Beatles, I'm sorry but Elvis Presley came down off my bedroom walls and the Beatles went up.

I love music, in any way, shape or form. I get very emotional when I'm singing. I can come out with goose pimples on my arms. I tell you where I do get very emotional, when I'm singing in church, I'm Catholic, and if we're singing the hymns in church, I can only get halfway through it. It must be something psychological from when I was a little girl. It evokes such memories.

Professor Wilfrid Mellers came to York in 1963 to start up the music department at the new university. He was one of the first academics to take popular music seriously and amongst a number of books he has written, are volumes on the

Beatles, Bob Dylan and female jazz singers. He is now retired and an Emeritus Professor at the university. He recalls:

The invitation came from York, to found the music department in a brand new university, and that was something I couldn't have turned down. I really did have the chance to make a music department, in my own image, as it were. And it did become quite famous. One of the reasons was that we co-opt from the popular music, as well as classical. And the reason for that was not a blazing clarion call, it was just that I thought an enormous number of original things that are called 'music', some will be bad and some will be good, and my job, as a teacher, was to at least have opinions about what was good and what was not good.

And the staff that I appointed, I had an absolute open book, and so I did appoint, on the whole, people who were composers, real composers, not academics who composed a bit. David Blake, for instance, he was a pupil of Hans Ivor, who had been a pupil of Schoenberg. I always did a jazz course every year, and we had a very good jazz pianist on the staff.

My daughters would play Beatle music all the time. I was interested in jazz, I was perfectly prepared to think it would be a good thing, and I thought the Beatles were very well worth writing a book about. Lennon and McCartney, they were the really creative two. I did a course on Bob Dylan in the context of American country music and I taught the Beatles course. There were very long queues for that, stretching over campus. I wasn't trying to be trendy. I taught the Beatles because I thought the music was good.

I knew the Dankworth jazz musicians quite well. I wrote a big piece for Cleo, [Cleo Laine, Mrs Johnny Dankworth], *the symphony orchestra, and three different kinds of jazz combo, the primitive kind, an Ellington kind and an avant-garde one. It was the biggest piece I've ever written.*

With music I don't think you can separate your head from heart, you certainly can't listen to Bach and Beethoven, without a heart. [With some pop music] *there's not enough substance in it to survive, it just titillates you while it's going on. And maybe that's the purpose, it's one of the functions, one shouldn't ban it. When I was teaching at the university, the kids who were interested in pop music would come and tell me, 'You must listen to this', and so then I was kept in touch.*

But you had to listen to the Beatles, and you certainly had to listen to Mr. Dylan. Joni Mitchell, to mention a woman, I thought she was very good.

Another popular band at this time was the Corvettes. They started playing in 1962 at the Blacksmith's Arms at Seaton Ross, a pub which had been the local

The Corvettes c1963. L to R - Dave Plues, Adrian Kaye, Ken Mason, Ken Newbould, Bill Mason.   *(Courtesy Ken Newbould)*

for many airmen and women stationed near there during the Second World War. The landlord was Bob Mason, who had run a dance band in the 1940s, Bob Mason And The Piccadilly Music Weavers. The original line-up of the Corvettes was Richard Stark on lead guitar, Johnnie Gaze on rhythm, Bob's son Ken Mason on bass, Bob's brother Bill on drums and Les Tomlinson on vocals. Johnnie Gaze went to New Zealand and Les Tomlinson became a policeman in Bermuda and the line-up of the group changed with only two founder members still playing, Ken and Bill Mason.

Ken Newbould came to York when he was 15 in 1963. He answered an advert in the local paper to join the Corvettes:

We had a residency at the Imperial Hotel, in Clifton and played one weekend out at Ken's father's pub at Seaton Ross, the Blacksmith's Arms really, but they called it the Bombers' because all the ceiling was made out of aircraft wings. He had a fish and chip shop in the barn at the back so about ten o'clock he'd come through and say, 'Right lads, we're fired up', and disappear out, go and get the chips, and come back in for the last one.

I had a Burns Split Jazz, a Stratocaster shape, but split sound, you could split the treble from the bass, and for things like Shazam you could have the real low bass notes, and high shimmering treble notes. There was virtually a group for every pub in the centre of York. On one occasion I think it was with Brian And The Easybeats, I've never seen anything so funny in my life. He got absolutely smashed, and fell off the stage, and just laid on the floor with a mike in his mouth, just laughing, and everybody was creased.

The Corvettes packed in, and when the Swingalongs folded, half of them came to join us and the Impacts was formed. We did have a bass player at one point that played trumpet as well, a bloke called Pete Richardson, and a drummer called Mick Richardson, but they weren't related. But it was nice when Norman Hughes got on sax, and Pete got on trumpet, because you could do more soul numbers. Norman was terrific when he was with the Swingalongs doing things like Johnny And The Hurricanes numbers, you got a mike stuck down the sax, and it sounded just about right. The Impacts went into a six or a seven-piece, and then it became more a showband in a way, and then we went on to the Dawnbeats.

Adrian Holmes joined the Corvettes as lead singer:

Adrian Kaye And The Impacts c1965. L to R - Ian Dearlove, Bryan Pearson, Adrian Kaye, Ken Newbould.   *(Courtesy Bryan Pearson)*

Linda Wood.   (Courtesy Linda Wood)

Adrian Kaye And The Impacts. 1965. L to R - Ken Newbould, Norman Hughes, Ian McLaren, Adrian Kaye, Steve Bennett, drums, David Plues, guitar.

(Courtesy Bryan Pearson)

I was 15 and lived in Acomb and knew lads who were older than me, Christopher and Malcolm Miller and I was keen on motorbikes and they had big Beezer Road Rockets, Triumph Bonneville, and used to take me all over on the back of the bike. And one Friday they took me to the dance hall at Pocklington. And this chap says, 'The group's downstairs, and the singer hasn't turned up'. So Christopher says, out of the blue, 'Well this chap can sing'. So I said, 'You must be joking'. But we went downstairs and they strummed the guitar and said, 'Just start singing'.

I thought I'd be booed off. They put this red jacket on me, and they're playing Blue Suede Shoes and Living Doll and I've never been so frightened in me life, but I started to sing these songs, and everybody seemed to enjoy them.

Adrian was asked to stay with the group and he became Adrian Kaye:

I'd only done a few sessions, and somebody knew the music teacher at Bootham School, and I went along to see her. She had a metronome and a piano in her lounge, and she said, 'Start singing, and I'll just start playing. You sing in tune, you won't sing out of key'. And when you're 16 that doesn't mean a great deal, but she told me, 'Your timing's very good, but you could

92

improve, don't try rushing it, just calm yourself down'. When you're nervous you tend to throw yourself in, 'Let's get this song over with'. But if you watch anybody that's been singing for 30 years, say Gene Pitney, they come on, and it's a breeze, because they're doing it five nights a week.

I went into town and people kept coming up to me, and saying, 'Will you sign my piece of paper, we saw you...?' I was walking down Coney Street, and a little lad got hold of me, and said, 'My mummy says are you Adrian Kaye of the Corvettes?' and they were really capped with this. I'd dance a lot, that was my personality, and always get somebody up on stage. I'd pick one out, put them on me knee, and sing Little Children by Billy J Kramer And The Dakotas, and I found that went down a treat, everybody loved it. I've seen top artists, they do more talking than they do singing, it's the rapport they have with the audience that makes them the star.

They're good at singing, and good at selling records, and they look good, and present themselves, but their rapport with the audience, and the way that when they're singing you think they're singing to you, that's a skill. I'd get down off the stage and walk amongst the audience, but we didn't have the microphones that they have today, so you had to be a little bit careful, you didn't have much length. Girls would still dance in a circle, and they'd come to the front of the stage, because they wanted to look at the group, and I'd get down, and ask, 'What would you like me to sing?'

We knew about 60 songs towards the end, and we always started with Never On A Sunday which was a popular theme and I knew when that came to the end, I was going to be introduced to come on to the stage.

I got myself maroon suits with velvet collars, slits up the sides, and a pair of red shoes. Somebody gave me a hat, and I'd walk around and people said, 'There's that chap, in that group'. When we'd do a new song, we'd say, 'I can't see the lady now, but she's over there, is it Maureen and her friend Christine would like us to sing Loving You?' Well they didn't at all, but we just needed to get this in, because we were running a bit short so we'd repeat a few.

The talent shows were Ken Mason and his father's idea. The theory was, the more jobs we did, the more people would get to see us, and that was the whole idea, to be seen. You'd do three numbers, a well-known song, a ballad, and finish off with a rip roaring rock 'n' roll song. We were very successful, we went in for six or seven and won every one.

I remember the gymkhana at Bilborough, and a talent show, and they wanted me to give some prizes out. At the Rufforth one, they had a very small village hall, and two or three of the likely lads of Rufforth, found at the end of the hall the main switch for the power, so when I started to sing, they would flick the switch and aagh! We'd check the equipment, and all of a sudden, after this happened two or three times, it dawned on us, that these chaps, that were eventually thrown out of the hall, were turning the power off.

Our fan base was in the Seaton Ross area, Hull, Beverley, Pocklington, Melbourne. It was an ideal place to go on a Sunday, people would stand outside and look through the windows, up at the stage, because you just couldn't get any more people in. Jimmy Savile was to come to Holme-on-Spalding Moor to the dance hall. He had some friends that run it, so they said, 'Would you like to appear with Jimmy Savile?' It was a good venue, it held a lot of people and we could fill the place. He said he would come and compere a show, and this was all arranged, and it was a big night, when people get dressed up. That's why people like entertainment, they get dressed up, they feel great, they go out and want to enjoy themselves. We'd done the first half but when I came off, 'Jimmy Savile's not coming, there's just been a call from his secretary, he's dreadfully sorry, but he's with the Rolling Stones in France'. And I said, 'Who's gonna tell all the people this?', and they said, 'You are'.

Jimmy Savile did appear at a later date there with the group and made an impact when he drove up in a lilac Rolls-Royce:

We did the Rialto a couple of times. Neal Guppy arranged it. Unfortunately my trousers split on that occasion. I don't think the Lord Mayor was too bothered at my trousers splitting, but his 14-year-old daughter and his wife weren't impressed. They had steel caps [on the stage] that lift up where people plug their equipment in, and then you shut them down when they're not in use, and somebody had left one open. I used to dance around and my trousers were very tight, and as this piece of tin went in it split all the seams of all my trousers, and everything, but they didn't tell me. And one of the things I'd do was turn to the audience with my bottom, and wiggle about, and unbeknowing to me everything was showing, and the mayor got up and asked for his car to be brought down Fishergate, and left. Next thing I knew, the manager and Neal are shoving me in a car, and taking me half way up to Askham Bryan where I was out of the way.

On Monday morning I had to write a letter and explain that I was a young bloke doing it for charity, I didn't mean to cause offence, and I was very sorry. But it really livened the show up and my sister said, 'We were listening to the people around saying 'look at that singer' and me and me mother were just sat there thinking we don't know him'.

94

When we played in Selby Baths, the police came to see us and asked if I made a habit of it. I explained that underneath my trousers I'd wear rugby shorts and a pair of swimming trunks then jockey shorts. Then at the Empire, Mr. Shepherd said, 'I don't want suing, so make sure you're well covered up'. The stage was rather high there, with chairs along the front, and they'd stand on them, and make lunges at you. The finale was the Jerry Lee Lewis number, Whole Lotta Shakin where I'd go berserk. I'd say, 'Ladies and Gentlemen, I hope you've enjoyed the show, it's been wonderful being here with you, but I'm gonna do something now that will totally amaze you' and I'd take my trousers off. The first Monty. There was my rugby shorts and the girls would take my red boots off, and socks, swing them about and people loved it.

I got married at 19. From 16 to 19, that was my life, the Corvettes. That's what we did, we lived it, I couldn't have a holiday because somebody had booked us. I remember we were in Hull and I came home, and me mother and father woke me at eight o'clock on a Sunday morning and said, 'There's a girl here, she wants to see you'. This girl says, 'I was at the dance in Hull and I've

come to see you. I came on the train that delivers all the papers, I set off at five o'clock in the morning. Can you sing, Loving You by Elvis Presley to me?' So me dad and me mother says, 'Would you like some breakfast?' you know what they're like. Never seen this woman before but she stayed the day, and I put records on, I sang Loving You to her and I took her to the station, gave her a kiss, and she got on the train back to Hull, and I've never seen her since.

Ousebeat magazine 1964 showing the Morvans near River Ouse. L to R - Dave Nettleship, John Morrell, Bill Tunnah, Pete Marshall, Peter Bland.   Below - the Cheavours. L to R - Pete Allen, Don Gargott, Alex Blaydon-Hill, Paul Blanchard and Dave Crabtree.   *(Courtesy Trudy Luker)*

Pete Morgan, the acclaimed poet, was living in York in the 1960s and edited the non-establishment pop magazine Ousebeat which ran to four issues in 1964 and reflected the scene very well. The magazine included interviews with national groups, like the Hollies, the Searchers, Swinging Blue Jeans and the Rolling Stones, as well as interviews with local musicians. There were reviews of concerts, pop films, all the

Mick Jagger at the Rialto 1964 reading York Ousebeat mag.   *(Courtesy Tony Adams)*

Advertisement for Enterprise Club (known as Guppy's) and the Morvans from Ousebeat magazine 1964.   *(Courtesy Adrian Holmes)*

latest gossip on the local scene, fashion pages, letters, and specialised articles, such as the one on amplification by guitarist Ian McClaren who had a GCE in music and certificates in physics and electronics. The most popular page was probably the beat group poll, where readers were invited to write in and nominate their favourite local groups. The top five in each issue included Tony Adams And The Viceroys, Barry Adams And The Swingalongs, Steve Cassidy And The Escorts, Gerry B And The Rockafellas, the Cheavours, the Morvans, Mal Dyman And The Tycoons, with brothers Barry and Tony Adams battling for first place each time.

Pete got involved because:

I'd found things that were happening in Germany, on an underground music scene, which were exciting, and a new form of music that I hadn't come across before. And when I came to York I was surprised to find it happening here, it was in pubs and clubs, it wasn't widely advertised. Nobody seemed to know where any particular group was. Some of the local groups were so good, and playing a very original form of music, that I decided we needed something.

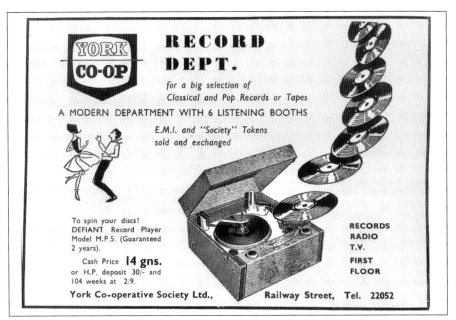

Advertisement for Co-op Record Department from Ousebeat magazine 1964.
(Courtesy Tony Adams)

It was their freedom, not just freedom of expression through music, but through fashion. And you can imagine, after years in the army, when you're not allowed to grow your hair, when you all have to look exactly the same, wear the uniform, it was that wonderful freedom of expression, I found it invigorating.

They were loud, a lot of them were writing their own material, and it was imitative in that the Beatles had presented this area of freedom, that songs didn't have to be about softly falling in love, and the whole world being wonderful. I'm a poet, so that interested me, and I found a poetry in their song lyrics.

Producing the magazine wasn't easy, editing it, putting it together, sub-editing, how we were to produce the whole thing. The design was assisted by the quality of some of the photographers. One photographer, Pete Jackson, died very young. The logo was based on an aerial view of the city walls. Once we'd got it printed, it became very difficult to distribute it to local newspaper shops, because we weren't an official publishing house. As well as editing it we were hanging around where the gigs were taking place, and actually selling it on the night of the performance. It meant we were working on it during the day, and selling it at night. It was too full-time. We sold around the three thou mark.

I met the groups and got to like them, and they became friends. One of the thrills was interviewing people like Jerry Lee Lewis, Chuck Berry, because you were always allowed access to their dressing room, an added bonus really to actually meet Jerry Lee Lewis, and appreciate the man. We were very persuasive though Mick Jagger didn't take much persuading to pick up the Ousebeat and stand in front of the camera.

So we had to keep an ear to the ground. And of course they came to us as well because once Ousebeat was out, they wanted to be in it. You didn't get press releases then, the groups were saying, 'Can you come and give us a review?' It was all highly experimental. When these lads got together and formed a group, they didn't know whether it was going to take off or not, where they were going to play. There were some bands that wanted you to go and see them, and they weren't all good. Some of them were not my cup of tea at all. But you still had to tell people about them, then they could go and make up their own mind. You weren't there in editorial judgement at all, you were telling people what was happening.

We had no office that we were able to use, it was one guy's private address. All the time this was going on I lived in Coffee Yard, which was wonderful, but you couldn't reveal it or your house would be full all the time.

Garry York And The Scorpions from Ousebeat magazine 1964. Back L to R - Phil Calvert, drums, John Makin, lead. Front L to R - Garry York, vocals, Ray Morris, bass, Tim Rothwell, rhythm.

99

STACEY BREWER

talks to

OUSE BEAT'S

Russ Lamond

Stacey Brewer. Ousebeat Magazine 1964.   *(Courtesy Tony Adams)*

Bobby Hirst, the pianist, helped us as an advisor. I was a bit of a kid really and if I needed to know about how to do this, Bobby would know. And Bobby was a good drinking pal. We would meet him in the bar and chat.

In late 1964 when Ousebeat folded, the Evening Press started doing it, and I thought, 'Aye, aye, they've started their own column. It's by this guy Stacey Brewer, there's a pseudonym if ever there was one. But I read Stacey, and thought, 'Mm, good, he writes well', and when I met him I really got to like the guy. There was a magazine in Hull as well, and that took us over, then after a while they reduced us to the 'York page', and it was at that time I had to say farewell. We didn't have any full-time staff at all. It wasn't our full-time job. We weren't at that stage where we could get an income from it, we didn't feel safe enough to be able to pack up our jobs.

CHAPTER SIX. GOOD VIBRATIONS:
The Beat Explosion

In 1960 National Service ended and the last batch of conscripts were called up that year. The young people in the 1950s still had vestiges of their parents' generation, but those growing up in the 1960s wanted to move away from those attitudes and embrace their own freedom. Some called it a peaceful revolution, and their slogan was 'Make love not war'. The world seemed an exciting place where anything was possible.

Ella Hirst, daughter of jazz pianist Bobby Hirst, describes how she felt during the 1960s:

When the Beatles came along it changed the world. There was this atmosphere, you could feel it in the air. In my dad's time I suppose jazz was just bursting on to the scene, whereas it had all been crooners, and he just got caught up in that. You could feel the change, and at 16 years old you were delighted to get up on a morning. You and your friends were into a new thing, and it was like a revolution because old people were absolutely horrified. I worked at a place called Raylors, and in the middle of August, it was so hot, and me and my friend Katie, Pete Morgan's wife, would wear black wool dresses, black stockings and leather boots. We were roasted but we

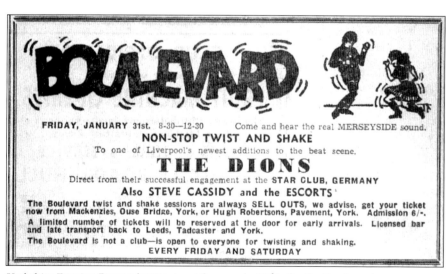

Yorkshire Evening Press advertisement from early 1960s for the Boulevard.

(Courtesy Colin Carr)

were not going to let that image slip. And we used to iron our hair. I had long red hair down to me waist, but it had this kink in it, and I couldn't do with that, so before we went out on a night I used to lay with me head on the ironing board, and Katie put brown paper on it, and ironed it, until it went absolutely straight. And your fringe had to be just on to your eyelashes. We'd wear really pale lipstick, and had these great big black eyes like Dusty Springfield. We were so affected we put blobs of paint on our jeans to make people think we were at art college. I remember having a pair of jeans with P J Proby painted down the side.

I remember the atmosphere, you were going out into this world and something new was happening, and you knew it was just for you. We'd meet in the Starre Inn, Stonegate, and in the Punch Bowl. We'd no money, we'd sit all night with half a lager, but you had to be there. If somebody said to me, 'You can have one day of your life again, which would you choose?' I would choose one of those days when the Beatles were on the up, and we'd started wearing the gear, and the lads had got their hair cut like that. I met the Beatles. John Pick [a local freelance reporter] *was doing a story on a girl who spent all her holidays in the Cavern in Liverpool. She knew about the Beatles before anybody. It was 1963, I was 16 and my dad found out that John was gonna do this story and take her into the Rialto. He got hold of my dad and he said, 'I owe you a favour, I'll take Ella as well'. So I took a day off tech college. At the Rialto, all the girls were screaming and shouting outside but there was just me, this girl, John Pick and the Beatles.*

It was every girl's dream. I was very slim and had red hair, and Paul McCartney said, 'Doesn't she remind you of Jane?' 'cos he was going out with Jane Asher at the time. I had to sit on his knee for a picture, and he's got his arm round me, I think it was on the front page of the Daily Express. So I go back to college, and the headmaster said, 'Why were you off school yesterday?' 'I had bronchitis'. 'Mm, you weren't poorly enough not to go to the Rialto with the Beatles on'. I could have died. It never occurred to me it would be in the paper.

I'll always remember I was in London when flower power really hit, and I was outside Buckingham Palace, and there were a load of girls stopping taxis, and giving everybody a daffodil and there were a row of soldiers with guns. And these girls were popping a daffodil down the barrel of each rifle, and there was this real old sergeant and he said 'I'd like to see 'em charging with a bunch of... daffodils'. But it was like that, we thought we were gonna save the world.

No matter what social activity was going on, it was always for the music. If we were going out it was to a dance, or a club, to listen to the music. Or we had to have Beatles records on, or Stones, it was integral then, it was absolutely necessary.

As the 1960s progressed, the number of groups increased. 1964 was the peak with perhaps 100 groups playing in the York area. Musician Mal Luker says that in that decade the crime rate in York went down because every young person was either in a group or watching groups.

As in the early days of dance bands in the 1930s, people wanted to hear music, wanted to be where the music was, wanted to dance. Older musicians accuse the 1960s young people of playing the 'three chord trick', but W C Handy, the great blues guitarist, said that it was 'a simple form with endless possibilities'. Knowing the basic chord shapes would mean that guitarists could play 50 or 60 chords from an original three. Of course, the Beatles changed everything by doing things which had not been done before as Pete Willow explains:

It worked even though it was unorthodox. With an art form, anything works. Look at an abstract picture, it's art to some people, it's rubbish to others. You can't standardise music, you shouldn't standardise art forms, they should be open ended.

The main claim of the 1960s songs is that they were largely happy and cheerful. In the last two years there have been many 1960s songs used on television advertisements, because their upbeat sound creates a positive feeling for the listener. There are those who say if you can remember the 1960s you were not there, an allusion to drugs. But many people do remember the 1960s and very vividly, and though the atmosphere is hard to explain to someone who wasn't there, it is obviously a wonderful memory for so many people in York today.

The success of the beat shows at the Mecca, led to other venues opening their doors to the new phenomenon. On September 27, 1964, York Theatre Royal was to stage its first beat music show with the Merseybeats and Little Eva heading a number of acts. The innovative director Donald Bodley made the decision to hold the show and said that if it was successful, others would follow. He claimed to be 'a beat fan myself'. Two days before the show it had to be cancelled. The Merseybeats were apparently 'exhausted from the strain of touring' and Little Eva announced she would not be appearing.

The Evening Press of September 1964 reported that a number of detectives had combed York pubs and coffee bars with the aim of smashing a drug ring. They had been tipped off that teenagers were smoking marijuana and hashish. Apparently a pusher came from London fortnightly to sell the stuff around the

Stonegate-Petergate area. This was big news at the time as was the thought that teenagers were taking drugs. Most 1960s musicians say that they never tried drugs and don't even remember being offered any, because their 'poison' was always alcohol.

In 1964 a trick was played on four York groups, the Rockafellas, the Swingalongs, the Strangers and the Ray Duval Trio. They were all sent letters, purporting to be from E Passey, Entertainments Manager for the North West Region of the BBC, inviting them to audition for the 625 Show on television. They all turned up at the Coach and Horses and waited for an hour but no one came and when they showed the letters to the landlord, he knew that it was a hoax. On ringing the BBC, it turned out they had never heard of Mr Passey and there was no such post as Entertainments Manager.

In May 1964 York opened its first fully underground youth club in the Kavern in Micklegate, in the basement of the Labour Party headquarters, which had begun in 1963 as a coffee bar. The young people wanted to decorate the place themselves and had a fishing net over the dance-room ceiling and the walls filled with cartoons and other graffiti. The dark atmosphere was ideal for a beat group in the corner and dancers squeezed in together in a small space. The local authority and the fire service were not happy about this, because in the event of a fire, the situation could be disastrous. One of the first groups to play there was the Boneshakers, with Timothy Newcombe on lead guitar, Roger Myers on bass, Grant Robinson on rhythm, and John Henry on drums.

In July 1964 the Evening Press featured a two-part article 'The Beat Groups Boom in York' and included details of the Morvans, Tony Adams And The Viceroys, the Cheavours, Mal Dyman and the Tycoons. The Cheavours had only been together six months, with Alex Blaydon-Hill on vocals, Paul Blanchard on lead, David Crabtree on drums, Pete Allen on bass and Don Gargott on rhythm.

After all the publicity in the Press about lack of amenities for young people, in October 1964 a York businessman, Ben Sugar, (who initially remained anonymous) said he would be willing to lease some central premises for over-17s to use as a meeting place and coffee house open every night of the week. With the help of local man C P Wiles and others, the Attic Club was to open in a block of rooms in Clifford Street, to be run by teenagers themselves. About 30 young people worked on decorating the premises, but unfortunately the idea was abandoned in February 1965 because of the expense in converting the building and meeting the fire and health regulations was prohibitive, and the lack of supervisory manpower in the building work and enough people to do the actual work.

In October 1965 the Pretty Things were due to play at the Zarf Club in Stonegate but were two hours late in arriving due to the van which held their instruments

Ian And The Shifters c1966 at Ripon Training College. L to R - Keith Coffey, bass, Charlie Abel, drums, Ian Nicholson, vocals, Bob Mallabon, guitar, Tony Skiera, guitar.
(Courtesy Charlie Abel)

being in a crash. Local group Gideon's Few, who were the support, stepped into the breach by playing a much longer set and then lending their gear to the Pretty Things. Gideon's Few set a record for playing for ten hours non-stop in December 1965. They began the marathon at the Zarf Club one Saturday at 3pm and played until 1am the next morning. The Few comprised Mike Matthews on drums, Deke Hughes on bass, Mick Fallon on lead and the youngest, 17-year-old Dave Alderson, on rhythm guitar. They had been playing together since the autumn of 1964 and had got the idea when they played at Liverpool's Cavern Club and found that the Merseybeats had played a marathon of eight and a half hours. By March 1966 the group had become professional and went off on a tour of Europe.

In September 1966 tragedy hit the York beat scene when Ian Nicholson and Bob Mallabon, both aged 19, of the group Ian And The Shifters, and their two teenage girlfriends, were all killed in a plane crash in northern Yugoslavia, when 92 of the 117 people on board, who were all British, were killed. The four are buried side by side in Fulford Cemetery and the upright row of white stones makes a moving sight. Although the rest of the group were devastated, they tried to keep the memory of their friends alive by continuing with the New Shifters, Jeff Booth, Mick Ward, Keith Coffey and Charlie Abel, but Charlie felt:

It just wasn't the same, we carried on but it wasn't the same again, you couldn't do it.

We always went down well, Bob [Mallabond] played a Gretsch guitar and we did a lot of Cliff Richard stuff with Ian [Nicholson]. He was the front man, you need somebody up there that's got a bit of charisma, or pulling power, it's got to be an image of a sexual nature especially with an all-male band because girls go to it. The guys listen to the music. With music it's got to be immediate. Soon as you walk on stage people have made their mind up, as soon as you walk on they're half way there. But as soon as Ian came on it was all, 'Ooh'.

Graham Sanderson started out at the age of 14, playing in a skiffle group. At Melbourne Youth Club, he graduated to a beat group:

It was called Garden Gate. We only had about three songs which we'd practised for weeks and the youth club leader said, 'Right lads what about playing?' They had ABC Minors on a Saturday morning and we actually got booked to play that as well, so after that you thought, 'Great, we've done it'. It wasn't all that good but it was a learning curve. We played youth clubs and then gigs out of York like Stamford Bridge Memorial Hall, Terrington and Huby.

Later there was a big agency from Scarborough came through and after we'd finished our set, he said he was looking for young, enthusiastic bands and would we be interested in signing up. We thought it was absolutely marvellous, like a dream. So we signed up under sole management and agency with Peter Pitts and he projected us into all different areas, all the north east. There was a thing at Bridlington Spa where all the big groups played and he was always promising to get us on there as support. He rang up, 'Fantastic news, I've got you on supporting the Sweet'. Then unfortunately they went to number one with Blockbuster and wanted twice their fee so we ended up supporting Family, which was very progressive. It wasn't really us but we still did it and there was over 2,000 people there, you were literally sick before you went on. We started to play and our public address system broke down so their roadie shouted to us and we stepped over and were on their P A which was marvellous. Near the venue, there was a massive placard about 20 feet high, 'The Family and support Garden Gate' which was great.

The music scene was really buzzing then, and a guy at the Yorkshire Evening Press, Stacey Brewer, ran the Night Scene [column] and we'd pop in there and he'd say, 'Where are you playing lads?' and give you a little write up. The drivng force was our drummer Steven Heggarty, a lot of ideas came from him. He was a big Troggs fan. We'd go to Banks and copy out words and some of the music, but if we felt flush we'd buy sheet music. We wore loons and high boots, sheepskin-type long waistcoats and the drummer had bright orange jeans. It was quite fashionable to have gonks hanging off the end of the guitar.

Everything just revolved around music. I worked with the lead singer and that's all we'd go on about all day, just music, music, music. We went out and we'd either be practising or go for a pint and talk about music or go and see groups. Apart from kicking a football on a Sunday afternoon. But come night time we'd be practising again, with dreams and aspirations that we were going to go on to big things. York seemed to have a special scene at that time, it just used to bubble. We'd go to other towns and it was not as lively, but in York every corner you turned there was a group starting up or a van went past with a load of lads on their way to a gig. We wanted to be part of that. You'd hear a song on the radio and as soon as we got the music for it, we'd be having a go. There was friendly rivalry, wherever you played you'd nearly always get other group members hanging about listening. We'd get on well and chat with each other, about amps and the strings on your guitar.

I had a Vox Phantom pear guitar. I got that from Gough and Davy and my dad went down to sign as guarantor, and I got a Marshall stack, I started out with a Selmer one and went on to Marshall and we had an H & H PA system.

We played Malton Community Centre with a group the Mandrakes. It'd start out basically quiet, a few dancing out there but as soon as you kicked off, their faces would be peering at you and there'd be loads dancing. Music had a rawer edge to it then, but now I suppose it's a bit more note perfect. Technology's gone on but I don't think there's anyone around who are better than those in the 1960s. A lot of people like Oasis but I think, 'We were doing that type of thing bashing around just warming up, at practice night'. I've heard it all before.

Murray Addison also started out at school, learning a few chords and playing skiffle in 1959:

Then at 16, I met the Swales Brothers, Rodney and Mike, and Peter Marshall. I joined them as a lead guitarist, so we played on the stage at the Empire for the first time and it went from there. That was the Courtiers in about 1961.

The Lowther had a big room upstairs and we practised there, but there was fierce competition, if anybody got a better job or if somebody nicked somebody's drummer or guitarist. York was very vibrant, had a lot of groups in a lot of pubs. Line-ups did change. I was once accosted by another group, because I had a van, and they didn't, and transport was of paramount importance in those days. People had bikes but if you could get around in a van, could throw a load of equipment in and go and do a gig, you were a star, whether you could play an instrument or not. I worked for Radio Rentals and borrowed their van sometimes. Then I went on to play with Ray and Tony Broadhead, the Beatboys, and then the Ousebeats.

The Empire was an old theatre, owned by Ernie Shepherd. He'd turned it into a roller skating rink then used it for wrestling. He found that if he put some guys on the stage and all the kids could jive, because they had a coffee bar downstairs, it was very popular. Then he started employing professional bands, and putting on shows. He got the idea from New Earswick's Bop For A Bob, which got a tremendous following. They only played records on a Tuesday night, and this place was heaving, people would come from miles around just to dance. So Ernie did that in York, with records initially and then as pop groups were starting to emerge, he paid them to stand on a stage and everybody would jive.

There were Teddy Boys with leather jackets and motorbikes, there's always a rough element everywhere. But in the early days rock 'n' roll music was exciting.

But alongside this there were still proper dancebands at The De Grey Rooms. Huby was a venue which was loved by many, and that was a proper dance

Gerry B And The Rockafellas 1964. L to R - Barrie Wood, Gerry B, Murray Addison, Mick Robson, Robin Illing. *(Courtesy Murray Addison)*

band playing on a Saturday night. Whether you were waltzing, foxtrotting, or bopping, it didn't matter, you did what you wanted to do. Village halls had proper dance bands in, and they were still very popular at the same time as the groups were coming on. The dance bands weren't that stuffy actually, they played some lively music. Towards the end of the evening all the couples wanted was a nice slow waltz so they could have a kiss and a cuddle.

I think I played with the Rockafellas longest of all, and then with the Tycoons. The Rockafellas were up at the Wild Man, there was Ron Goodall, Barrie Woods, Johnny Newcombe and Robin Illing. Gerry B was seconded into that. He had charisma, he was very funny, and made us laugh a lot. What started as a rock 'n' roll band, copying Beatles and Stones, turned into a cabaret show. He'd dress up, impersonate people, and he got very good at it. I think Barrie had the idea of the ultraviolet light. Gerry used it on stage, would get dressed up as P J Proby. Proby at that time had only made two records, and we'd do these, and then he'd go off and impersonate somebody else. So we're talking to the landlord in The White Horse and Gerry says, 'Why don't we have P J Proby in one night, we'll advertise it, fill the place, we'll only charge you XYZ, you know, he'll do two numbers and then he'll go?' I said, 'Do you think it will work?' 'Yeah, but in the advert in the Press we'll spell the name wrong'.

Which he did. Gerry did the advert, 'Appearing one night only, White Horse, Coppergate. Don't miss the great P J Probie, singing his latest hit'.

So we nipped down there at half-past six and come quarter past seven you couldn't move in Coppergate. It was terrifying, there was hundreds of people down there, in the street, they were everywhere. The landlord was getting quite worried, because there were so many people he couldn't serve beer. He was doing all right, he was taking as much as he could. All the band was worried, except Gerry. 'It'll be all right, the landlord's gonna turn all the lights on, you start playing, on comes the UV light, I'm coming out of the toilet. I'll do a number, we'll only do one, we're not gonna do the two, because if the lights come on between, somebody might suss it out'. So they got the big build up, somebody introduced it, very professional, drum roll, lights out, we start playing, on comes the UV, Gerry comes out of the toilet, and he looks really good.

Full white suit and a wig. Did this one hit, and absolutely brought the house down. He left the stage, went back into the toilet to get changed again, they put all the lights on and somebody made an announcement that this guy had to go off and do a big gig in Leeds. I was very worried that we would get lynched that night. But we actually got away with it!

There was absolutely no jealousy in the band, we were the band, and he was the star, and that was it. It was clear to everybody that he was very talented but it was only when the band folded that he decided to go off and do a one-man show, become Dustin Gee, build up a repertoire of jokes, dress up and do impersonations. Later we went to see his show at the Westfield Country Club, and we were gobsmacked at the change that had come about in a short space of time. You've got this professional comedian, and tears were rolling down our faces, he was so funny, and he wasn't even dirty.

I remember seeing Gerry B and his group when I was about 13 at a dance in the village hall in Bishopthorpe. I went to Mill Mount School and he worked at Shepherd's next door to the school. He was doing design there and he sat beside the window so we would wave to him and sometimes even knock on the window. It must have embarrassed him, yet later he became a big star so perhaps the early adulation left him wanting more!

Murray remembers:

He always had a lot of ideas. Everyone else would turn up and play and get the money, and be quite happy to drink and meet girls. He was very artistic. He worked as an architectural draughtsman, and in addition he was artistic as a performer, and always looking for something new to do. We were quite happy just to learn the latest Beatles' hit, to play it as an exact copy of the record, but he wasn't happy with that, he wanted to do something different. So he had the creative spirit that we didn't have and that's why he got on and we didn't.

Steve Cassidy And The Escorts were very good musician-wise and very professional. Colin Berriman was brilliant, without doubt the best drummer that York's ever produced, and the guitarist that played with them was Ian Early, the best guitarist around at that time, he was a music student, and eventually went off to play professionally in Manchester.

With Colin Berriman [in our band], we'd walk off stage and he'd do a 15-minute drum solo, in five/four time, and that is not easy. Now and again a bass player would walk back on just to play the bass riff again, to keep him where he was, and they would do Take Five. He was very much respected by all the groups in York. Charlie Abel was also a very good drummer and Phil Calvert was excellent.

I think any musician going to listen to another group of musicians, would enjoy it if they played well, and they'd certainly give them credit for it, 'cos they might have done their own arrangement at one time. Then you'd go and see somebody really professional. I remember in Leeds, Joe Brown And The Bruvvers had come up from London especially to play in the bus warehouse there, and as a guitarist he just knocked me out. How could anybody play a guitar that well, while he was talking, singing, and jumping around the stage?

We had an agent in Castleford, and we started playing some of the West Riding clubs in those days, because the Miners' Welfare Clubs were wealthy clubs. The miners like a pint of beer, and they'd take their families down at weekends, and most of that money was retained within the club because they were non-profit making. They would organise trips to the seaside for the children with the spare cash, or they'd give a Christmas party. They usually had a resident pianist, organist and drummer who could back any singers that came along, and it was well organised. So this agent came along and within six months we were playing seven nights a week and sometimes on a Sunday we were doing a lunch-time session and evening. I was still working five and a half days a week at the time in my proper job, and the average time for getting to bed was about two o'clock in the morning!

Murray's wife Avril worked with Gerry B:

He was always coming up with bright ideas, and he decided, 'Let's put a light bulb inside this drum, so that every time the beat goes it would flash'. He'd

*do a stencil, lay it on paper, put light through it, and you'd be able to cut
letters out. It was mounted on a piece of cardboard and cut through, and you
would just get the name. It got so that loads of groups had these drum fronts.
I'd make them, they were only cardboard, they didn't last long, but I'd spend
ages doing these drum fronts and cutting them out with a craft knife. I know
the Tycoons had one, I know Gerry had them.*

*We used to go to see loads of groups. [When we saw The Who], I was sitting
on the third row from the front and the noise was deafening, and I was
worried, 'cos I was a few months' pregnant and Keith Moon clocks me with
my fingers in me ears, and he was deadly with a drum stick. He threw them,
it didn't hurt. But I kept Keith Moon's drumsticks!*

Joan Gaunt, neé Bainton, worked for Ernest Shepherd at the Empire and booked
all the groups there in the 1960s. She became friendly with many local
musicians like Murray Addison and Gerry B. She had lots of parties at her
caravan which were a great success :

I started there probably 1962. On Saturday we ran a bop and we'd have a

*group. That's when we first met
Gerry B. He'd have a white suit on
and do his Gene Vincent turn with
his group and the kids loved them.
He went on from strength to
strength then. It gave local groups a
good start, because there were such
good crowds.*

*I enjoyed those years, they were
exciting, and there were nice people
who worked there. Ernest was young
at heart and always rushing about
getting involved in all sorts. He was
well known in York, and he always
worked at putting on what he
thought everybody would like, things
for the youngsters. We had a Senior
Service show once, which ran for a
week. The compere was Bill
Maynard, when he wasn't a
'Greengrass' type, he was a very
young and handsome man. They're*

Joan Bainton, later Gaunt, at the Empire. c1964. *not allowed to do it now but they*

112

The Innominates 1965. L to R - Dave Rowntree, Colin Smart, Steve Jackson, Gary Barnett, Chris Birch. *(Courtesy Steve Jackson)*

were giving away Senior Service cigarettes, and the whole Empire was decorated with the logos. They did a concert and quizzes and you won cigarettes.

Johnny Kidd was ever so nice. It's not very long after he came to the Empire he was killed. We had some good parties at the caravan, we just decided to be silly and we did Cinderella. Gerry was the dame, and every time anybody was lost for words, he would come on and do a funny turn. We had a little jazz group played down in the Empire coffee bar, it didn't overlap into the main theatre. It was locals who got together and said, 'We'll come and tinker in your coffee bar for a few hours'.

Teenagers didn't ask for as much out of life as they want today. They were quite happy with a little local rock group, a few cokes and a packet of crisps. Now they want to go to Ikon and Diva until three o'clock in the morning, that costs the absolute earth.

Steve Jackson, a drummer, was the youngest member of his first group in the early 1960s:

The first gig I ever did was at the school Christmas party, we played trad jazz stuff. One of the guys played trombone and we had a banjo and a pianist.

113

About six months to a year later, I thought, 'I'd like to carry on with this', so I got a bit better kit. I had it sent up from Bell's Music in Surbiton, an Olympic which was a cheaper version of Premier drums. And I did an audition for a band in York, the Innominates. I got that and started playing clubs and pubs. The first booking I did with them was at Layerthorpe Boys' Club. I was really nervous in this room with about 50 people but it went down well and I was chuffed to bits. I'm actually playing with a band! We were playing in Hull at the Skyline Ballroom along with a London band called the Riot Squad who had drumming for them Mitch Mitchell, later Jimi Hendrix's drummer, and he had this beautiful green Ludwig kit. I'm there with my Olympic kit, I think, 'I want one of those'. I didn't get a green one but I got an oyster blue pearl one like Ringo's. I was made up with that. We had ideas of going professional and that never really worked out. But it was a good starting point.

Later I got into another band called Ansermet Swing. They had big ideas but we seemed to get stuck playing at the Zarf Club and a few bookings like the Folk Hall and the Riley Smith Hall at Tadcaster. John Loughran, who's quite a well-known guitar maker and repairer, suggested that we form a trio with Cliff Wade [from the Roll Movement]. We did quite a variety of material, a few Byrds things because John had got hold of this Danelectro 12-string guitar which sounded incredible. And we'd play at the Enterprise Club in Walmgate, more-or-less had a residency there. It was a great place for sound for some reason, just a concrete cellar but it sounded good. We were called Cucumber.

It seemed then like everyone was in a band. People in the next street were in a band, you could go out and meet people that were in a band, every pub had a band. The 1960s was such a time for music. I still love that music. I think a lot of people still relate to it, it takes them back, they're happy songs, they last forever. I'm glad to have started playing in that era when music was good. I don't enjoy drum solos. I'd rather play backing music. I love the sound of a nice solid groove, and other musicians like that, if they've got something solid to play against. You always get asked back if you can lay down a good tempo and keep good time. Some musicians might laugh at this, but the drummer is really the main part. If you've got a band with a drummer in it, everyone looks to the drummer. You can't hear the bum chords and stuff, but if a drummer makes a mistake, everyone looks round. 'What's going on?' So you've got to be really on the ball, it's a hard job. The Kinks drummer, Mick Avery, and Adam Faith's drummer, Bob Henritz, I thought they were both really cool. I met Bob Henritz a few years later when I was playing with another band, it was nice to meet him, and swap a few stories.

The next band was Red Dirt in 1969. I met Steve Howden who had played with Cliff Wade in Roll Movement. He was living near Market Weighton and he said, 'Why don't we get a band going? I know a couple of guys and I know this record producer called Geoff Gill'. He'd been the drummer in Smoke and worked at Morgan Studios. He said, 'I can get us a record done through Geoff'. And so we got Ken, a bass player from Bridlington, and Dave Richardson, who was a multi-instrumentalist, really talented guy from Hull. Played everything, keyboards, guitar, violin, harmonica. We went in the studio to start this album and we hadn't played a live gig. We just rehearsed a few numbers and went in. The studio was one of the most popular at the time. We went in and Donovan was just coming out. 'Have a nice session, lads'. None of us had been in a proper recording studio before and we had Andy Johns engineering who engineered the Stones. He just happened to be working that night and we had a lovely session with him and we did about three or four tracks in the night. 12 o'clock until about six o'clock in the morning. And he got us a really good sound. It was a great studio, the sound was there. But he made it really easy did Andy Johns. We'd go down to London every couple of weeks and do an overnight session, do a couple of numbers and mix them. And it turned into an album which is collectable now. The band became Snake Eye and we did a lot of work all over England. Travelling around in the back of a van, doing tours supporting people like Mott The Hoople, Wishbone Ash, Stray, Status Quo. We weren't getting much money but we were playing all these rock venues supporting big bands and that was great experience.

That was the first band that I thought we were all of the same mind. We all just wanted to get better and better and when you're playing all the time you get better without really realising it. We were playing all the rock clubs, the Marquee in London, the Speakeasy, trying to get a bit of interest going. We had management in London which got us all this work. We had reviews in the Melody Maker and Sounds and people would come and say, 'That was brilliant'. I think we got Cleethorpes Winter Gardens with a band called Caravan who were quite well known at the time and they said, 'We just played Reading Festival last week and you're better than most of the bands who were on there'. But we're still doing all the, what they call now toilet gigs, the clubs, back rooms of pubs for next to nothing. We knew we were good but it just didn't follow through. We had this management but the work was gradually tailing off.

We all had more-or-less the same influences musically and we all had personalities, we could get on with each other which is the main thing in a band. But after all this work we'd come to absolutely nothing just through bad management in London and I was at a real loose end. I knew a drummer called Dane Morrell and he said, 'I've seen an act at Hull Bailey's last week and they're after a drummer'.

The act turned out to be the Paper Dolls who had a big hit with Something Here In My Heart. They had three girl singers and four male musicians. Steve got the job of playing with them:

They did a show and I couldn't believe it. It was a big cabaret club and it was completely different to what I was playing like rock music and self-written stuff. All covers but incredible routines, dancing, great guy front singer, four piece band. That was the best band, apart from it being really hard work playing for routines all the time because obviously the tempo has to be a certain way. Dance routines always have to be fast, if they can do it faster it makes it easier for them. Really professional people and I loved working with them. Every night right through the year. This was when I really started playing and learning. I had learnt a lot about playing in Snake Eye but I learnt about professionalism, it was a brilliant act, one of the best cabaret acts that were going around England at the time. Everywhere we went, we were top billing. We did the whole chain of Baileys clubs and just went from one club to another. You get good when you're doing that. The band was great, the dancing was great, and we all got on well. In 1975 we did a summer season at the Isle of Man at the Palace Lido. It was massive, held about 2000 and it was busy all summer. That was the best time I've ever had socially, in the Isle of Man. Everyone was nice, it was a lovely island and everyone chilled out, nobody rushes about and the weather was brilliant every day.

The band split shortly after that, due to personal reasons and Steve spent the next few years playing professionally with Sweet Sensation and the Dallas Boys:

The last year with the Dallas Boys, we did the London Palladium twice, playing with a full orchestra, a bit nerve-wracking! But a brilliant experience. They had parts for the whole orchestra. And we had to go through a whole band call so that they knew the show. If you're all on the same level musically, you can have a great night together. You all get high on the music.

In the 1960s it was a tremendous time. Your first influences are always your most important I think. That's where you come from. I've had a lot of different influences, soul, blues, different drummers that I've liked, but I still like playing 1960s music even after 30 odd years.

Some nights I've been playing and I'm thinking, 'I'm not doing this, somebody else is doing it'. I've always felt that I've been looked after. Obviously I've played one or two bad gigs but I've been able to assert myself and get through. So I always think there's somebody looking after me. I've got an angel somewhere taking care of me. I believe in that, it keeps me going.

Phil Calvert came to York as a young child in the late 1940s:

I remember me dad taking me to military parades, and they were quite exciting, all the services marching past, and you used to hear the band in the distance and your excitement would increase, and it would be packed, crowds everywhere, but the thing that always interested me was that big bass drum. It would hit you in the chest as it went past.

Phil remembers hearing a local group play which sparked off his interest in drums again:

Within a few weeks I was in our shed trying to make drums. I got a couple of apple barrels and went into the City Leather Company [in Church Street], and got a chamois leather. You stretch it over and wrap some wire round and get biscuit tins. Me mam used to play hell because there were all dents in the bottom of her biscuit tins. You know the curtain wires, you put through your nets at the top, you used to roll 'em all round, and force 'em in, and it would rattle, like a snake. And I had a coal skuttle lid for a cymbal, and I'd sit in the room with records on for hours and hours, it was all I wanted to do. And when I hear people now say, 'Oh, I want to be a drummer' and parents say, 'Do you think he'll stick it?' I tell them, 'You'll find out, 'cos that's all he'll wanna do, and he won't come out of his room, it's all consuming'.

I made a bass tom once, I got this great big barrel, and attached it to a post on a stand and it must have sounded terrible. Eventually, me dad cottoned on and bought me a kit from Leo Burrows, he played at Clarence Club. He had a 1920s kit with this enormous bass drum. There was a high hat, big bass drum and that's all you need to start with, and it had a set of skulls. That didn't have a snare drum, so I had to go for some more chamois leather from the City Leather Company and stretch it out. I'd probably be 15, and I was listening to the Shadows, Ventures, Ricky Nelson, Duane Eddy.

Then Phil saw an advertisement for a drummer by a group called the Scorpions and he plucked up the courage to go for an audition :

It was at West Park in Acomb, there's a church with an upstairs balcony and there was so many drummers set up on the balcony, about 20 and I got there with this awful kit, this big gold glittery bass drum. But I could play Shadows' stuff because I'd played for years. There were all these fancy kits, and I nearly went home. I was quite shocked to find that they picked me out of this lot.

We played at Acomb Hotel, and an experience I had in there once. I had a pair of drum sticks with nylon tops, pressurised on. I was playing away, and one of these tips shot off, like a rubber bullet, and I saw one of these big hard men in this pub flinch, it had hit him on the head, and he seemed to know where it had come from but nothing happened. We had a break, then half way through the last set, this pintful of beer flew across, and smashed on the wall at the back of me.

As soon as we started to get a little bit better, Neal Guppy invited us to play St. Chad's Church Hall, at one of his dances. He was honest with us, and he says, 'It was all right lads, but just slow down you're playing everything too fast'. And if you listen to young bands, that's what they do, it's excitement.

Eventually there were five of us in the Scorpions, Tim Rothwell, rhythm, Ray Morris on bass, John Makin lead guitar, myself on drums, and Stu Harrison was the vocalist, known as Garry York.

Sunday nights at Our Lady's all revolved round Father Murphy. He was one of the first people who was connected with a proper organisation, like the church, who I'd ever seen coming out on the side of young people and encouraging them. He'd come on stage and say, 'We've got a band for you tonight, you're really gonna enjoy this. What you gonna do for us lads, what's your first number?' 'It's Glad All Over, the Dave Clark Five'. And he says, 'The boys are gonna do a number called Feeling Gladys All Over'. It got busier and busier, more and more gigs, and one night we were playing Our Lady's and our rhythm guitarist, Tim Rothwell, collapsed on stage, and it all came to a sudden end. They had to call an ambulance and he'd got exhaustion. Then Garry York packed in, he'd got a serious girlfriend. We got a girl singer for a while, Linda Cook [now Wood] was the main singer, and she was really good. She sounded like Diana Ross with the Supremes, and we got Mick Colley on guitar and vocals.

It became a different sort of band, but we had the hard edge to it, because Mick Colley would sing a few Beatles things and we got quite a lot of work. Linda left next, so it ended up with just the four of us, and we went round as the Four Shades Of Black, that was it.

Phil left the band soon after the name change. Several groups asked him to join but he chose the Tycoons :

They were changing their whole image, they'd all changed their hair and were starting on a new repertoire completely. They loved the Hollies and all those lads could harmonise, they'd learned their craft for years. We decided we were gonna rehearse for a month solid, and then our first night was gonna be at the Buckles. Saturday and Sunday nights, Taddy Road was where it all happened in York. The Wild Man, The Buckles, Boulevard, Caribbean

Club, and we were resident at the Buckles. It really was a class act, and the harmonies were spot on, things like Eight Days A Week by the Beatles. John Olive, he was not only one of the best rhythm guitarists in York, he used a Gibson Jumbo electric acoustic, and you didn't see a lot of people using acoustics. He had a great high harmony. Ron Allpress was a great bass player. Dave Nettleship, great guitarist, he had this very Beatley sound, George Harrison was his idol and he sounded like him. Mal Addison was the singer, he called himself Mal Dyman. Great singer, great mover on stage, women liked him, the band really had everything.

We got to a great standard before we even did that first gig, and had a big following at the Buckles, it was packed out to the doors. We'd even gone out and bought shiny mohair suits, light grey and really smart. Waistcoats, really hot, with being called the Tycoons we had pocket watches with fobs. We came out this particular Sunday night and absolutely knocked this place out. We got an agent in Bradford. He got us a lot of work all over the West Riding, some big rock clubs, like Ikon and Diva. We started to really learn our craft there, it was timed to perfection. You were behind the curtains and they'd give you this big build-up. You were supposed to behave like stars, you had to create an aura. And we were told, 'Don't bring any women with you because the women out there like to feel they've got a chance with the guys in the band'. I started to learn what this was all about, we went into like a sausage machine, all totally professional.

Then we started writing stuff. I wrote quite a bit and there were a couple of numbers we put in the set. One number people would request. One Saturday we had an audition at the City Varieties and this was run by a guy who was a BBC2 producer. He had an agency round the back and if you got on there, you got all the military and air bases. And we'd gone to try and get on in his agency, so we were there in the horrible dressing rooms at the back and these strippers were just peeling off, with their boobs out, and one says to me, 'Would you like to stick me stars on?'

We did three or four numbers, and one was a really nice version of Will You Still Love Me Tomorrow? That was our 'slowey', what you call a 'bum feeler', that's the musical term for it. And we finished off with this number I'd written, and it was like you see in films when the theatre's empty and seven or eight people are sat in the middle, and this guy says, 'What was that last number? I've never heard that'. 'It's one we've written'. He says, 'I like the band and I'm particularly interested in that 'cos not a lot of people are writing stuff. Get me a demo recording and I'll take it to London, I'll virtually guarantee I can get you on with Columbia', which was a top label then, Cliff Richard And The Shadows were on Columbia.

Nowadays everybody's doing demos, there's recording studios in people's garages but to make a recording in those days was big stuff. There were only big studios about, and I found one in Newcastle, Morton Sound, where the Animals recorded, phoned them up, and got a date for an audition. But to my utter dismay, a few days later, the lead guitarist and the bass guitarist decided they wouldn't go professional. They'd both got professional exams to take. Dave Nettleship was an architect, and Ron Allpress was studying to be an accountant. That was a blow because they were irreplaceable, vital to the sound of the band.

We did a few gigs for this guy, and when we did Menwith Hill, it was like little America. They had all the American cars, we rolled up and were frisked. Everybody out of the van, and we had a couple of girls with us, the lead guitarist's fiancée and someone else, and these Americans said, 'Who are the broads?' Tight security. We got on the base and they wanted us to play from nine to three in the morning with very few breaks. By the time we finished we were absolutely knackered.

I think there's a lot of passion in music, and a lot of passion in youth so it's youth and music coming together. I think the bond still stays between musicians. I've always been passionate about drums, and about rhythm. What killed it off eventually was discos. Originally there were dance bands, maybe 20 people, then groups in the 1960s, then musicians on their own like Michel Jarre.

In 1966, pirate radio swept the country and Radio 270 broadcast from the Dutch boat Oceann 7 docked in Bridlington Bay, a feast of pop music from 6.30 am to midnight every day. Because pirate radio was illegal it had to be registered in Honduras, a country not signatory to the International Radio Convention. By July the Government had published a Bill suppressing pirate radio and making it illegal to broadcast, install equipment on the station, supply tapes and records or advertise on the programmes. The Bill finally became law in August 1967 and the radio station had to close despite a petition for Radio 270 to stay open, with 500,000 signatures on it. The station signed off at midnight on August 14, playing Vera Lynn singing Land Of Hope And Glory. As a 14-year-old schoolgirl, I remember listening to 270 at a time when I could not afford to buy many records, and enjoying the music played constantly. It was so different from Family Favourites and the programmes our parents listened to. The BBC brought in Radio One later that year but it wasn't the same, it was 'the establishment'.

Stacey Brewer called the pirate radio 'swashbuckling adventurous radio... we were not pirates who plunder and steal, we were pioneers'. In the 1960s Stacey ran first Trend and then The Night People, columns in the Yorkshire Evening Press. In 1966 he was asked to run his own show broadcasting five nights a week on Radio 270. He also appeared on BBC radio programmes like Today and Voice Of The North, and began broadcasting with the British Forces Network. He retired in 1990, having received the MBE the year before, after more than 40 years with the Evening Press.

Ricky Royle worked on Radio 270, as well as at various dances in the York area. His nickname was Ivan the Terrible. He recalls:

We were on the ship for two weeks on, one week off. And then the tender came to pick you up and take you to shore. When it shut down they had the farewell do at the Assembly Rooms in Blake Street. They had the group Simon Dupree And The Big Sound and Mike Hayes, one of the Radio 270 DJs. It was packed out with people and a very good night. But a very sorry one as it was the end of an era. Hopefully pirate radio will come back, but whether it'll be in my lifetime I don't know.

Ricky also worked as a freelance disc jockey. The Heartbeat Club had a session for youngsters on Saturday afternoons:

It was adjacent to the Cat's Whiskers up the side, we'd go and entertain the kids from two till five, absolute madness. But I do enjoy it, I love entertaining. Nothing more pleasurable than me doing a show and having a complete dance floor absolutely buzzing away like I don't know what, with everyone having a darned good time.

In September 1968 an appeal was launched for a new Arts Centre in the redundant St John's Church in Micklegate, which had been the home of York University's architecture department. The aim was to have a venue which catered for less mainstream theatre and music in intimate surroundings. The centre opened in October with a membership of 600 people and over the next 20 years would regularly present live music. The same month the university's Music Department announced that the Lyons Concert Hall would be opening in March 1969, and members of the department moved from their Micklegate premises, transporting 18 pianos, kettle drums and a record library to the new building. All the teaching rooms had pianos and stereo equipment, and all practice rooms had mirrors so that string and woodwind players could study their technique. One room in the hall was set aside specifically as an electronic studio and the use of computers attached to a 12-channel tape machine was already happening. The financing of the new hall was due to a gift of £110,000 from the businessman Jack Lyons. At the opening ceremony, Wilfrid Mellers said that music was a 'a basic necessity for the mental well-being of mankind in all

Wilfrid Mellers, Emeritus Professor at University of York.   *(Courtesy Wilfrid Mellers)*

ages and races'. His composition of Life Cycle, a cantata for young people, was performed at the ceremony. The hall has gone on to present a wide selection of classical concerts, and popular concerts performed by the University Jazz Orchestra.

CHAPTER SEVEN. A SONG FOR THE ASKING:
The Folk Music Revival

Folk music enjoyed a resurgence in the 1960s. Eight students from St John's College, York, formed a folk group with guitars, harmonicas, violin, mandolin and banjo under the name of the Garden Street Philharmonia International, which later became the Exiles. Soon they were appearing in pubs, clubs, universities and prisons, some of them for charity, but when they finished at college in the summer of 1965, the group had to break up, although one of them, Allan Armstrong, stayed to teach in York. They were invited to appear on Opportunity Knocks in December 1965 and so they came together again from all over the country for that. Two more York folk groups made up of college students were the Crimple Mountain Boys and the Pinewood Ramblers. Neal Guppy ran folk nights at the Enterprise Club and would put local groups on, as well as more famous ones:

On one occasion I had the Spinners perform in the cellar, because although they could fill a hall of 1,000 people for a concert, they were prepared once a month to go to a proper folk club, to support folk clubs because that's where they'd come from.

I moved from my own premises because one of the shortcomings in 1965 was I didn't have a bar and the tradition with folk groups is that you meet in a pub so I had the first of the folk nights at the Black Swan. By 1970 I'd got my own bar so I carried on folk nights then. The McPeake family came, they were

Members of The Exiles Folk Group performing at the Enterprise Club c1965.
(Courtesy Neal Guppy)

very famous. The Crofters and the Exiles were from St. John's College. So were John Hayes, Griff Roth and Tony Heald. Training colleges seem to get folk singers because they pontificate do us teachers.

An article in the local press in August 1968 called it 'a boom time for folk' in York, with York Folk Club regularly packed to the doors. In September 1968 the York Folk Festival took place, with national artists appearing at the club's regular Friday night spot, the Lowther. On the Saturday of the weekend festival, there was a folk competition in King's Manor with three sections - traditional, contemporary and instrumental - followed by a grand ceilidh featuring the Fettlers, Al Stewart, Mike Cooper and the Wagoners. York Folk Club always had a number of performers, including a star guest, resident guests and local singers, with a big weekly audience. However only 11 days before the festival took place, the folk club split. The Lowther club, which had a membership of 150, disbanded. Tom Davis, licensee of the Lowther, accused the committee of the club of 'cloak and dagger tactics' and he stopped the club after five years of smooth running. The Lowther Folk Club reformed and the rival faction named itself York Folk Centre and moved to the Castle Hotel. The Lowther staged its first concert on August 29 with only 30 in the audience. The occasion was reported in the Evening Press with the headline 'Breakaway folk club accused of childish tactics'. The new club had an audience of 80 at its folk night, and Tom Davis accused them of 'spreading rumours that his club had disbanded, cancelling his advertisement in the newspaper, picketing the Lowther, advising people to stay away and interrupting his concert'. The secretary of the new club denied this and said that there was enough interest in folk music in York to support two clubs.

A well-known traditional folk group in York was the Foresters, whose member Brian Oxberry wrote some of their songs. One was a protest song for the Bishophill Action Group who were formed to oppose the planned multi-storey car park in Bishophill. The Foresters were resident at the Hopgrove Inn on Malton Road. Other local songs composed by Brian were about George Hudson the Railway King, the Bacon Cinema Club in Acomb, and another about Swift Nick Nevison, the highwayman who rode from London to York.

East Yorkshire and Humberside had and still have a strong interest in folk, with annual festivals in Whitby, and clubs in Driffield, Cottingham, Holderness, Beverley, Scarborough, Grimsby and other places. York has had a smaller folk tradition but a strong one nevertheless. Traditional singer Alwyn Wilson recalls getting interested in folk clubs in the 1960s:

I was chased out of a ballroom dancing school, and there was a folk club round the corner and I wandered in. And after you'd seen Tony Harper in a mini-skirt, dancing on a bar table, with a pair of clogs, you wouldn't wanna go anywhere else. I was 17. I went every week, it was a cracking night. This was the York Folk Centre, which had just moved to the Castle, in Nessgate the week previously. I spent a lot of my childhood in Whitby, 'cos my grandparents were from there, and Whitby Folk Festival was on the go, so I'd heard and seen some dancing and some music.

We had a really good chorus line in the York Folk Centre, some lovely harmonies, and the singers' nights were a treat, just a glorious sound. This was 1967 and I'd never really been to much live music before and this was definitely live. There was traditional and contemporary, a fair old mix, Steve Flanagan used to do a lot of blues, Graham Metcalfe would do traditional songs and ballads, Pat Niblet who died a few years' ago, he had a lovely deep rich voice and sang traditional songs as well.

The songs, or narrative ballads, were mostly about working class people, and it always struck me as being amusing, because when I started thinking about it, most of the people that went there, they wouldn't be labourers, they'd be more middle class. I was probably the only fella there that used his hands, who was a manual labourer. I went with Jed and Jim [Morris] on one or two of their bookings, we went to the Processed Peas Club and the Lonely Celery Hearts Club outside Driffield, and Jed and Jim were being paid to sing there, and they persuaded me to sing, I think it was Dido Bendigo. I'd heard the Watersons sing it, I said, 'I'll sing it, if you'll stand up with me' so I stood up and sang it, and I turned round, there was nobody there.

We learnt songs from books and recordings. Topic was a good label to get recordings off. Groups like the Watersons, and Derek and Dorothy Elliott from Barnsley, were quite generous with their material. And also a tape recorder was a good thing to have. I got one for my 18th birthday and I recorded a lot in the folk clubs. That's how I learnt some of the lyrics, songs with 14 or 15 verses! There are little tricks to it, but it's hard work. Trial and error mostly. What does help is that most of the songs have a story, and I'm convinced that the modern songs that are being written now, will eventually go into the bank so to speak, they'll be sung in future years. I like the new songs, especially comic songs, and songs of events, because let's face it, this is how they were written in the first place. Someone would get hold of it and write a song about it, whether it was a murder or a mining disaster, and there are still people writing.

There was our club the York Folk Centre on a Friday, the University Folk Club that met in the Talbot on Wednesday, the Black Swan Folk Club on a Thursday, and several clubs outside York as well. A good one in Bubwith on a Saturday night, Selby on a Sunday night and one in South Cave, maybe Tuesday night.

I was going to a folk club every night of the week, I had a little motorbike to get about.

One of the biggest nights we had at the White Swan was with a lad called Mike Cooper, who played the National Bottleneck style. There was Diz Disley, the Coppers, and Fred Jordan was a frequent visitor, he'd come up with his leather gaiters on, and horse muck still on his boots, straight from the farm! Yet he'd always end up with one of the prettiest girls in the room on his knee, he wasn't daft! He was still doing that up to a couple of years ago. He died this year.

Alwyn likes the informal nature of folk clubs, where performers mix with the audience:

I think the heckling was a big part of it as well, which doesn't seem to go on so much nowadays. Some of it was not very polite!

I'm not sure whether the Lowther actually booked any artistes, or just had singers' nights, but there were a good few singers around at that time. An artiste might come from Leeds, Barnsley or even further afield, and they'd get a bed for the night if it was too far for them to travel home. I think the understanding was it was a straight fee, plus expenses or a bed. We moved from the Castle to the Talbot and then to Vickers Social Club. We had Don Partridge one time, which filled the place, that was a couple of years after he'd had big hits with Rosie and Blue Eyes. I don't know exactly how much he charged, but we managed to cover it, which was the main idea and you would use the singers nights to finance that.

After Vickers we went back to the Talbot for a little while and then to the White Swan in Goodramgate. Had some really good nights in there, and then for some reason it became unpopular so we moved to Thomas's, and that was a smaller room, we left there and went to the Bay Horse in Gillygate for a couple of years, then ended up at the White Horse in Bootham. My social life was built around folk music at that time. I never actually put anybody up, but you did get to meet people like the Copper Family. They were traditional, from Rottingdean in Sussex, and the whole family came up and stayed in the Station Hotel.

I've a great deal of time for singer-songwriters and old blues as well. There's some nice instrumentalists around. Folk music is music of the people. That's how I would define it. Accessible, with no class barriers, and not much of a barrier between the audience. Like having somebody in your front room doing a concert for you, that's the closest I could come to it.

York Folk Festival 1967. Performers L to R - Jed Morris, Packie Byrne, unknown. Back row seated - on left Chris Brownbridge, second from right Jim Morris. Front row seated - girl with banjo unknown, on her right Pat Niblet, Sue Rawson, Richard Inns.

(Courtesy Alwyn Wilson)

Graham Kennedy at the Lowther Hotel c1969. *(Courtesy Graham Kennedy)*

We branched out into ceilidhs at the Folk Centre, we had Martin Carthy in King's Manor Cellars. You'd have a couple of sets of dances and then an artiste would sing, and then more dancing. A lad called Richard had been looking forward to seeing the Copper Family for years, and when we actually did get them, we'd been on the beer on the dinner time and we put Richard selling sandwiches and he fell asleep over the sandwiches and missed the Copper Family.

The set-up with the folk club was, the MC would do a song, and then you'd have some singers from the floor, regulars, then the artiste would do half an hour, then you'd have an interval, and then the same in the second half. We'd finish about half past eleven.

The regular MC was Jumping Jed Morris, a very lively character, he hopped about a bit. There was Judy Dinsdale, Graham Metcalfe who is now in Oxford, Bill and Fred Evers, Bill played the accordion, Chris Brownbridge, he was unaccompanied. A lad called Alec Graham did a lot of Phil Ochs songs. Martin Carthy was revered then, and he's still on the go. He and Nic Jones, they were the two. Everybody wanted to go and see them. Martin's still doing the same songs he was doing 30 years ago, and doing them just as well. The songs have been around for a while, I know of ballads from 1845 and the 1790s, they've stood the test of time and people still sing 'em.

Nic Jones he played York and Selby quite regularly, and he was always greatly admired,. He played the fiddle and his arrangements were so good. His guitar style was excellent, I couldn't fault it, you couldn't believe that there was just one person playing the guitar.

Nic Jones had a dreadful car crash in February 1982. The folk musicians rallied round and sent tapes of his music to his wife and she played them to him when he was in a coma, which aided his recovery.

Nic moved from the Fens to York as he recovered from multiple injuries. In April this year (2002) he played in public for the first time since his crash. He accompanied his son Joe on guitar at the Black Swan Folk Club after his great friend, the singer Tony Rose, was forced to cancel a gig.

Graham P Kennedy, who originated from Wales, was billed as singing 'blues and contemporary folk in York':

I started performing when I was a student at St John's College in 1965. I could play harmonica and a fellow student called Chaz Scott played guitar, so we formed a duo based on early country blues like Sonny Terry and Brownie McGee and we practised in our rooms until we thought we were good enough to play at small concerts within the college and then we stretched our wings and went down to the Lowther Folk Club run by Stan Norman and to Guppy's Club. When we left college I continued to play, I moved to Doncaster and learnt some more material and returned to York and went back down the Lowther and played as a floor artiste for some time.

At that time the university had a June Ball at King's Manor and I got booked to play and on the same bill was Elton John although I can't remember all that much about that night. Joanne Kelly couldn't turn up and she was due on at three o clock in the morning, and I'd done my set earlier in the evening and about midnight they asked me to play again. The booze was free for artists and I'd had my fill and more, and by three o clock in the morning I couldn't remember what songs I had played so I just did the first set again and no one really noticed by that time in the morning!

I remember singing with Dave Gibson, a teacher at Nunthorpe, Colm McCabe, who moved down to Reading, I've seen him since and we sometimes have a reunion at his house and play all the old songs. Then Phil Cerney, who was from North America, when he arrived in York he was quite surprised that the audience knew some of his songs because, unknown to him, I was doing some American songs.

There was a Sunday night out at Stamford Bridge, the Corn Mill. If you got a booking there I think that was a fiver a night and that was big money. The audience were less than appreciative but because you were getting a fiver, you kept going and just played to amuse yourself, it was work and a chance to practise some of your new songs. I'd sing what I preferred to sing, I wrote some of my material and adapted blues songs to my style of playing.

I did a session for Radio Humberside. We'd travel across to Hull and to the Processed Pea Club at Etton which was a little pub in the village but a centre for folk. We'd borrow a car from the people we worked for and fill it with a few support singers and come back in the middle of the night and be up in the morning ready for work.

Nore Hull enjoyed folk music from a young age. Her father sang in music hall:

The house we lived in, although it had an inside toilet, there was no electric light and because the children couldn't walk down the stairs in pitch dark, we had chamber pots. There was a big family of us and in the morning grandma would come through with the bucket with a lid on and she'd look around at all the children quite knowingly, and say, 'I'm going to make the beds'. That meant we had to stay sat where we were. Then grandma sang, just to let us know that she was on her way down, and we hadn't to go near the stairs. And she sang this song,

With a li-fajilly-faloreum, they put some muck in me mouth by gum,
I left it there till a copper come, with a li-fajilly-faloreum.
With a li-fajilly-faloreay, they thought I was awake, said Jay,
I picked up me clogs and I walked away, with a li-fajilly-faloreay.

And then we just knew that she was down the stairs and clear. She came from Flamborough Head and she had some wonderful songs [The above song is a phonetic transcription from the taped interview].

I was born in 1927. There was no work and my father went into music hall, it was a way of making a living. He had a beautiful voice, he'd had it trained and he'd sing a lot of Paul Robeson songs. But he could take George Formby off brilliantly. He was a great banjo player. He appeared at the Empire several times, the Tivoli at Hull and Blackpool and Scarborough. He used to tour all the time.

We were evacuated at the beginning of the war then my father found this house in York. My Mum played the piano at the chapel. The whole family was steeped in music. My son Pete and Gil Stapleton ran the Lowther Folk Club for quite a few years. I sang in other places at the sing-around and at the Black Swan once or twice. You're just sat round in a circle and they stand up where they are and sing. And you get some really good talent.

There's mandolins, guitars and the fiddle's very popular. The bodhran, the squeeze box, the bigger accordions. It's something to do with being mobile, it's usually just something they can carry. I'm sure there was singing down Walmgate in the old days, there must have been 'cos you can't stop the Irish singing can you? I've been to Ireland a lot and every pub you go into in Ireland is a folk club. It's just naturally there. The Lowther was a mixture of traditional folk and contemporary.

Jim Elvin, he goes around the country collecting songs, a lot to do with the seafaring life, Heave Away To Trawl and Pull For The Shore, a song about Grace Darling which is really nice, the Barleycorn Song which I'm sure everybody knows, Where Is My Wandering Boy Tonight? and that is very traditional. It's stories, murders and love affairs, just life, that's what folk music is. Jimmie Rodgers, all his songs are stories about the railroad like The Liners. Go to Newcastle and you get an awful lot of songs of the pits. And there's agricultural songs and different industries. It's just telling the stories of their lives and the work. I love it, to me, it's the only music worth listening to.

There's Yorkshire songs like My Girl's A Yorkshire Girl, and farming songs. But York's a very cosmopolitan place, it's a bit of a one-off like that. There isn't a [specific culture]. It's this ancient city steeped in the past.

At the Lowther you never knew what was going to happen, how many's going to turn up, but it was usually quite full. Different people would roll up with a guitar. I'd be on the door. They'd say, 'Can we sing?' and sometimes your heart sank and you thought, 'Oh no!' but you had to say, 'Yes'. Pete and Gil would start it off because they sang together a lot. Pete would perhaps do the odd blues and probably a couple of quite cheeky ones and then Gil would sing one on his own. We did get a lot of the university lads came. And a lot of talent came with them.

Dress is always very casual, and I think a lot of the folk people were the ones with long hair. You weren't allowed to have a guitar if you didn't have your hair down your back then. There was one guy, great singer and he played the squeeze box, Jim Younger, and he wore a full-length woman's fur coat and a Homburg hat. And he looked great, beautiful hair down his back. He was at the university. They started wearing a few beads and fancy scarves, it probably originated with the folk people. One thing I do think in all the years I've gone to folk clubs, I've never known any trouble. I've always found it about folk music, it's like being in your own front room singing, like a family.

They would make an awful lot about the gore, and blood and death. Poor women being downtrodden, some of the mill songs would break your heart.

You get the right sort of singer and it does affect you. You're there with the poor little kids going down the pits and into the factories and the mills. You'd get one singing one of these really sad songs and the next one'd be singing something quite happy and funny. Vin Garbutt is one of my favourites. He can really tear your heart out when he sings, yet he's the funniest man. He's a real comedian as well but if he does sing tragic ones you really feel it.

Proper folk, traditional folk, should be acoustic. I hate it when, at a folk club, you see all these amplifiers set up. The Black Swan doesn't need amplifiers. You get a good folk singer in and he'll just pick up the mike and shove them at the back. To me this loud music takes all the goodness out, all the naturalness.

I can remember from being really tiny, my dad would practise in the parlour where the piano was. I loved to sneak in there and sit quietly. I could listen all day. I'd have hated life without music.

John Whittle got involved with folk clubs in York in the 1960s:

I saw away at a fiddle, and pick at a mandolin and things like that, but I'm not very good. I used to do a bit of singing, and I was the treasurer of the first York Folk Club when it set up in about 1963. I heard that a family called Sheridan were coming over from Harrogate to do a sing-song in the Woolpack opposite the Black Swan. Loads of us were vaguely left-wing and CND background, we packed the pub out, and John Sheridan sang and played with the rest of his family. And that was the first of any kind of folk music of a semi-organised nature that I can remember in York. From that the York Folk Club was formed.

I think possibly a lot of people felt that it was a little gauche, or passé, folk music and the traditional stuff wasn't as interesting and lively as dance music. I can remember the Maple Leaf Four on the radio. Canadian barn dance was okay but English folk song wasn't. At the first York Folk Club, the name that I particularly remember was Barry Slater, a student at St. John's who played guitar

FAMOUS FOLK ARTISTS

appearing at

THE ENTERPRISE CLUB

56 WALMGATE — YORK

8 — 11 p.m.

THURS 14th OCTOBER **DAVY GRAHAM**

TUES 26th OCTOBER **COLIN WILKIE & SHIRLEY HART**

TUESDAY 9th NOVEMBER **JOHN PEARSE**

TUES 23rd NOV **MARGARET BARRY & MICHAEL GORMAN**

WED 15th DECEMBER **THE SPINNERS**

TUESDAY 4th JANUARY **LOUIS KILLEN**

TUES 18th JANUARY **THE WATERSONS**

Enterprise Club poster c1966.
(Courtesy Neal Guppy)

132

and sang. And there was Paddy somebody, who'd sing Kevin Barry every week, religiously.

It only ever met once in the Woolpack, and the club proper started going in the Sea Horse in the upstairs room where they played table tennis. We had the tables removed to the side, and we sat in there. I particularly remember Ewan McColl and Peggy Seeger, they visited us, that kind of personage didn't come often, it was mainly regulars singing.

The Lowther is probably the best place it's ever been. It was a wonderful room for singing in, a great sort of glass pyramid at the top of the room, and it echoed all round, we didn't have to try at all!

I think that quite a lot of people who went to the folk club would be equally interested in jazz, a lot of the skiffle musicians in fact turned to folk. The kind of people that went to the Folk Club were the kind that had enough respect for their ear drums not to venture into pubs like the Burns where they had these amps going at about 146 decibels, and you were blown out the door.

My experience of the years in folk music, going back from 1960, to fairly recently, is that for a lot of people who were performers and singers, there's a heck of a connection between church and folk, the interchange back in the Middle Ages between secular and religious music, and huge numbers of the people that I've come across were in the church choir. A lot of 'em got their feeling for harmony and stuff from that kind of early life experience, and you're looking at that self-made enjoyment and entertainment. In some ways York was too self-consciously middle class for a lot of that to be around. You'd got Archbishop Holgate's, St. Peter's, Bootham, all these sort of places which were looking for stuff on a higher plain! The words and the music for really traditional singers are so closely interlinked that you go back thousands of years, where oral history was, you had to remember it by rote, and you had a chant to it. It is the music of the ordinary man.

If you read some of the commentators like Willa Muir, on the Border Ballads and the more traditional stuff, they're talking about a distancing between the narrator and the events. They're describing really quite horrific stuff, in a matter of fact way. This is life, this is what happens, this is what we expect to happen, no surprise about it, it's tough. A bit like the Greeks, if you were unlucky people were a bit sorry for you, but kept away from you. There was hardly any kind of input or inflection of emotion in these words, and Muir found that much more telling than all the pop singers nowadays breathing hard, or trying to put the emotion into every word. She felt that the smoothness of it all, and the distancing of it, had much more impact. I tend to agree with her and you even find that judges at singing competitions will be looking for you pushing the emotion into it.

There was a strong current of the kind of people who would be interested in leftish-wing politics, but the apocalyptic stuff, like Bob Dylan, nobody took that too seriously. That was very poppy I thought anyway. There is always this ambivalence, between the contemporary and the traditional in the folk scene. I've run across clubs where they wouldn't have anything contemporary at all and you even had to pass an audition to get up and sing on a singers' night. Some of them were very snooty!

Most folk song is very accepting, it details the injustice of this dreadful world that we live in, but sort of resignedly in the last verses says, 'Well, there we are mates, that's it, you rich people have pity on us'.

The folk scene was just a group of people who vaguely hoped that they could strike a chord with others. Some of them enjoy performing, there's always gotta be an element of somebody wanting to show off to get up there and sing, but basically it was to have a good time, sing songs, play music, and have a congenial social atmosphere which was relatively safe. I never felt very safe in the Big Coach, or the Burns, you never knew when a glass was gonna come flying. So we were probably the wimps! But I was going along because it's the next best thing we have to those family get-togethers that once existed. I want people to be part of it, all enjoying it, all contributing. I think it's fair to say there is an unbroken thread that goes all the way through English music, and one of the things that ruined it for local musicians, was when those wretched Victorians bunged organs in all the churches. It was the village band that played in churches until then. They document this very much in one of Thomas Hardy's books and it was a loss of status for the village musicians. So they nearly broke the thread, and a lot of it was overtaken by more popular forms of music. But there was a fresh impetus from America in the 1950s and 1960s, Pete Seeger, the Weavers, all those people bringing stuff back that had gone out there 300 years ago.

Graham Metcalf started out playing guitar in beat groups but later moved into country music. His first band was the Pathfinders when he was 16. One night he was persuaded to sing Do You Want To Know A Secret by the Beatles, and he found that he enjoyed singing and others enjoyed hearing him. Graham also makes guitars:

Members of the Pathfinders were Derek Waugh on drums, who later played with Tony Adams And The Viceroys. Then we got Bob Adams. We had Dave Jackson on bass, another school friend who'd been dragged in to help us out but didn't stay long and Mick Blackburn occasionally sang with us. This band played at the very first dance ever organised at the newly opened York University in 1963.

I was badly in need of a decent guitar. I was playing a home-made one when we did the youth clubs. I'd got some wood from school and carved myself out a Fender Stratocaster from a solid piece of wood and the only things I bought were the pickup and the tuners. I built a couple of guitars before I could afford a proper electric one. We went over to Leeds to buy an amplifier and the assistant brought out a pink Fender which was £55 and my friend said, 'That looks really good on you!' I got it and kept it for 25 years and eventually sold it to a collector! In the local youth club there was a portable PA system which consisted of an amplifier with bare valves sticking out, no cover and a couple of horn speakers that you see on racecourses. The big flared horns made of metal. It was a huge square thing, four feet wide, five feet deep and about 18 inches high. And we took this thing in a taxi to the Burns Hotel and set it up in the middle of the stage and it actually sounded quite reasonable 'cos you didn't need a lot of power to drive it.

About 1964 I progressed to join a group which had been more established, and been getting better work, a well-respected band called the Morvans. It was getting more towards the Tamla Motown sound so we were doing a bit of that sort of stuff, getting work in Leeds, Dewsbury, and a couple of gigs at Bradford University.

In 1967 I had a bit of a break from music, decided it wasn't for me as a career although I still liked it, listened to music a lot, still kept my guitar but sold everything else, and finished my apprenticeship and college courses. But I missed the music and I wanted to get back into it when I'd got all these exams out of the way. By this time, the folk revival was in full swing with Bob Dylan, Peter, Paul And Mary, Gordon Lightfoot, Simon and Garfunkel. I especially loved Paul Simon, some of his early acoustic stuff. I bought an acoustic guitar, taught myself finger-picking, and folk style and started looking around for people to play with. At the local folk clubs you just turned up with a guitar, waited your turn, sang a couple of songs and then sat down. It was nice but not really what I was looking for. I was at Hull college by this time, and a friend who travelled with me every day, was a technician at York University and we got talking and he'd worked with a lot of bands doing the technical side of things, sound and lighting. He was very clever. And I happened to mention I'd like to get back into playing, and he said, 'I'm involved in a country music club in York, but it covers all sorts. Come down'. Eventually I went to this club in a pub in the centre of York which is now McDonalds.

It was originally the Half Moon, but everbody called it Hennekeys 'cos it was one of the Hennekey Inns at the time. I turned up one Wednesday night, in November 1969, and I was amazed to see a bunch of guys of all ages from 21 to 65 year olds, singing with guitars. Hank Williams and Johnny Cash songs with very little equipment, just a tiny PA system, a single drum with a pair of brushes. I hadn't been in the place more than ten minutes when I had a guitar thrust into my hand and I'm told to get up and play with these two who were to sing. I thought, 'If we can get away with it, it won't do any harm', and that was it, I'd met up with a couple of partners and we formed a new band. We went out as the Western String Band for about a year or two until the bass player decided he was moving to Australia and it left the two of us, Joe and Graham, and we started getting decent work in country music clubs.

I'd heard of Hank Williams and I'd heard of Don Gibson and various people like that but I'd not really listened to them in a serious way and I'd no great attraction for that sort of music but eventually came round to liking what we were playing. When I listened to it in greater depth and some of the instrumental work, some of those guys can really play, the Nashville musicians. So I'd heard this wonderful instrument called steel guitar and I asked, 'How does that thing work, how do you play it?' 'It's got these pedals on it, and knee levers and loads of strings and you don't play it with a plectrum, you play it with finger picks. It's easy, you just do this, press this pedal and this wonderful sound comes out'.

So I bought myself a pedal steel guitar and immediately became known as a pedal steel guitar player 'cos there weren't many of us around and eventually, after a year or two, I got the odd recording session and I worked with other bands as well. The duo with Joe Mollan, Ventura Highway, stayed together for 20 odd years, but he sadly died some five years ago.

We occasionally augmented the duo to a four-piece band, sometimes with a bass player and drummer, and sometimes with acoustic instruments. A couple of friends from Bradford, one played mandolin and fiddle and the other one played banjo extremely well and we teamed up with these two lads on occasions, and formed a bluegrass band. I bought myself a banjo eventually. I just had to have these instruments, I was always interested in how they worked and how you got the sound out of them. I could not believe how these banjo players fitted in so many notes, how they played them so fast.

Graham eventually wrote some of his own songs and made some tapes:

In a lot of ways the music scene hasn't really changed. The music may have changed a bit but the actual scene I don't think has. You still get bands playing for their own enjoyment and a bit of pocket money.

As well as acoustic country and folk music, many pubs had sing-songs:

I remember the Acomb Hotel on a Saturday night when I first started there, there were sing-songs at the end of the night. Everybody in the pub would just sing, no accompaniment or somebody would get on the piano. A bit of a traditional thing that had gone on for years. You don't see it now..

Like Graham, John Coleman started out playing other music and moved into the country scene:

I think it was Donovan, and Bob Dylan that started me off and I'd had a guitar since I was about nine, but I just pretended to play it. It wasn't till I was about 17, I learnt a few chords and started playing Donovan, and Dylan and the Seekers and learning folk songs.

We went along to the folk club at the Lowther, most weeks, just to listen. And this particular week the artiste didn't turn up, so they said, 'If any floor singers want to get up and sing, feel free' and a neighbour of mine says, 'Oh, John'll get up, he'll sing'. 'No, no, I aren't getting up'. 'Just do a couple, it doesn't matter how bad you are'. So I did a couple of songs, and that's how I got started. I played at Hennekey's, and the Black Swan.

Soon John was asked to sing and play at medieval banquets at the Black Swan:

You got a five-course meal, and drinks all night, and a fee for doing it so I did that for four or five years, and then we did 'em at the Merchant Taylors, Merchant Adventurers and the Castle Museum, in a fake medieval costume, home-made doublet and we sang folk and comedy songs.

Then there was an advert in the Evening Press for anybody interested in country music, from Mrs. Smith, she had a music shop in Tower Street, and she wanted to start a country music club. The first meeting was in a pub down Burton Stone Lane, the Corner House. There was a guy called Tony Upton, Tony's son and his wife, Joe Mollan and a guy called Dave Middler, massive guy, like Giant Haystacks, he had hands like shovels but he finger-picked a little Spanish guitar, so sweet, and what a lovely voice. We started the country club at Butcher Terrace in about 1966, at what was the Sub-Aqua Club, with Mrs. Smith running it, and booking different artists from all over the place. When they knocked that place down, we moved to the Woolpack on Peasholme Green and the Cross Keys in Goodramgate, the City Arms and then it finished up at the Hospital Social Club, in Haxby Road. When it first started, it was just acoustic, fiddles, banjos and guitars, and even the ones that had gear, it was very primitive, AC30s and one mike. We booked Mike Harding two or three times to play with a guitar and a squeeze box, and now if you

(*Courtesy John Coleman*)

Country Style - John Coleman and Graham Metcalf in 1970s at Dunnington Sports Club.

see him he's got an articulated lorry full of lights, amps, eight or ten guitars, four or five squeeze boxes, sound technicians and roadies to set all his gear up and he doesn't sound any better. He's still good but he was good before.

At the first club, we'd meet on a Thursday night, and anybody who wanted to sing, listen to that for a while, it was just an appreciation of various forms of country music. I could play and Tony Upton and his son did a duo, they finished by having a five-piece band, Tony And The Comancheros. Then Graham Metcalfe came and joined. He's an incredible musician, he plays pedal steel guitar, lead guitar, banjo, and whether he's playing folk, country or rock, he's as near as dammit to the record.

When it first started out they just came in ordinary clothes and then one or two started coming in cowboy hats and boots, and it finished up they were bringing guns in, and if you played Ghost Riders In The Sky, you couldn't see across the bloody floor for gunsmoke.

There was a guy who was a pensioner, about 70, and he came every week, with a kiddie's cowboy outfit with a black waistcoat with fringes on, and a sheriff's badge, and a big hat. And he enjoyed the music. Some of them would pay £50 for a pair of boots, and nearly as much for a hat, then some of the shirts they started wearing were really good. If you played at a country club then you were expected to wear something they could identify with country music and the songs that you were gonna sing. In York clubs in the interval they'd have bingo. But up in Hartlepool and round there, it was Quickdraw contests, they'd draw names out of hats to see who's gonna go against each other, 'Tonight we'll have Black Bart and the Ringo Kid'. And these two would come out, face each other with six guns on, and they'd have a balloon in a metal holder, and the bloke would say, 'Now' and they'd draw and shoot and burst this balloon. They were good with what they did, but at the end of the night all the guns were going off, and you get choked with smoke. But it all added fun to the evening.

I'd been booked at a wedding, over near Malton, and it's in a fabulous big marquee. And it was all under drawn in silk and they had a floor and proper chairs round, and flower arrangements, and I thought, 'Oh this is a posh do this, I like this'. They said, 'If you'd like a drink, go over to the bar and help yourself, just tell the guy'. So went across, 'Three pints of bitter please'. 'Sorry we haven't any beer'. 'Oh, it's a right posh do', I thought. 'We'll have three whiskies then'. 'Sorry, we don't have anything alcoholic, Methodists don't drink'. They toasted the bride and groom with orange juice and coca cola. Then this lady came across, 'Do you think you could start with the Dashing White Sergeant?' 'Sorry, don't do that'. 'Who's your caller?' 'I haven't got a caller'. 'You are country square dance?' I said, 'No, no, we're a country and western group. Look, you've obviously booked the wrong act, and we've obviously come to the wrong venue for us, so if we go, you don't have to pay us anything for the inconvenience'. 'Oh no, you'll have to stay', she said. So we stayed and did our three sets, and after each song there was a polite little ripple, and nobody moved off their seats, nobody spoke, nothing, we tried to get 'em to get up and dance and nobody would move so that was a long night!

John's speciality became comic songs:

This is what sticks in people's minds now, because lots of people did the country stuff, lots of people did folk, but there wasn't anybody else doing the comedy songs. If it was a country night and you put a few comedy songs in, that went down great. If it was a Sixties night and you put a few comedy songs in then that went down equally well.

I loved every bit of it, every stage that I've sort of gone through, I lived for folk, or for country, I've met a lot of wonderful people, and been invited to all sorts of places that I would never have gone to if I hadn't been playing guitar. I'm not a particularly good singer, and I'm not a very good guitarist, but I can entertain, and there's a vast difference. There's people who are better musicians, but I can entertain as good as they can, if not better than some.

I'd get involved with the audience, and they like that, they like to feel a bit special, and if you can do a request for somebody then it's nice isn't it?

Mrs Doreen Davis talks about her husband Tommy who became landlord of the Lowther Hotel. He played drums at the Empire for many years:

And then it closed. Ted Lewis, he was the trumpeter, he'd pawn his trumpet every week and take it back out on a Monday. And Fred Kell was the conductor. But Tom's music was the main thing, nothing else mattered. He played everything, vibraphone, xylophone, tympani, glockenspiel, tubular bells, the lot. He was well taught in the army and he played at the Edinburgh Tattoo.

We went in the Lowther in 1958, I should think we'd been in about four or five years when the music started. This man came along, 'Could we practise in your big room upstairs?' That was Gerry B And The Rockafellas. They were a regular item. Then we had the Late Night Lowther with Tom Baker and Laurie Taylor, they were at the university together. They did plays, music, and this company came to see it one night and booked Tom Baker as Rasputin in Nicholas And Alexandra.

*But then someone said, 'Can we start a folk club here'? Now that was terrific,
it was every Friday night, and you couldn't get into that big room upstairs.
We had all the university, we had all the crooks, and there was never one
scrap, they all mixed with each other. The police would come in and say, 'We
want somebody for identity parades, 10/- each' and they were all dashing to
go, 10/- was a lot of money. And then when we got flooded, it was a folk night,
everybody still came and half the students were carrying them in and going
straight upstairs and of course we were on bottled beer because the cellar was
flooded. I don't regret one minute in the Lowther, I enjoyed every one.*

York folk group Prussian Blue, was formed by Dick Sefton, a teacher at
Burnholme School, and included John Bird on guitar, Barry May on guitar and
Roger Pattison on bass. They appeared on BBC's Come on In, in July 1973.

A Christian folk group based at Heworth Parish Church called the Psalters was
formed in 1968 and they sang at many colleges and church groups. In 1971 they
brought out an LP which featured 12 songs, 11 of them the group's own
compositions. Brian Wilson was the oldest of the group of four, and he recalls:

The Psalters folk group 1971. L to R - Richard Walden, Brian Wilson, Chris Walden.
(Courtesy of Brian Wilson)

They say that if your mother sings to you in tune, you're liable to be able to sing in tune later in life. I remember listening to the Ovaltinies on the radio, and as a child I imagined they were all little people inside the box. At seven or eight I joined the choir at Heworth church and sang the occasional solo.

In the 1960s Brian began to lead a young people's group at his church. Most church music at the time tended to be choral or organ music, but when he met three young men, Paul Nolan, the vicar's son, and brothers Chris and Richard Walden, who had been at the Minster Song School but who were influenced by folk music, they decided to form a group and met each Monday evening at Brian's house:

We played Peter, Paul And Mary stuff like Blowing In The Wind, songs by Joan Baez and Simon And Garfunkel. Paul Nolan was influenced by a Christian singer, Graham Kendrick, and the whole Liverpool beat scene. When we had the centenary service at Heworth, David Watson [a charismatic York vicar who is known for increasing the congregation at St Cuthbert's church from seven until it was overflowing and they had to move to St Michael-le-Belfrey] *was one of the speakers. By that time we were proficient enough to sing in the service. When David made his first radio broadcast, we were asked to provide a song with guitars. We sang one from Youth Praise* [songbook] *called Can It Be True? That was an experience recording with BBC technicians. Then David asked us to go to outreach meetings at St John's College.*

The big influence in York musically then was York University [music department]. It uplifted all the choral societies in York and the music standard started to grow at that point. The group make-up was Richard Walden on bass, Chris on 12-string, Paul on jumbo guitar and I had a little ordinary one which they'd only occasionally let me play. Paul sang the melody and the rest of us sang harmonies. Chris and Richard made up their own harmonies and we developed that way. If it was a folk song like Blowing In The Wind the harmony was limited, but if it was a thing like All My Trials, it lent itself to strong harmony. My strength was Negro spirituals, Paul Robeson was my idol, things like O Sinner Man and Michael Row The Boat Ashore.

Paul's father, Rev. Nolan, had a strong connection with the Mission To Seamen and we went to Filey to support the Fisherman's Choir. We sang in the interlude, and not long after that Paul came up with the song Fishers Of Men, his own composition. We were looking for a name, and I thought fishermen are known as old salts, and a psalter is something you sing from, so thought of Psalters. We recorded the LP on a tape in my house and sent it to a studio in the Dales and they sent back the cut disc. I put an advert in the press for an open day to listen to the record, and it was quite successful. I finished up eventually with only two records left. From my point of view, and theirs, it was the Christian outreach of it that was the main thing. People wouldn't listen to the Christian message unless you sang it and the spirit of the time was that older people had to get used to the change from Bing Crosby to the group music. My only composition on the record was The Summer Is Ended. We did an open-air service with David Watson in the Museum Gardens, with loud speakers going out across the gardens and across the river. It was an inclement day and when David started to speak, it started to rain, so Chris put his big umbrella up and I thought, 'That's good, he's going to hold it over David while he speaks'. But no such thing, he put it over his equipment.

A lot of music appeals to the heart and that's where you start with the Christian message. C H Spurgeon [a Victorian preacher] *said 'the best music is that which plays the heart strings most'. You've got to find out the music that will reach people where they are, to get their attention and awaken something within them.*

CHAPTER EIGHT. FLOWERS IN THE RAIN: Psychedelia

By the late 1960s, the period of happy-go-lucky songs, and bops, was over. Groups became bands, and it was cool to like progressive or underground music, from bands who did not play chart music, but albums which had tracks with long drum solos and lead breaks.

The three main York bands in this category, who all became professional and made records, were the Roll Movement, who had started out as a mod group, Angel Pavement and the Smoke, who progressed from the Viceroys and the Shots.

John Cartwright played guitar in a group called the Misfits at the age of 15, then he and drummer Dave Williams got together with two others to form the Roll Movement:

It would be 1965, we formed with Cliff Wade and initially Johnny Fielder on bass. They pushed us in the newspapers as 'York's first mod group'. We practised in a butcher's cellar on Bishopthorpe Road. We played soul, progressive, unusual bands like the Doors, and always the old faithfuls, the Beatles, the Who, the Small Faces. Eventually I started trumpet, when soul music was beginning to drift in. We took it very seriously and did lots of rehearsals in that cellar, we were very keen and very dedicated and wanted things exactly right. One of the first tracks we ever tried was My Girl. The trumpet was amplified so it sounded like more than just one brass instrument. Cliff was a very good all-round musician, lead guitar and he could play bass, he had a good voice, and we started doing some of our own songs which Cliff had composed. I think the first gig was for the Evening Press, in a hall in the centre of York, and we came away feeling pretty good. Then the university gigs in the King's Manor which was like playing in a cave. A lot of the York bands started off their apprenticeship in the pubs but then moved on fairly swiftly if they were reasonable bands. There was some good talent around in York, there was no question about it.

Johnny Fielder left the band and was replaced by Pete Shaw, and in June 1966 the group entered the Melody Maker Beat Contest:

That was very pleasing and a shock to us that it took off so quickly from doing a number of gigs for a few months. Suddenly we're thrust into the heats, and we moved up to the semi-finals in Brighton and beat a band who went on to become famous, Mud, to get through to the Palladium for the final. It was about August 1966, but a band called Eyes Of Blue from Wales actually

The Roll Movement c1967. L to R - Pete Shaw, John Cartwright, Dave Williams, Cliff Wade. *(Courtesy John Cartwright) won the contest. We took several coaches of fans and had a lot of support. A fan club was created by two ladies from Tadcaster, Chris and Jean, and they kept in touch with the band all through its existence and travelled with us all over the country when we started going national. We did go professional in 1966. I remember giving up my job, and that was a very exciting time but risky. There was the prestige of playing on the famous stage for the contest, everybody had seen the Palladium on TV, and we had great celebrities judging, including one of our heroes, Stevie Winwood.*

When we went to gigs in York and Leeds and the Scarborough area, a lot of scooters would turn up with flags up on the long aerials. Dave, our drummer, had one and a classic parkah, he was very much into the mod scene. But we moved on eventually. We weren't going to be just stuck in one particular groove.

Some of the York shops were trendy. We would try and pick things that were fitting the image. Odd times one or two of us went down to London to the inevitable Carnaby Street for bits and pieces. We'd wear horizontal-striped jumpers and trousers went through the different styles. Eventually they became the bell bottoms or stripey trousers. [Flowered shirts] came a bit later. The hair had grown a little, and we'd moved into a progressive era. Bands like Pink Floyd were around, and there was the influence of psychedelia. We designed and painted and crayoned on our clothes. Most uncomfortable some of them were, because they were very stiff with the paint, but they looked quite good. It was purely stage gear, part of the image. The others were very much into necklaces and beads, mine was more the hand-painted smoking jackets and jeans painted with psychedelic swirls. One of the first times we played in York was the Assembly Rooms, a regular gig for decent top-name bands. I remember feeling really good when we did go out on the stage in all this gear. It was a very colourful time. Roll Movement started in 1965 and came to a halt in 1969, but in between we played all over the country, supported lots of big name bands, like the Who and Pink Floyd, in all-night sessions in an old tram shed in Leeds. We supported Cream at Matlock in Derbyshire, and at the same gig supported Family on another occasion. They were one of the most exciting live bands of that era. We did a summer season in Blackpool, about eight or ten weeks in l966, probably in the build-up to the National Beat Competition and worked at the Twisted Wheel in Manchester. They were complete drug dives. Dave Williams and I would often travel there to see live bands, like Georgie Fame And The Blueflames, and some of the excellent soul artistes that were around. Most of the audience was completely stoned. Purple hearts were very much the vogue of the day, and you'd go in the toilets and there'd be tablets all over the place. But we didn't go for that kind of stuff, it wasn't our scene at all.

We once played Bradford with Soft Machine and a band called Tomorrow. Keith West was a very good singer, and Steve Howe on guitar later went on to join Yes. You always aspired to some of these bands that we used to kind of worship. They were so polished and exciting to watch, you'd take influences from other bands and adapt things, and some of that came through in the songs. We were Small Faces style, they were a very innovative band. It got more sophisticated, more advanced and more proficient. But some bands about that time were a bit self-indulgent and went on a bit, a drum solo might last ten or 15 minutes which is probably pushing it a bit. When we supported Cream, they were tremendous musicians, but some of the solos were extremely long.

Sid Hartas was our manager. He lived in Penley's Grove Street, in York, and once we got attached to him, we started rehearsing in the back of that building. He eventually coupled up with an American chap called Charlie, and they produced the Tinned Chicken Club [at the Folk Hall, New Earswick]. We knew Geoff Gill, the drummer, [from The Smoke] he lived very close to me, and had connections through his excellent band with Chris Blackwell, who formed Island Records. Through Geoff's negotiations with Chris Blackwell, we received a letter saying he'd be interested in meeting us. At the time we were happy with our management, and so we didn't go down that route, but an interesting thought really.

We played wherever the manager got us gigs, church halls, universities, colleges and specific clubs, there were quite a lot in West Yorkshire. There was a place in Chesterfield, the Black Daffodil, which had a tremendous atmosphere, the Mojo Club in Sheffield, and a place in Boston, Lincolnshire, called the Boston Gliderdrome, an old RAF hangar, it was huge. We played there once or twice and had a good reception so we were invited back and got a lot more money the second time. The Key Club in Newcastle was a superb gig. It was down a cellar, and a great band at the time was resident there, Skip Bifferty, they were just superb. And the Newcastle Club A GoGo, the Animals started off there. There was a circuit of certain really cool gigs.

It's good to travel round the country and have a good name, and to have audiences that really appreciate you. That was excellent, to be tuned in to the audience. But I guess the ultimate for any band is to achieve fame with records.

The band was approached to work with other musicians on a performance of a song cycle based on four Chinese poems, which was quite unusual:

We had ten or 15 minutes of a little production thing, and we tried it once or twice at one or two gigs, but it wasn't danceable, so I guess that didn't make it very popular. But some bands were doing very unusual music at that time. Some of the soul music we played before we got more into the progressive stuff, you always had the audience up and dancing, and really enjoying themselves, that's why soul will never completely lose its popularity. We had a PA system, which for its time, about 1967, was very cutting edge. The Ike and Tina Turner revue were coming from America, and had some problems on the aircraft with losing equipment, including the PA system. Our manager, Sid, received a phone call, could they borrow ours? Pete Stringfellow who was running the Mojo Club in Sheffield, with his brother, knew we had this decent PA, so we all trekked across and we were very honoured to have Ike and Tina Turner singing through our PA system.

Sid was always one to try and think of publicity stunts for us, got us all into a boat, on a day when the seas were extremely rough, and we tried to go out and board the Radio 270 ship, to take over the broadcasting on the last day of its existence, for a bit of publicity. But it was so rough, we couldn't safely board the ship and we had to turn round and go back. Once we played on the Scarborough cruisers and we went round Scarborough, and had all sorts of signs up in the van. I was blasting my trumpet through the window as we drove round to attract people's attention that we were going to be doing this gig on the boat.

It was a strange balance being professional. On the one hand it was very exciting because it was doing something that was not really anti-establishment, but it felt like that. Parents saying, 'Get a normal job', all of us had heard those kind of statements, and here we were making a living, getting by and doing music professionally. But it was also very tiring. You're travelling up and down the country, sleeping in a rather noisy, smelly van, with fumes, and sometimes being in some near-miss crashes as well. We were in the Peak District and you can get pretty bad weather. One or two members of the band had become a little bit disillusioned in the months leading up to this, it was snowing, and I remember us going slowly down this hill in the van, and suddenly we lost control completely, and were sliding, and then we careered through one of these stone walls. The front of the van folded under, all the equipment came crashing on to us, and Cliff got his leg trapped, and he was hurt a bit. That put the cap on it really, that was in 1969, and it just made the decision and the band split. Some of us were wanting perfection in the songs, and some were more laid back. It's just all different personalities thrown together, and when there were some slight changes in the line up, you might click for a while and create some good music, but sometimes personality comes to the fore, and you get little break-ups and disagreements.

But certainly in the original line-up of Pete Shaw, Dave Williams, Cliff and myself, we stuck together for about four years.

In 1969, things were changing and the idealism of the early 1960s began to wane and disillusionment set in. The stabbing of a fan by Hell's Angels at the Rolling Stones concert in Altamont, marked a turning point:

Before that you had Woodstock and everything seemed beautiful. But certainly the Stones concert was a watershed in many senses. We split up and I went off and worked at Butlin's, then went down the King's Road, and spent lots of money on nice clothes and got a few jobs. In 1971 I was approached by members of the Angel Pavement. Their rhythm guitarist was leaving, so I took up the offer but we were only together in that line-up for about two years, before the Angel Pavement folded. Some of the gigs we did would have bands of all kinds, some playing straightforward rhythm and blues, ourselves playing a mixture of progressive, soul and our own material and you might get something completely different, almost akin to jazz.

It's a time I look back on with no regrets, whatsoever, it was a rare opportunity for a young person. In my adolescence to go off doing professional musician's work! From the early 1960s, the first plucking of a guitar, until about 1973 when Angel Pavement folded, I packed in a lot of very enjoyable times. Some stressful times as well, but mostly it was good memories.

Alfie Shepherd came from a musical family, his father being a Minster choirboy. His older sister played 78rpm records of rock 'n' roll, particularly Elvis Presley:

I was having piano lessons, and I think my father would have preferred that I pursued that but I was keen on learning the guitar, and I started jigging piano lessons. Used to trot off as if I was going, hide my music case under a bush and go and play football! I bought my first guitar when I was 13 for the princely sum of £11 from Hugh Robertson's, about 1960. Buddy Holly was the person who influenced me. I was self-taught, but I could read music and transpose what I knew to the guitar. We practised in the youth club, the Four S's. Then we became the Jetsons, which was a cartoon series. Baz Starkey's cousin John joined us on the vocals, so it was Johnny Starr And The Jetsons. We had a lot of fun. Then I went through O-levels in 1964, started work. One or two pals would come round and we'd play together, and that was the beginning of Wesley Hardin's Shotgun Package, Neil Webster, Brian Thorpe, Al Reeve and me. Must have been about 1965, that's when I got my first Fender Stratocaster. We played soul and I wanted to get into West Coast sounds, and multi-harmony. About 1967 there were some changes and we

Wesley Hardin's Shotgun Package c1967 at County Hospital Recreation Hall. L to R - Brian Thorpe, bass, Alan Reeve, drums, Neil Webster, vocals, Alfie Shepherd, lead and rhythm.
(Courtesy Alfie Shepherd)

ended up with Paul Smith, Graham Harris, myself and a lad called Dave Smith on rhythm guitar. Then we got Mike Candler, Candy, on drums and changed our name somewhere along the line to Angel Pavement. We started writing original stuff and our bookings were getting more diverse.

In 1968 we went to Mexico, we had to turn professional at that point, so we all packed our jobs in, and spent a lot of time up and down the M1, knew every blade of grass on the motorways, but we were quite finely honed by then. A lot of original stuff and good harmonies. The idea of going off for six months appealed to us and we made a lot of use of that. Because we were away we didn't have any diversions, five of us were thrown together, and we literally lived and breathed music. Over there we got to know local groups and Mick Fleetwood popped in to the hotel to see us on one occasion and we weren't there. When we got back, he'd written on the telegram paper, 'Hi there, Mick of Fleetwood Mac popped in to see you, sorry I missed you guys, make lots of dollars'. From there we had chance to go to San Francisco to play at the Purple Onion Club, a breeding ground for groups like the Byrds, and

150

Angel Pavement 1971 at the Hypnotique. Back L to R - Graham Harris, Mike Candler. Front L to R - John Carwright, Paul Smith, Alfie Shepherd. *(Courtesy Alfie Shepherd)*

Buffalo Springfield. We thought this was great but Candy was too young for a work permit, he was only 17. They were quite strict on employment legislation, so we had the plan where we would go minus Candy, and he would join us when he was 18. But we'd come that far together, so no, it was back to Britain, and meanwhile we'd got a recording contract.

We started on the university circuit gigs again, second billing to name groups. In those days recording companies would get together with the new releases, and decide which one would get all the plugs. The same week our single was released, Blue Minx's Melting Pot was released on Fontana, the same label, so it got all the airplay.

Alfie recalls John Cartwright joining the group in 1971:

John was an excellent arranger, he could take something that was very simple, and make something quite complicated out of it. There were some creative individuals in the group.

As far as York groups go, I like to think we were a bit different. I certainly remember people came along to listen to us because we were doing avant-garde West Coast stuff, by groups that a lot of people had never heard of, apart from John Fielder who knew every musician and every band all around the world. He'd come and see us because we did Moby Grape stuff, Buffalo Springfield, and Love. We did different material to a lot of the other groups and very rarely chart type stuff, we weren't into that. There was close harmony, all five of us sang, not necessarily on stage, but certainly in the recording studio. We were able to swap lead vocals, there were three of us that would sing lead, in different songs. We recorded at Morgan Studios, and BBC tapes at the Playhouse Theatre in Leeds for a series, The Family Of The Seventies, we actually did seven recordings. We all got on well. When we weren't playing together we were often crammed in a Transit van and so it was quite intimate, we knew each other's secrets, and respected each other's ability. When it came to music, we were free to criticise each other, and sometimes did. If somebody had something to say about a particular piece, we'd say it. I don't think we ever really had a falling out about music.

Alfie does not agree with the assertion by older musicians that music in the 1960s was just a 'three chord trick':

I would say that's not true. It's rather an old-hat attitude. There were people who would pick a guitar up and bash three chords, and there were plenty of people like that who had a lot of success. Bruce Welch reckoned he'd travelled the world on three chords. He's an excellent guitarist. Anyone with any ability would produce some good music. In the 1950s some people would damn rock 'n' roll as 'awful screeching', and some of it was but there was also a lot of talent. A lot of guitarists who played in backing bands were excellent. Lonnie Donegan was a very good banjo player. Everything seemed suppressed in the 1950s, people were coming to terms with being able to do what they wanted to do, and money was tight in the post-war years. So the 1960s was a kind of explosion.

Early on in the Labour Government, the Wilson years, things became easier, education became easier, the idea being that if you had the ability you should go to university. And that's where a lot of music bred, a lot of groups went to the university scene. People could do what they wished, too much so probably, because I think we're paying the price now, but it was a decade that I can't see being repeated in my lifetime. My own daughters say how much they envy us living through that. They're keen on the music of the era, there was a lot of live music then and you could see the artists easily.

The Beatles had a lot to do with that, and they kind of dictated fashion. I remember having Beatle boots with three inch cuban heels, and crippling myself trying to walk in the winter snows of 1963. And winklepickers, chisel toes, loud clothes, loud colours. After the war there were depressing colours and when we got into the late 1950s, bright yellow socks and Teddy Boys. People just wanted to express themselves and had the freedom to do it. I bought a tasselled jacket in Mexico in an Indian market, handcrafted. People travelled more widely, they could buy clothes abroad. I remember walking about in a bright bottle-green velvet jacket. Older people would say, 'What's up with him?' People didn't start wearing their hair long until about 1963, even the Beatle cut was just a mop cut, it wasn't all over their ears, and shoulders. Then in the early 1970s there was glam stuff, effeminate clothing, like the Sweet.

Nothing lasts for ever. The whole magic thing of the 1960s and flower power, the hippy era, you can't keep that sort of thing going, it just ran out of momentum. Then you got glam rock, and punk which was just raucous, discordant to me. Next thing comes rap which was certainly different. But just reading a book to a drum machine isn't music, there's nothing creative about it. In the 1960s there was melody and there was melody in the dance bands of the 1940s.

Our family's musical. If there's a moment's silence in our house, you can guarantee that one of the daughters will put music on. It's always there, it's a language of its own. Been a very important part of my life, I'd have been a boring accountant without it but earning more money.

In November 1968 Angel Pavement were playing in Sibyllas discotheque owned by George Harrison, in London's Mayfair, when they were approached by the manager of the Hotel Aristos in Mexico City and offered a six-month contract in his nightclub. Alfie was 20 and the others all still teenagers. The group found it was cheaper to go via New York and buy equipment there rather than pay £1500 to ship it out. Their first performance was to be March 6, 1969, and a TV appearance was also lined up. During their stay they did open-air appearances to audiences of 8,000.

Graham Harris remembers:

In about 1963 at Nunthorpe, Eric Wragg was an absolutely cracking musician and he had a six string guitar. He persuaded me to get a bass guitar so that we could mess about in my front room. It was the period when they went from double bass to electric bass. Elvis was double bass but if you listen to his style change, it became electrified. You'd gone suddenly from the big band sound to the little band sound which made just as much row as the big band.

I couldn't afford an amplifier so Eric worked out that if you got one of the old radios with valves, bared the wires at the back and got an ordinary guitar lead, took off the plug and bared the wires on that and put them together you could play guitar through an old radio. The first group was the Screen, with me and Eric, and three other lads from Nunthorpe. The drummer had a Salvation Army bass drum so our first ever gig was in Poppleton Church Hall, and all the local girls thought we were brilliant but we didn't exactly threaten the Beatles.

Then Graham joined with Alfie Shepherd to form Angel Pavement:

We did all the working men's clubs with Angel Pavement which must have done them good because of our following. It was the Pink Floyd era. They used a hot wax thing between two sheets of glass, projected behind them so it looked like amoeba, and they also had smoke. We had a road manager who worked at the hospital and he borrowed this projector and slides for the coloured water, and he moved it around so it looked like amoeba. Cracking! The amoeba worked very well but the smoke was a bit of a problem and we cleared the place, they all went out as if someone had thrown tear gas.

We went all over the country, we had a white double wheeled Transit, the group's first main form of transport. You knew you'd made it when you got a double wheeled, long wheel base. We put a partition in the back and some bus seats behind the driver's seat and that was luxury. We played Scotland, Inverness was the furthest north and then in Cornwall. If we were in the south, coming back up there was Don's pie and peas stall in Leeds and he

Gideon's Few 1967. L to R - Mick Fallon, Dave Alderson, Deke Hughes, Mike Matthews.
(Courtesy John Cartwright)

didn't open till midnight so about three or four in the morning we'd be charging up the motorway gagging for pie and peas and a sauce bottle full of mint sauce.

Our name came from the book by J B Priestley, Alfie thought of it. I thought the Roll Movement were better than us and I'd go to see them. Pete Shaw was the bass guitarist and I thought, 'Why can't I get a bass sound like him?' cos they only had bass guitar, one guitar, a drummer and a trumpeter who later on joined us, John Cartwright. He had this home made speaker in a big box with a union jack on the front, and I bought it off him eventually and I couldn't get anything like the sound that he got. Roll Movement were really great and they had a good following in York. Gideon's Few were pretty good, the bass guitarist had a Rickenbacker before I got my Fender.

We rehearsed at the club in Micklegate, near Walkers Bar, but it was always a major problem, where to rehearse. Especially when we turned professional. You could sit in someone's front room and do your harmonies, but not many people wanted you 'cos of the noise, so we used to beg, steal and borrow. I always liked anything with musical harmony in it, Hollies, Beach Boys, Fifth Dimension. We had Mal Spence as manager, really laid back, he came to Mexico with us.

Alfie Shepherd wrote a bit, we had about six original songs. We recorded in Morgan Recording Studios in Willesden, and we got put on to it by Geoff Gill who became our recording manager. The first song was a backing track now on a CD called The Best Of British Psychedelia, with strings and orchestra. And the Roll Movement are on that and the Shots. We'd always get midnight recording sessions until about six in the morning. We recorded a whole LP and two singles. The two singles were published, the first one squeezed into the top 50. Kenny Everett played it every Saturday for six weeks, a song called Baby You've Got To Stay, and the only other one he played six weeks on the trot was a Beatles song. He said, 'I really like this song but who are the Angel Pavement, I've never heard of them, let me know'. So me mother phoned in six times! On the strength of that, I really thought I had made it 'cos we went to Philips studios in London, and Scott Walker of the Walker Brothers, came walking through.

We got to Mexico City and had a six-month contract in this nightclub, £30 a week each, and a flat. We were like stars out there, it was in between the 1968 Olympics and the 1970 World Cup. After five months we got a bit bored playing the same place. So we said to the manager, 'Can we go home?' and he said, 'I've got your return flights booked but they're in a different season so it will cost me more. I want to open a hotel in Juan Juatto which is about 200 miles north of Mexico City, a silver mining town and it's their festival. If you go and do a concert up there, I'll pay for your upgraded tickets'. So we got on a jungle bus, chickens on the back seat, cows on the roof, and at one stage they actually put a coffin underneath the space and we ended up in Juan Juatto, and the first night we went to the local theatre 'cos they were having a festival evening and we got in one of the boxes and everyone stood up and applauded and shouted 'los angeles', the angels, 'cos we were megastars! Next day we went to where we were to play, on a dam in a park facing the lake. We turned up that night and there were thousands of locals round the lake and on rowing boats so we started playing away and after about six numbers the rhythm guitarist Dave Smith nudged me and said, 'Look at that' and we had a huge board to plug all the amps into and the lead for it went up into the mountains. It turns out they'd got this local in a house on the hill and unplugged the TV in the lounge and put in this three pin plug. So sparks were coming down the wires. I threw my guitar down and everyone else did, the drummer threw his sticks away. And eventually they fixed it and then that evening they said, 'The mayor of the city wants you, they are doing a reception for you, and he'd like you to be there because we always got on well with Queen Elizabeth'. So we got there, we had a few pink gins and he made a speech. We had dickie bows on and he did a talk about Queen Elizabeth, the two countries and everything. Then at midnight, 'We're in a silver mining town so that the band come and go round town so we'd like you to join them'. We went outside and there was this band, miners with their torches and candles. Battered trumpets, bass drum with one skin on and it sounded brilliant so we joined on the back, and ended up at the bandstand in the middle of Juan Juatto. I saw a European looking girl so we were dancing away. It turned out she was an American nurse who had been to the concert. We were dancing and then all of a sudden she started screaming. And all this band were sort of groping so I dragged her back down a street and into a bar where the mayor was slowly getting topped up.

After about half an hour this fellow came in, bandolier, local policeman and he said, 'Mr Harris, telephone call for you'. I thought, 'How does my mother know I'm here?' It was our manager and he says, 'Are you still alive?' I'd disappeared with this girl back to the bar and the rest of the group had started dancing with the local girls. Alfie had long straight hair and Candy the drummer had long red hair so the girls were fussing over their long hair and the fellas got slightly annoyed and had got knives and hatchets and chased the lads. Luckily we had a minibus that was driving us round and they made it back to the minibus but as Paul Smith got in his seat, a dagger came through the window and he shut the window on his hand. It was actually quite a dodgy situation. They never saw me disappear so they thought I was dead in a gutter somewhere and eventually I turned up back at the hotel! We did what we had to do in Juan Juatto and got back home. An amazing experience.

I think the production of music is brilliant now, the production of the Beatles was superb, that's why it stood out, they had everything right, the songs, the talent and the production. Technically songs are better but there are a few things I hate, the main one is electronic drumming. The main riff of the 1960s was 12 bar blues and some of the popular songs have come full circle and my kids say, 'How do you know that dad?' I say, 'It's from the 1960s'. The best groups have got a certain style of their own, they can play whatever they want and you know it's them.

Music's there in everybody's life, I'm a whistler and a twitcher. I go into work on a morning and even if the radio is not on, I hum and twitch. I don't know whether anybody in the Jacobean or Medieval era would have done the same but maybe they did whistle Greensleeves on a morning.

In November 2002 Morgan Studios are to release an album by Angel Pavement called Maybe Tomorrow in a limited edition of 1,000. The group have something of a cult following in England and abroad. Eight of the 14 tracks are mostly by Alfie Shepherd.

In the late 1960s Graham Harris became manager of the House (Mick Miller, Steve Rogers, Pete Shaw, Eric Wragg and Tony Lea). The group appeared during a York Theatre Royal production of A Midsummer Night's Dream, and ten new songs and the music were composed by Lea, Wragg and Graham Harris in three weeks. They had to dress in appropriate costumes and make the music 'light and airy with a vague medieval sound to it'. The play had good reviews and the group played during the performance from a box. They went with the play when it toured to Darlington. Graham has fond memories of the period:

My lad, 20 years old, said to me the other week, 'Dad I'm so jealous, you grew up in the 1960s'. I think that's a general thing with the youth today but we didn't think at the time we were in a special era, we enjoyed what we had but we didn't know what we had got.

In early 1964 five beat groups, who had won the five initial heats, competed at the Mecca Casino in York for the area final of the National Beat Contest. They were Tony Adams And The Viceroys, Gerry B And The Rockafellas, The Flintones, the Cheavours and Johnny Starr And The Jetsons. Tony Adams And The Viceroys won. The contest was very popular with more than 1,000 fans present. One of the things that fans liked about the Viceroys was their ability to present a full stage show, and include their own arrangements of standards such as Summertime. They were also famous for a rendition of Jack The Ripper in which Tony dressed up and scared the audience. In April the group had secured an audition with Decca but did not win a recording contract.

On May 4, the group went forward to the country's final of the Beat Contest at the London Lyceum. The posters in York read, 'Follow Tony Adams And The Viceroys on the Ousebeat Bus, depart Exhibition Square at 8am on May 4th'. By July they were playing dates in London and the south coast. On Friday September 11, the group played with Danny Adams And The Challengers, Brian And The Easybeats, the Cheavours and the Vampires at a Five Star Beat Ball in an aircraft hangar at Shipton-by-Beningbrough.

Tony Adams is well-known in York music circles :

In about 1958, I had my first taste of singing in public. My brother Brian had been in the army and was well into the Everley Brothers harmonies. But of course you can only sing harmony numbers with someone else. He was home

Tony Adams And The Viceroys 1964. L to R - Mal Luker, Deck Waugh, drums, Keith Hunt, Zeke Lund, Tony Adams singing at front. London Lyceum 1964. *(Courtesy Trudy Luker)*

on leave, and he says, 'How do you fancy trying out harmonies on Bye Bye Love and Wake Up Little Susie?' So we attempted Bye Bye Love and we were taken aback at how well it went. I think we were both naturals, because we found it easy. We went to Holgate Club. I'd be about 14. Brian had taken his guitar and said, 'Come on, we're going to do a song'. People tend to warm to a younger performer but I think we did a good job. The audience reaction to one song was enough. That's where it all started.

My friend Keith Hunt and I were both extremely musical. When we became interested in pop music, he got himself a guitar and joined a skiffle type unit at Carr Lane Youth Club. He knew about this group at the Acomb Hotel. He said, 'It's only up the road from you. Shall we call in?' There was Bobby Adams, the original drummer, Mal Luker, Steve Puckering, who was the singer and John Lund, Zeke was his nickname. And they were wanting a rhythm guitarist. Keith had had an accident at work and cut a tendon in one of his fingers, so he now had to play as if he was left-handed. Mal was the one that wanted a musical career, this wasn't a hobby for him. They got a few numbers off and they were given this spot on the Saturday night, and I'd been to a couple of their rehearsals, earwigging, and on this night, Steve

159

didn't arrive. I ended up singing. I was taken into the band and we practised at Mal's gran's in Scarcroft Road. My brother Barry had organised himself a band, the Swingalongs, and they were playing in the Burns Hotel. To get a residency in a pub in town was the bee's knees. I don't know how it had come about, but I'd actually got up with our Barry's band for a very basic rock 'n' roll number. And then Barry got laryngitis, and I got this message, 'Can you get in touch with Ron Cooper at the Burns Hotel?' I'd probably learnt ten songs altogether. It was a bit scary. He says, 'You can do the same songs all four sets, it doesn't matter. But we need you to play'. So I did it.

Tony Adams being congratulated on receiving the winning cheque from Bob Gaunt of Gaunt Brothers, National Beat Contest 1964. *(Courtesy Tony Adams)*

Walls and Mecca were two of the companies who decided to put on a National Beat Group competition. I went down to the Mecca bingo hall in Fishergate with an application form for Barry's group to enter. However, he was approached as an established band, to make a guest appearance. That meant they had an opening, so we took it. It all started off as a giggle, and it snowballed, and we won the north east. We failed miserably when we got to London because we were so green, and were wet behind the ears. We were dealt a raw deal because each band was given three songs to sing. After the second song I had to disappear off the side of the stage to put this top hat and cape on to come back and do Jack The Ripper, originally done by Screamin' Lord Sutch. Because I'd actually left the stage, the people who were operating the revolving stage thought we'd finished and turned us round, so that didn't help our performance. It was a great learning curve. A group that was very similar to the McGill Five won the competition, simply because they looked like them and dressed like them. But because we won the north east one, that gave us huge publicity and we were very successful, managed to get a residency at the Boulevard Club, which was another prestigious thing. There must have been about 50 local bands, all trying to get somewhere to play. We had work every weekend.

It was like a cauldron of local music and revolutionary 'cos you've got to remember that before this, pop music was provided by top American stars with huge backings, they'd take an orchestra around with them, whereas now, you'd got condensed. You'd have four or five people who were making their own music with their own instruments and amplification. You could get it all in the back of the van and go anywhere.

Mal and John were really the people that directed the band the way they wanted to go, we were a pot-pourri of different kinds of pop music. On the one hand we were doing Satisfaction by the Rolling Stones, or something similar. On the other hand we were doing You Were Made For Me, by Freddie And The Dreamers. We're talking about a raunchy sort of rough R & B man at one end and a prissy little man with glasses on, dancing around as if he's PeeWee Herman at the other end. And because of my performance stature, I was also being these people from one end of the pendulum to the other. All we were doing was providing live versions of the records that people knew anyway. Geoff Gill became our drummer then.

Tony Adams And The Viceroys on roof-top with York Minster in background. 1964. L to R - Tony Adams, Keith Hunt, Zeke Lund, Mal Luker, Deck Waugh.
(Courtesy Trudy Luker)

Half way through this, Mal and Zeke decided, 'Let's not just cover singles. Let's cover album tracks', which was fine until we realized we'd covered every single track of the Stones' first album, like Route 66 and Walking The Dog. And that's the route Mal and Zeke took us down, the R & B route. We got our name because Mal's gran had a paraffin heater called the Viceroy and that name was in by the time I'd joined them at the Acomb Hotel.

It happened to me because I was in the right place at the right time, actually entertaining others. It was their hobby to go dancing, or be entertained. It was my hobby to do the entertaining. Not many people get that chance. I think if you have an entertainer inside you, it's brought out in other ways. If somebody else thinks I'm good, I'll do it again. You've got to have an ego, anybody who says they haven't, they're either in the wrong business or they're lying. And that's what it's all about, it's that appreciation from an audience, without a doubt.

I was happy with local fame. I've got my group audiences, then I became a popular DJ with Mecca, at the Cat's Whiskers for five years. I was a successful, professional DJ in a club in Harrogate. I came back to York and worked at Mecca bingo. And all these people recognize me at some point, and are always very friendly. I wouldn't have liked to have gone down the avenue of the small fish big pond, which is what London would have been I think. I've been lucky enough to do it on a local scale, and I wouldn't have wanted to have got any bigger 'cos you see traumatic results of what can happen to people who can't handle the publicity machine.

Mal Luker lived in York with his grandmother, May Passmore, who had worked in music hall in the early part of the 20th century, (see volume one of this publication). His mother Trudy Luker was an international jazz pianist and singer, so it was quite natural that Mal would want to get involved in music. His grandma recalls:

Malcolm was very much like Paul McCartney. I remember John [Zeke] and Malcolm were coming up Fishergate and there was a line of girls waiting to get into the Rialto for the night show. Somebody said, 'There's Paul McCartney' and the two boys started to run and they ran after them. They went down Kilburn Road and up Edgware Road and opposite was my driveway and they got round before the girls knew where they'd gone. They told me the different things that were taken out of their dressing rooms, what they were wearing and everything like that.

I only saw the groups that played at the Rialto when they entered that competition. I was amazed at the way the girls went on, at the end they all went down to the front and they nearly shook their heads off, I couldn't believe it. I remember girls would ring me up and ask questions about Malcolm, what kind of pyjamas he wore and things like that.

In late 1964 three members of the group, Mal Luker, Geoff Gill and Zeke Lund, decided to go professional and merged with Mick Rowley and Phil Peacock, members of a Scarborough group, the Moonshots, to become the Shots. With a strong determination to succeed, they left the north and arrived in London with only a few pounds and a van full of equipment. After four months, they had written 35 songs but were not getting anywhere. Geoff was working as a dishwasher, Mal served in a coffee bar, Zeke worked in a record shop and Mick Rowley became a cleaner in a block of flats. Mal tells his story:

At 11 I was in my first little group, and played tea-chest bass. There was a couple of guitarists, one of the guys knew two chords, and the other guy knew the other one so we were made. That went on for a while, and then we started to get more and more serious, it was all we thought about. Each pub had their own band, and it was good fun, there was a lot of energy, it was positive stuff. I had a hell of a lot of support from my gran. She had this house in

Kilburn Road, and let us practise there, instruments and amplifiers everywhere. We religiously recorded everything we did, and the drums were set up by the telephone, out in the hallway, so that every time the telephone went, we had to stop recording!

It was a cultural revolution, and music played such a great part in it, a major vehicle to transport the whole thing that was going on. You didn't wanna work on the railway like your dad did, you wanted to do something else, and that something else was within reach, because the kind of music that was being played and made back then, was so simple, anybody could play it.

Mal Luker aged 11 with friend. Note the framed photographs behind of his mother Trudy Luker and his grandmother May Passmore. *(Courtesy Trudy Luker)*

We went off to London, and the landlady that owned the house where we were staying, in Swiss

163

Cottage, got us this thing with the pub next door in Adelaide Road. On Sunday afternoons, when the pub was closed, we could rehearse in there on the first floor. She knew this famous producer, Don Black, so he comes on the Sunday. Closing time happens and we all go upstairs and we'd written a few tunes so we played them to him. He says, 'Okay, guys, thank you' and we tried to let him out but we couldn't, the doors were locked. We had to lower him out of the first storey window, on a rope.

It was hard but we weren't intimidated, we had £14 and a van full of gear, we were gonna conquer the world. We realised how provincial we were after a while, when you see what goes on, but we had a few lucky breaks. It wasn't without opening your mouth, and asking for what you want, and that was it, to have more front than Woolworths. I'd be calling up record companies and saying things like, 'I need to speak to the producer in charge of the A & R department, Geoff what's his name'. I'd no idea who the hell it was, just so I could get through to somebody. I managed to con my way through to a whole bunch of people.

A few weeks later Don Black actually got us into the studio to cut some demos, and we did four songs we'd written, and he comes out, 'Well, it's all very nice guys, it's ten to one, I'll go for lunch right now so by two o'clock, see what you can do'. (Otherwise, forget it). So he goes off, and it was either Mick, or Geoff came out with this thing, 'I guess you've gotta keep hold of what you've got'. So we wrote this song Keep Hold Of What You've Got in 20 minutes. He comes back, 'Have you got anything?' 'Yeah, we'd like to play you this'. 'Why didn't you play this before?' 'We've only just written it'.

Bookings began to come in and the group got an agent and signed a contract. Then one night, they met the millionaire businessman, Alan Brush, who had the biggest privately-owned sand and gravel business in Britain. Mal recalls:

We did a tour with P J Proby and this bloke comes into the dressing room, and brings in a case of beers, and sits down and talks to us, and we got on with him like a house on fire. That was on the Saturday night, and then on the Monday we get this call, 'We've got a much better place for you to go and live, so you can rehearse, and we've got someone to invest in you guys'. So we packed the van up, and drove down to Morden in Essex. We spent that summer there, [at Alan Brush's place], rehearsed in the mornings, and went horse riding in the afternoon.

The group had a wonderful time. Alan Brush's partner, Jack Segal, signed them up, bought them new clothes and equipment and sent them to live in Brush's mansion in Essex to rehearse and write more songs. They lived in the 40-room mansion, with four kitchens, billiard-room, music room, five foot square television and 72 acres of land including tennis courts, stables and racecourse, as well as space for the Rolls-Royce cars and private helicopter. After two months, the group were ready to record and begin a nationwide tour. The recording contract was with Monty Babson, of Morgan Records, and their first single, Keep Hold Of What You've Got, was released on Columbia in October 1965.

But then they ran into difficulty when it was discovered that the first contract had been broken. It turned out that a signatory on the contract was one of the Kray brothers. Mal explains how the group met the Krays :

We played in their club, and they liked us. We had no idea at the time about them, they were always nice to us, and they had some involvement with this agent that we were with. One of the Kray brothers was on the contract. He showed up, he was as sweet as pie, 'You know boys, why don't you call me, if there's a problem we can sort it out'. And we scared each other to death, subsequently hearing stories about these guys.

The agent's lawyer wanted £750 to tear up the contract and as the group had not come up with the money, he locked their instruments in his office. Mal's gran, May Passmore told us how, when she heard of the situation, she raced down to London on her scooter and sat outside the lawyer's office, refusing to move until the instruments were returned.

While the problems were being sorted out, the group came back up to Yorkshire. By this time Phil Peacock had left the group and the other four became The Smoke and continued to write material. Eventually Monty Babson was impressed by a song called My Friend Jack (Eats Sugar Lumps) which was issued in February 1967. There was heavy airplay on pirate radio but problems linking it to the use of drugs meant it was banned and the label quickly dropped it. But the record had already made number one in Germany for seven weeks which ensured a tour of the continent. By January 1968, the group came 14th in a popularity poll of groups in Germany, only one behind the Rolling Stones. They had topped charts in Germany, France and Switzerland.

In June 1968 the Smoke were playing at shows with Manfred Mann in southern Germany, and being filmed playing on a boat trip down the Danube, with dates in Paris, Stuttgart and Venice, when they heard the tragic news of Phil Peacock's death back in Scarborough. He was only 21 when the car in which he was a passenger went out of control and through railings on Marine Drive. His body was swept out to sea.

The group were now based in Detmold, Germany and their new record Suddenly Gill's Fanciful Machine was doing well. But by September the group had decided to split up. They did not enjoy touring, as Mal recalls:

We just wanted to be songwriters at that point, and then we had this huge hit in France and Germany, all over the place, and they said, 'You've gotta go and do a tour'. We started practising again, having to get our act together.

Soon Mal, Zeke and Geoff returned to London to do session work, compose and arrange. Geoff Gill continued with Morgan Studios producing records, and was able to encourage a number of York groups to record. Mick Rowley stayed behind to work in Germany. Some years later Mal and Zeke also went back there.

In 1976 it was reported that Mal and Zeke were now big names in West German record production and had engineered albums by international stars. Ten years later in 1985, Mal had become managing director of a record company with studios in Munich and Sydney, having recorded many singers and groups including Michael Jackson, and the soundtrack of a Star Wars film. He won an Emmy award for his soundtrack of Peter The Great. The Record Collector magazine in 2000 described the Smoke as 'unquestionably one of Britain's finest psychedelic rock acts, still held in particularly high regard today'. Mal finishes the story :

Zeke and I ended up working for Morgan Studios, which Monty Babson owned. I'd met Mick Mason from Pink Floyd, and we were playing what we thought was country. It was so 'out there', that the engineer that was recording the stuff, after about two weeks of this, gave up. He said, 'Look guys, I can't handle this'. But it was dead simple, and I'd been recording all the demos for the band right from days in York so I just carried on doing the album. Then they asked us to do another one. One of the bands that we'd been touring with a lot, was the Small Faces, and Steve Marriott and I became pretty good friends. He'd formed another band with Pete Frampton and Greg Wrigley called Humble Pie. I was jamming with them. The first few days we were in the studio, it was all great fun, and Steve says, 'The Small Faces are starting back up again, and they've got this new singer, and they'd really love you to join the band'. And I said, 'Ah no man, if it was with you, cool'. By that time, my first kid was on the way, and I was wanting to do something serious. The singer was a Scottish guy called Rod Stewart.

When I worked at Morgan, I met a whole bunch of interesting people, and worked on some albums there, as an engineer. It really interested me, the technical side, it's like painting pictures with sound.

Then I moved to Germany, I was offered a great job, it was four times the amount of money. They had two studios and said I could buy whatever equipment I wanted, it was like Christmas. I'd been working on film music

The Smoke. L to R - Mal Luker playing sitar, Zeke Lund, Mal's wife Elenith, Geoff Gill. London 1966.
(Courtesy Trudy Luker)

stuff since about l984, Ewok's Adventures After Star Wars, the Lucas film, and then a whole bunch of big mini series and I met a lot of composers and directors through that. They were all saying, 'You gotta come to America'. And I decided to move there only about five years ago. They fly you around all over the place for different productions, 'cos not all of it's recorded in Los Angeles, some of it's recorded in London, some in Budapest, then jump on the tin budgie and flap home to Australia.

My introduction to the American music industry was when I'd got asked to record an album with a band called the Four Seasons, Frankie Valli. So we waited for 'em, an hour late, two hours late, three hours late, and then all of a sudden, my assistant and I were sitting in the control room, up high in the studio and we heard real heavy steps, two guys coming up the stairs. These two blokes walked through the door with full-length fur coats on, looking like Italian bears out of some mafia movie. It was unbelievable. And they didn't say a word, just looked at us, and we were completely and utterly stunned. Then we heard these other footsteps come up, and this guy walks through the door with a full-length mink coat over his shoulders and one of the guys says, 'Gentlemen, Mr. Bob Gordio', and there's only two of us sitting there, and it confirmed everything we'd heard about Americans.

If you wanna do something hard enough in life, you'll learn it. I deal with computers all the time, and we call it the bleeding edge of technology, it kind of gets beyond the cutting edge. And if any of my teachers could see what I do now, they'd never ever believe it in a million years. I started producing and I got more gratification getting others to do something that I couldn't. Coming from that side of it, to be able to pull the best out of other people, it's either a gift or frustration. Like working with singers, you've got all the phrasing, and you know exactly how it should go as a musician, and I found I did it okay. But nothing comes easy, you've gotta work damn hard for it. I'm glad to be doing what I'm doing, playing in the sandpit with the big boys. You get accepted, like in Hollywood it doesn't come in five minutes, you've gotta put your time in on that.

The whole thing that happened in York, I look back on it fondly. We had an awful lot of fun. We were young kids, and we were going around playing, it was cool. If it hadn't been for my gran, I don't think any of that would have happened. She was right behind us all the way, she was great, a super lady.

CHAPTER NINE. THE JUMPIN' JIVE:
Jazz from the 1950s to 1970s

The first jazz club to open in York in the 1950s was the York Jazz Club, at the beginning of 1953. By September it had been renamed the Studio Club as it met in the dance studio in High Ousegate. This was to accommodate dancers as well as listeners. But the club did not last. It was reported in the Press in July 1957 that a group of local people wanted to form a jazz club, Peter Forshaw who played the piano, Keith Laycock on bass, Ken Kenyon on drums, and Ken Turner on tenor sax. The Jazz Attic Club opened in 1958 in a candle-lit coffee bar on the top floor of a house in Petergate, above a restaurant run by Pete Madden. The opening of the club was due largely to a 19 year old male nurse and keen jazz fan and drummer, Colin Wilson.

In September 1955 the Gazette and Herald ran an article with the headline 'Nine York Boys blow their own Trumpet' about nine schoolboys who had formed a jazz band called the Minster City Stompers and had recorded eight pieces of jazz including New Orleans marches. They were so concerned that the school authorities would disapprove that they would not reveal either their names or the name of their school as it was 'not in favour of the band, partially because of the unsuitability of the type of music'.

Traditional jazz enjoyed a national revival in the 1950s and the Empire Jazz Club opened in September 1959 with Diz Disley and the Geoff Woodhouse Band playing. Ernest Shepherd was the president and the membership card stated that 'the object of the club is to promote good fellowship and further the art of music'. But once more the club folded after a short time. In December 1960 the Empire advertised a jazz session with the Roger Dean Quartet, hoping that Friday evening jazz sessions would be successful, with admission only 1/-.

At the same time a jazz club opened in the Clifton Cinema Ballroom and the first night featured the Burgundy Jazz Band. This seemed to attract greater crowds and over the next couple of years, many out-of-town bands played there including Chris Barber's Band with singer Ottilie Patterson.

In September 1963 another jazz club, this time called the York Jazz Scene, was started in Acomb Church Hall presenting traditional jazz bands every Friday night, with the Back O'Town Syncopators on the first night. The man behind it was Charlie Abel. Charlie originated from York. He had been working in the Midlands and gone regularly to jazz clubs there and when he returned to York, he could not understand the lack of provision for lovers of jazz. But by 1964 the

Spotted Cow Jazz Club 1975. L to R - Charlie Galbraith, trombone, Digby Fairweather and John Addy, trumpets, Dave Jones, clarinet, Norman Hughes, sax, Bobby Hirst, piano, Joan Whitehead, vocals. *(Courtesy Joan Whitehead)*

club had closed due to poor facilities. Later that year the jazz pianist, Bobby Hirst, organised a big concert of modern jazz at the Tempest Anderson Hall, where his own group played with several other Yorkshire acts and London saxophonist Don Rendell topping the bill. Another major jazz concert took place in December 1966 in St George's Hall, organised by Fred Baker, a headmaster from Riccall. Although jazz is regarded as a minority interest, there have been many individuals who have tried hard to keep jazz clubs going, only to find that venues and finance were a problem.

In June 1970 the Ardarth, York's new nightspot, this time on a barge held its private launching party, though it took another year before it became licensed. The barge advertised folk nights but it was predominantly a floating jazz venue. The regular band on Wednesday nights comprised Dave Harding, tenor sax, Jack Oliver, piano, Colin Baines, bass and Bill Eadie, drums. The barge kept going for a few years.

The place which did succeed in maintaining regular jazz nights was not a big hall, but a pub. In the 1950s, Joan Whitehead, landlady of the Spotted Cow in Barbican Road, employed a pianist, who played jazz-oriented music, but a decade later this evolved into a resident band on Wednesdays and Saturdays. She would get locals and professionals to appear as well as occasionally singing herself. Joan recalls :

It just seemed to swell until we formed the Spotted Cow Jazz Club, and had the T-shirts and everything, about 1972. We had guests like Eddie Thompson, he was blind and always had his dog under the piano. Wonderful pianist. Then Fred Hunt, Digby Fairweather, Roy Williams. Reg Sollitt was the first pianist, he was with me for years and then Harley Acton, he was with us until we retired, and the band moved to the Edinburgh Arms. There was Bill Eadie on drums, John Terry, Alan Craven, John Addy and Paul Acton.

Ron Burnett was part of the Cherry Tree Band, on a Wednesday night, that was more modern jazz. Music has been very important because I've made an awful lot of friends over the years. Depending on how busy it was, I'd call time and then I'd start singing. I feel the words I'm singing, you can with jazz, I like to put a lot of feeling in. If I can get their attention at the back of the room, I've done it. Everybody likes music, it's deep inside you. Tunes remind you of something in your life, I can associate people, or things or places with different tunes.

It was our own private club and it covered all ranges. Different types of people, a lot of the students and older people as well. And I've never known any trouble with jazz followers. Musicians always seem to be friendly. In a way they're all helping each other, when they're playing, it's like a bond.

Mick Brown got very keen on jazz when he returned from National Service:

It was in the RAF when I really started. I came back a Louis Armstrong fanatic. On the English scene it was Humphrey Lyttleton, I got all his records and tried to play like him. I went to St. George's Social Club, Walt Harrison was a big jazz fan and he was learning clarinet, and Phil Scott was also mad on jazz.

Bob Scott started this 59 club at Green Hammerton [see volume 1] and he'd heard we'd got this band. All real musicians he'd got, top class, Bob Scott himself, Bobby Hirst, Ray Philips, to us they were modern, because we were playing this old time stuff. He thought it would be a good idea if they had a trad band as well so he asked us to go and play. We'd get a coach at Exhibition Square on a Sunday, full of people going out to listen to some jazz.

We had a pianist by that time called Dave Plows, a banjo player Dave Storey, Paul Baines, Ernie Wilson and me. We didn't have a bass player, we got away without it, with a banjo. San Jacinto Jazz Band. It's an area around New Orleans.

171

Mick Brown playing piano at York University, late 1960s.   *(Courtesy Mick Brown)*

Jazz session at Black Swan c1962. L to R -
Bruce Adamson, Les Goodall, Greg Wadman.
(Courtesy Greg Wadman)

I remember we'd go to the local dances to see Johnny Sutton. I always admired Bob Scott and thought it must be great to be able to do that! Ray Cooper was a banjo player, he sat in with us, he played a phenomenal amount of instruments, saxophones, violins and others. There was a rehearsal band on a Sunday morning at the Black Swan, and they were essentially Ray Cooper's arrangements. Good jazz venue that was. We played in this café down High Petergate, Pete Madden had it, in this top attic room. We'd go up there and it was absolutely jammed. It must have been a fire hazard. But the number of people now who remember that band! I went to this party and a bloke came up, and says, 'You're Mick Brown, aren't you? You were my idol, I used to try and play trumpet'. I said, 'Yes, so did I!'

Jazz Quintessence with Ron [Burnett] and Al [Jenner] coming to York, that was the high spot for me really. My friend Eddie Johnson was the instigator, he knew I wasn't doing anything, and these two didn't have a rhythm section, so he got me and Ernie Wilson, and Mick Goodrick, put us together with Ron and Al and we formed a band and started to play at the Winning Post on Bishopthorpe Road. There'd be Bernie Cash on bass, a professional musician attending St. John's College, and Ken Kenyon, a lovely drummer. I loved going down and listening to them, really top class stuff. Quintessence played in and around York, and we moved into the Lowther and it really took off, we seemed to have a lot of fans.

Mick found himself playing with world class musicians, like Chris McGregor, South African Dudu Pukwana, and Louis Moholo, at the Old World Club in Stonegate:

The Geoff Woodhouse Band from Hull, who Al Jenner had played with, were in at the Empire once a week. I remember hearing this fabulous piano player and trombone player, the Pine brothers, Chris and Mick. Chris was one of the finest trombone players in the world. I actually got to play with them on trumpet, Eddie Johnson shouts, 'Can my friend play?' so I was sat in there and I played Basin Street Blues and I heard this piano playing, it was like Art Tatum, amazing, you could see they were world class. Mick Pine finished up playing with Ronnie Scott and they played here at the university. There was a girl we knew, she had a flat and we'd go there, and there was Ronnie Scott just reading the paper. And Eddie Johnson's mischievous. He says, 'I'll get this trad record out, see how he reacts', and he never turned a hair.

Colin Dudman was a really fine pianist, he'd been a musician in the army and came to York University and formed a big band there and I got roped in on trumpet. He went on to play with Barbara Thompson. I remember playing at Shipton Community Centre, and it was the night man landed on the moon and we played Fly Me To The Moon.

They formed this jazz club at the Rowing Club near Lendal Bridge in 1972, and I'd occasionally get called upon. They had visiting artists and they'd need a rhythm section and I'd find meself playing with Ron and Al again, and with musicians like Ernie Tomasso, who played with Harry Gold's band [and is now in the Cotton Club Orchestra]. *I remember one night, just sat there started up playing and saw this figure passing the piano, and it was Joe Harriott. Plays like Charlie Parker, absolutely fantastic musician, world class, walked in from nowhere and said can he play Lover Man! So we started playing, and he played the rest of the night, I couldn't believe it, me playing with Joe Harriott!*

When you take up an instrument, I did it because I listened to this music and loved it so much, I wanted to try and do it. You had this urge inside you. I could hear musical phrases in me head and I wanted to get 'em out. I've been playing at times and the only thing I can say is that the inner drive is almost orgasmic. You get this surge, really excited, when you're on a good night!

John Terry liked modern jazz and started to play in his early 30s:

I began to explore the possibilities of hearing more of this cool West Coast sound. I was really attracted to it. Most people came listening to jazz through the trad school. Delta music onwards and upwards, but I started in the middle. Eventually I heard Charlie Parker and that changed me again. A chap just round the corner from us, Derek Parker, had been a dance band player in his youth and he gave me a few lessons. We'd sit in his kitchen and he taught me the basics because if you don't learn the basics, there's a lot of steps to fall backwards down.

I gained some proficiency on the instrument [tenor sax]. *The Spotted Cow had music from 9pm on a Friday and Saturday. We went along and it just grew*

174

and we finished up with a quintet. A lot of the personnel came from Johnny Sutton's Modernaires who had played in the De Grey Rooms for dancing, and would go to the Winning Post for a little jazz blow in the middle to the late 1960s.

I much prefer the freedom of being able to improvise rather than read what's written down because you tend to get a bit mechanical. When you take a tune and you improvise, you're putting your stamp on it. It's like a painting. An artist gets a piece of paper, some colours and a brush and puts his stamp on that paper.

Eddie Johnson c1950s.
(Courtesy Eddie Johnson)

Eddie Johnson, originally from Bielby near Pocklington, was instrumental in getting the York jazz scene moving at this time:

I became a go-between, and that carried on for a good many years in terms of my enthusiasm. I've always wanted to get things moving so during that period I used to go and hear jazz all over the place. I was fortunate in having access to a car and we'd trek off to the Colton Hotel at Redcar, or we'd drive to Manchester, to the Sports Guild. We went to Hull on a regular basis, the Windsor Hall, they always put on good jazz.

My politics had shifted considerably, I'd been brought up in a very conservative background, and then suddenly through my association with Mickey Brown, and such people, I was exposed to different, new ideas, and so I'd become a socialist and I always took a very strong anti-racist position, mostly through my love of jazz.

Musicians often stayed with Eddie and this would mean little impromptu jazz sessions at his home:

I was renowned for giving people silly nicknames, so Ernie Wilson became Shadow Wilson, a famous American drummer. Ernie always smoked Gauloise cigarettes and I think they did a cigarette called Shadow. I got Ernie, Mickey Brown and the bass player, Pete Williams and we got a rhythm section together and went up to the Black Swan, and organised this session with Ray Crane on trumpet, and it turned out really well. And that was what became

Jazz session upstairs at the Black Swan 1964. L to R - Eddie Johnson, Paul unknown, Chris Boyes, Brian Eden, Len Rawding, Ray Cooper, Alex Boyd, Greg Wadman.

(Courtesy Ray Cooper)

Jazz Quintessence. The first regular blow of all was back at the Black Swan. The line-up was two trombones. Al Jenner was a very fine player, played instinctively. The band ticked over nicely, they worked out a few arrangements and it was good.

When I moved to East Parade, in 1964, there was a guy living across the road from me called Adrian Macintosh. He was in the other camp, I was deemed to be a mouldy fig, and he was a modernist. And he was quite friendly with some members of the Dankworth band. I don't know how, but I ended up with this long playing record of Ornette Coleman, Tomorrow Is The Question, very prophetic title, it seemed like it was avant-garde jazz, and it was just sheer cacophony to me. This mutual friend said, 'Adrian will take that off your hands'. So I literally went knocking on his door with this record, and from thereon we became very good friends. He introduced me to more modern sounds and more progressive sounds, and I helped him to listen to things which he'd overlooked.

Adrian was a great Goons fan, he had this penchant for ridiculous names, and would spend hours looking in telephone directories, and coming up with silly names, and he found a guy who was always writing to the Press, called

Fred Moth. When he told us this he became Adrian Moth. One night there was a gig at the Gallery Golf Driving Range on Wiggy Road, it had only just opened, and this big bill poster said, 'York's Finest Jazz Trio, Bobby Hirst, piano, Ken Kenyon bass, and the fabulous Adrian Moth on drums'!

Adrian moved down to London and is probably, with the exception of John Barry, York's most successful musician. He's performed with everybody, lots of great American players, and in 1982 he joined the Humphrey Lyttleton Band, and has stayed with them, as Humph's longest serving drummer. It's taken him round the world, and he's played at all the big festivals, with people who he himself idolised. I remember Adrian coming to the Lowther, and at that time he was heavily into avant-garde jazz, and he was nuts on Tony Williams, Miles Davis's drummer at that time, and I remember Aid turning up in kaftan and beads and knocking hell out of Shadow Wilson's drum kit. We put jazz on there, about four or five sessions, and it was going really well, 'cos it was good beer, and the room was ideal. You went up the staircase, people got jam packed in, comfort wasn't the order of the day then, it was all about atmosphere, if you were choking on cigarette smoke, and crammed into some sweaty cellar, that was all part of it.

Gill Fox was bowled over by the new rock 'n' roll in the 1950s although later, jazz became her great love and she wrote a jazz column in the Yorkshire Evening Press for some years:

Rock 'n' roll nearly blew my head off, I just thought it was fantastic. I learnt to jive at Mary Mac's, the first part of the evening was compulsory ballroom dancing, then for the last hour we were allowed to jive. There was Bop For A Bob after that, we'd go there on our bikes and bop our socks off.

No one thought of putting records on for people to sit and listen to. Neal Guppy's the first one I remember doing that, 9d it was, to go in the Woolpack. I don't remember there being a bar, but alcohol was not the priority in those days.

A lot of rock 'n' roll was based on jazz and blues, so there was an automatic link but I really became introduced to jazz when I got a boyfriend who was at the art college in York. We went to parties and listened to jazz and blues records, which I just thought were absolutely wonderful. I had a running book of orders at Banks' music shop. I got the numbers and took them in. They would take about three months to come sometimes, presumably from America.

The door at the side of the art gallery, which is now blocked up, that was the main entrance to the art school. There was a ground floor hall and we had a dance there every month, fancy dress which took quite a bit of organizing. I'd go as a Fire Nymph in hand-painted gauze, that my boyfriend Paul had painted. I was about 18, it was 1958, and people weren't that interested in jazz. If they did like it, they were listening to big band sounds. But then places started to open. There was one in the Clifton Ballroom, and the Burton Stone Inn had a jazz band in that back room with the big window. We'd go in there for one jazz thing, on to the Clifton, then Neal Guppy's, we'd dance all night to records.

Pete Madden had his coffee house in Petergate, up on the top floor, and whoever was there, me, Maxine Liversedge and Olive Adamson, mucked in and served the coffee. We'd have coffee and play our records. We'd sit discussing the latest books, we were keen on new writers and existentialism, we thought we were Beatniks, cool and trendy, part of the Left Bank. It sounds pretentious now but at the time, when you're that age and impressionable, it was world rocking stuff. I'd had this very conventional upbringing so it challenged everything I'd ever been taught, and music was a part of that.

Pete Madden was simply part of the institution when I met him, but I was told he was an ex-bomber pilot, very flamboyant, rather handsome in a dashing kind of way. He obviously liked young people, and he had this café with red & white checked tablecloths and Chianti bottles with red candles in. That was on the ground floor, of what is now Plunketts. And it was very much a place for the theatre people to go after the performance. You could have rump steak and chips which seemed fantastically sophisticated in those days, it was cheap as well. It was always a bit dark and mysterious, with bead curtains and was considered very chic.

It wasn't a private club, but Pete knew most of us by sight and we used to walk through the curtain to the stairs which he more or less guarded. We could take our own records which were usually jazz, but I remember we played Big Bill Broonzy's music and Cliff Richard's Living Doll, and anyone with a guitar would play, like Bruce Adamson, the brother of Olive, who was nicknamed Segovia.

Very long hair was de rigeur. My boyfriend was doing textile design and he painted fabric for me and we all wore stuff we made ourselves, the full skirts and everything. And white faces, white lipstick, looking as if we were at death's door. Big black eyes, the Dusty Springfield look before she was around. For the men, long hair was pretty new, and fairly avant-garde, they took a lot of flack for having it.

About once a month a band would come through, from Harrogate or Hull. It would be on the first floor which we didn't normally go into, a bigger room with bay windows, and I can remember one night when they were hanging out of the windows playing the trumpet in Petergate. The whole place was jumping. We danced to the big bands, they were lovely to dance to, wonderful musicians, they certainly knew their instruments but I think the new music was more creative. It left more room for experiment. The big bands never set your blood going round at 200 miles an hour. They belonged to another era.

When we were bopping and learning to jive, it was all full skirts and flat shoes and I wore something called the sack. We did a dance, the Creep, which meant you couldn't move in your clothes, and the boys' trousers were drainpipes, very tight. We'd pack our great big petticoats, with whale-boned corsets rolled up, pack our shoes, and cycle off to the De Grey Rooms.

I'm sure music broke down class barriers. It was so exciting, if you were young, and had blood going though your veins, you'd be hard pressed to resist it. There was a generation gap then. My sister was five years older than I was, born before the war. Had a different upbringing, and she didn't like it particularly at all. But it was a big turning point. A lot of things were happening politically at that time as well, which we all used to waffle on about, probably very misinformed.

Jazz is intimate music, it would be lost in bigger venues. A jazz trio, or six or seven, it's very intimate and intense, and the dark smoky venues go with it.

Adrian Macintosh was brought up on music, as his parents ran a dance band, Mac And His Music, and he started playing regularly in the City Arms. He went on to become a professional drummer with the Humphrey Lyttelton Band:

I'd made a few attempts with rehearsal bands, and was absolutely dreadful. My mother played drums in my father's band, so there was always a pair of drum sticks and a snare drum at home. But I'd play on a folded-up chess board, and I put a bit of brown paper over the chess board, and that was the snare drum, and I had a block of wood that was a cymbal so I'd play along with records. Peter Williams, who plays bass, he knew I could keep time, and there was a job came up in Haxby I think, and he said, 'You can do that, they need a drummer'. 'I haven't got a drum kit'. 'No problem, we can get the drum kit'. So I went along and did this job, and it worked out okay. I ended up doing another job and the third job along the line was with a trombone player called George Kingsley, Musicians' Union secretary for York, and Minnie Badger on piano. Strange trio. If you could have recorded that, I shudder to think what it would have sounded like. Then eventually I was getting so much work I went to Kitchen's in Leeds, and got an Olympic drum kit. I got some lessons too, and got to know quite a lot of jazz musicians. This was in the early 1960s.

1960, Johnny Dankworth's Orchestra was doing a tour of Britain, and I got to know the band, and the drummer was Johnny Butts. He taught me a few things, and he gave me a practice pad and so I picked things up at the 'university of life'. I was working nearly every night, sometimes until four in the morning, not much sleep was had in those days. I worked at a night club in Harrogate, four or five nights a week with a trio. But I wanted to play jazz and there was a club on Wigginton Road, Gallery Golf, and they started a jazz club. I worked there with Bobby Hirst on piano, Pete Williams sometimes or Mick Goodrick on bass, and Mike McNeill on guitar. Mike and I actually also joined a pop band called Tricycle. Sylvia McNeill was the vocalist, and I did my first broadcast with that band.

I left York in 1966 and ended up working with dance bands from the past like Lew Stone, Harry Roy and Victor Sylvester. I remember a friend had bought tickets for Benny Goodman's band at the Albert Hall. It was a band of my idols, Zoot Simms on tenor saxophone, Bill McGuffy on piano, Mousey Alexander on drums and Bucky Pizzarelli on guitar. We were sat right next to the band, and Zoot Simms looked over and smiled, and passed the time of day. The following night I did the very first gig for Victor Sylvester's Band, in a hotel in London at the back of Marble Arch, and who should be staying there, but the Goodman Band. I walked in with my drum kit, and Zoot Simms and Bucky Pizzarelli were in the foyer. They said, 'We saw you last night, are you playing tonight?', so I said I was, and, 'Perhaps we'll come in for a blow later'. Well of all the bands I'd played with up to that point, lots of jazz groups, and the one night I worked with Victor Sylvester I sort of fronted with Zoot Simms!

When I first left York, I was very friendly with Bobby Breen, the singer with Dankworth's band and within almost a week of being in London, he got me a job, six nights a week, at a jazz pub in Bermondsey, called the Lilliput. And the piano player was a legendary player, John Taylor. It was mostly singers but occasionally you'd get famous soloists coming in, so I got to know a lot of people through that. And it was good to be employed on a regular basis for two and a half years, and then I joined Val Doonican for about a year!

In 1982, Adrian was asked to fill in at the last minute one night with Kathy Stobart's Band in a jazz club in Aldershot. It was quite late and Adrian almost turned it down, but managed to get there in time. He thought nothing more of it, until a while later when Humphrey Lyttelton was looking for a drummer and approached Kathy to ask if she knew any. She recommended Adrian and he has been Humphrey's drummer ever since:

Humph phoned up and said, 'I've got two jobs, one is Aston University in Birmingham and then, can you go to Monte Carlo for a week?' And that first week, in Monte Carlo, we worked on the Tuesday morning, we did 12 minutes, Tuesday evening we did 30 minutes and the same on Friday. And the rest of the time we were in a five star hotel with a suite each and champagne breakfasts every morning.

You pick up things. One of the essential things for a drummer is to work with good players, and for many years I wondered why I was getting terrible backache, and shoulder ache. It's because you're straining to keep the time, if the bass players weren't strong enough. For the last goodness knows how many years, I've been lucky to work with some of the best bass players around, and the difference that makes, it's like gliding on air; you let the sticks do the work for you. When I see these drummers flailing about and struggling, I just look at them and think, 'You're wasting all that energy, you can get all that sound without doing half of that'.

I remember Thomas Beecham was once talking about piano players, and saying if you watch the great players, you see that they pull the notes out of the piano, they don't pound their fists into the keyboards. And I've noticed that with great drummers. I've spent many an hour watching my idols, like Billy Higgins and Art Blakey, who had this ferocious sound but he actually pulled the stick out of the cymbal, so his wrists were hardly moving. The stick would just bounce off the cymbal, and you could play as fast as you like and you'd hardly notice it.

Ron Burnett originated from Hull but came to York in 1966 although he had been playing music in York much earlier:

I went to art college in Hull, and art colleges have traditionally been training grounds for all sorts of musicians. John Lennon, a famous example, Pete Townsend and so on. We're talking about 1957 when the trad boom was in full swing. Kenny Ball, Acker Bilk, Humphrey Lyttleton, they were all up there. So this was the natural music in the same way that nowadays kids would try to follow Oasis, or in the previous generation, the Beatles. Our mentors were

Ron Burnett and Al Jenner - late 1960s. York University.   *(Courtesy Mick Brown)*

Dave Kendall on banjo, watched by Denis Goodwin, 1970s.   *(Courtesy Dave Kendall)*

Kenny Ball, Chris Barber, these people. We adopted Acker Bilk style waistcoats, morning trousers, straw boaters, or bowler hat, for our particular music.

At that time jazz fans travelled around from Hull to Scarborough, Bridlington, York, Leeds. If you heard there was something on, you'd go. Particularly if it was a name act, one of the big touring American groups. Jazz fans were willing to tour around and find their music wherever it was, so we found a lot of people were coming to Hull from York and before too much longer they were inviting us to play in York. The first time we played in York was 1958 at Pete Madden's Café, we'd play there regularly. Another place was the Empire, the coffee bar there, and we'd come over to the Clifton Cinema late night jazz sessions, very well attended. You'd get a couple of hundred coming.

We got invited to come over by York Art College to play their Arts Ball in the Assembly Rooms. Everybody in fancy dress, a big end of year event, jazz bands playing. None of us had cars then and the only transport we could find, one guy borrowed his uncle's horse box, a big closed wagon full of hay. We had a nice job and all the young people were dancing and I noticed a chap who stood out from the crowd. He was in his 60s, grey hair, very distinguished, wore one of those smoking jackets that the aristocracy wear, red velvet, and he was smoking a cigar and holding a short glass of whisky. At the end of the event I thought no more about him, but he came up and said, 'Would you chaps like to come back to my house and play?' It turned out he lived at Norton, near Malton, and his name was Percy Legard, he was a racehorse trainer. So young lads keen for adventure, we followed him along these country lanes to Norton and we turned up at this big house with a swimming pool, played there and wended our weary way back to Hull about 6am.

And he invited us back regularly over the summer, so we'd finish up there every Saturday or Sunday night playing for his assorted guests, a mixture of aristocracy and showbiz. At that time all the coast had shows on and live bands. So as well as us going and playing, a lot of other musicians were there too, and it was interesting to play along with professional musicians at this rather sumptuous, decadent private party, sat on the side of a swimming pool.

At this time, Eddie Johnson got us together to form a band which played regularly at the Lowther. The publican was Tommy Davis, a very skilled percussionist who played all the pantos and shows at the theatre. We started a weekly residency in the top room playing Dixieland. The highlight of the Lowther season, was one York Festival which would be 1968. Laurie Taylor was Professor of Sociology at the university at that time, and a great jazz fan and we were always pleased to see him come through the door 'cos it meant that there'd be a huge team of acolytes with him, beautiful girls and young men, about 30 people would follow him around. So that ensured that we would have a good audience.

The thing that changed popular music once and for all, was the coming of The Beatles. Either you were with 'em or agin 'em, and we were never against them, 'cos I loved their music, but it scuppered the jazz thing, and kicked it firmly into touch, and replaced it with this new phenomenon, the first Brit pop wave. So jazz again went back to being a sideline in terms of popular taste, had its followers, but they were by no means a majority. The interesting thing is how it's survived and prevailed, and sustained itself over 100 years. The same kind of music is still being played as it was at the turn of the 20th century in New Orleans, Memphis and Chicago. I suppose folk music survived in the same way. It's a kind of oral tradition. Jazz musicians would listen to the records, copy the ideas, and then work out their own ideas from that. So the kind of jazz that we're playing tends to be popular jazz, rather than grand art and is recognised as the only original 20th century art form. Jazz as an art form was quite an innovatory thing in the hands of people like Duke Ellington, Miles Davis, Louis Armstrong.

In the 1940s in America, Charlie Parker and Dizzy Gillespie were moving the music in a new direction. They were observing what had gone on in Europe and what was happening in the avant-garde scene with people like Stravinsky. People were impatient playing the same old tunes over and over and wanted to try something different. They had to be supremely in command of their instrument, to know music inside out, and even when they played a popular tune, when it came to the improvisation section they would put in substitution chords and different lines, and counter harmonies.

Geraldo was a band leader, famous on the radio but he also had a franchise for putting bands on the big ocean liners going across to America, so Geraldo's Navy were the dance band musicians who played on board liners going across to Boston, Philadelphia and, of course, New York, with a chance to get off the boat for a day and go and hear these legendary new people like Parker, Gillespie and Charlie Ventura; the first time in the flesh to get the real spirit of it, and bring it back to England. Ronnie Scott is one of the people who did it, plus a man called Johnny Rogers, a wonderful alto player who finished up being a signal man at Grosmont up here in North Yorkshire.

Music very firmly is a scene setter and it's actually opened quite an interesting market for us as jazz players in what I call 'wallpaper music'. In other words you're booked, not to be the main attraction, but to be an ambience, a background. Music is there to make people happy, to set the scene, to give them an enjoyable experience.

Phil Scott was keen on jazz from an early age:

I was only 10 or 12, probably influenced by my elder brother Bob, he started playing and all the records came in, the old 78s. The main interest was big bands. We played in a skiffle group, Mickey Brown and Affie McClay on washboard, me on tea-chest and Walter Harrison on clarinet. I always remember being at St George's Youth Club and you could get AFM and this guy would come on and say, 'Sounds a bit cool in the megacycles', and it was Shorty Rogers modern jazz from San Francisco area. And somebody said, 'You can turn that crap off for a start, Scottie'.

I remember Derek Dunning's bass player, he was a little old guy and he adapted a cart for the back of the bicycle, which he could strap his double bass on to ride into York. That was when the City Garage was open in Blake Street and you could go dancing and you could go on your bike and park it there for 1/-.

Derek Dunning, tenor sax, Bobby Hirst, piano, jazz session 1950s.
(Courtesy Angela Dunning)

The Modernaires met in Thomas's for a drink and to stop me paying 6/- for the ticket, I'd meet the lads and take the instruments in. One week it would be my brother's trombone, the next week the tenor sax, a few of the drums in for Ray Phillips and even the double bass for Mick Smith. I'd get a bottle of beer and a pass out, and the doorman, a council employee with a uniform, says, 'I wish I was as bloody clever as you'. I said, 'Why?' 'You're so versatile, I didn't know a bloke could play as many instruments as you can'.

When I started work we sort of drifted away from the youth club and there was a group of us from the carriage shops used to meet and have a bow-tie night. Bow-ties in those days were only to be worn with evening dress, but everybody had a lounge suit, and in winter a Crombie coat, or a Raglan with the

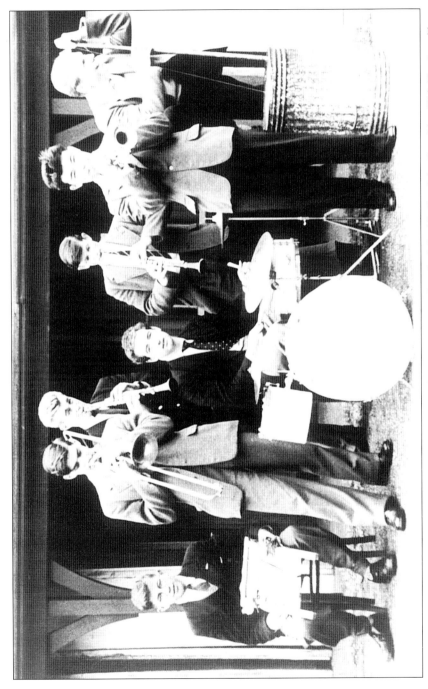

The Skiffle Group from St George's Youth Club at Wenlock Terrace c1957. L to R - John McClay, John Partridge, Walt Harrison, Tony Gillian, drums, Paul 'Tiny' Baines, clarinet, Mick Brown, trumpet, Phil Scott, dustbin bass.
(Courtesy John McClay)

shoulders on them. I had a big tweed one because I was on a discount with Isaac Walton's. All the best suits, Daks suits and everybody had a tie on. Then we would say, 'Right tomorrow night, bow-tie night' and you couldn't wear a black one, you had to wear a colour one, but there weren't many coloured ones available. They made it a ruling that you had to go and find yellow ones and pink ones, and can you imagine walking down town and going in the Burton with any of those on?

As for jazz and drugs, on the national scene there probably was. But locally it was pints of John's. That was your stimulant. I can remember going to a symphony orchestra at the Rialto and seeing the whole of the brass section on the second piece that was played, get up, walk off the stage, come down the steps, out through the fire door, and across the road to the Edinburgh Arms, knowing that they had a good 25 minutes. It isn't the strings and it isn't the wind section, it's nearly always the brass section seem to work up a good appetite for thirst. The only one of the strings who used to drink heavy was the bass player. Mind you when you're pulling one of them things around all night you do need a pint or two to get yourself back again.

Paul Acton is the third generation in a family of musicians. His grandfather, William, was a band leader in Manchester in the 1920s and came to York in 1938:

He sang, played bass, violin and saxophone. He never actually played instruments other than bass once he came to York. He got gigs playing with Bert Keech, Derek Dunning and, briefly in the 1960s, at the Society Club with my father. It was like a cabaret. He was still doing gigs occasionally in working men's clubs right up until 1967 when he died.

Will Acton won the 'best individualist' prize as a bass player in 1947 in a Melody Maker dance competition. Paul's father, Harley, began playing piano when he was quite young, and Paul followed in the family footsteps when he played jazz at the beginning of the 1970s:

I think he was 18 when he got called up for National Service. He was quite a good piano player and he broadcast for the British Forces Network whilst he was stationed in Hamburg. When he came back to York he did gigs with various bands throughout the 1950s and had a residency at the Chase Hotel.

I was a late-comer and didn't start until I was about 21. At school I had a good music teacher and he was into jazz and he played us some records, Dave Brubeck. I thought it was great. When I went home and told my father he couldn't believe that I'd shown an interest in jazz. He did everything he could to encourage it. We started going to jazz concerts in Leeds, and buying records. I liked the 78s that my father had left from the war, so it was always ingrained. It's like learning to speak isn't it? My father was always playing piano, so I knew all the tunes. Then he got it into his head that he might play bass, so he bought all the gear and we met John Terry who was playing at the Spotted Cow, and they were short of a pianist 'cos Reg Sollitt had left. So my father got the job as pianist. Then the bass player had to leave. I'd practised with my father at home a bit but I didn't want to actually go in front of an audience. But he said, 'Come along, do a couple of numbers, and if you're no good we'll tell you to sod off.' So I went along, scared to death, and the first number was Take The A Train. The sweat was absolutely pouring off me, but it went down all right. The drummer, Bill Eadie, bought me a couple of drinks, gave me quite a lot of encouragement, and the night seemed to fly by. And from that I was there for 15 years! And I thoroughly enjoyed it. I couldn't wait for the weekends to come around.

In York then, most of the live music had gone, the discos had killed it stone dead. In 1971 I can only think of the Spotted Cow, the upstairs room at the Black Swan, the floating barge club, and perhaps the John Bull. If you had live music it was a novelty but the older people were glad to have it back. And that's why I think it was such a success at the time.

My grandfather was more of a dance band musician but my father was a jazz musician. At the Spotted Cow it was fantastic. You could never get the band started, but you could never get them off once throwing out time would come along. There'd be people sat in the other bar waiting for the music room to open so that they could get a seat and by half time you couldn't find a square foot of floor space. It was absolutely packed out and they stood in the corridor, up on the stairs, shouting and screaming. I've never known anything like it.

It was pretty cramped on the stage as well because there was a fireplace still in and Mike Dann, our drummer, was half in and half out of the fireplace, and on one side were customers at the bar elbowing him. Jim Davidson, our clarinet player, he couldn't read but one night there was some classically trained clarinet player in and he was at the front table listening to Jim wondering how the hell he did it. He just couldn't work it out and Jim couldn't tell him either 'cos he had a special fingering system all of his own and he got results. John Addy was the front man, he was indispensable. People do come to see a singer. It's more entertaining for them. My father used to write a lot of stuff out for the band, there were about seven of us - my father and myself, Mike Dann quite often on drums, John Addy on trumpet, John Terry on tenor sax and Jim Davidson, clarinet, sometimes Denis

Goodwin on trombone and later Alan Crane on baritone and alto. Joan Whitehead would sometimes sing, she was good.

I've known quite a few bands split up because of personality disorders. And musicians, when it comes to personality disorders, there's plenty of them! But there was no problem like that. People couldn't believe how that band stuck together really. We had a good following, a range of ages from 18 to mid-70s. Jazz is that sort of music you see.

I got a lot of satisfaction out of playing with my father, we were pretty close anyway and it was a common bond. We had the same musician's sense of humour, cynical and mickey-taking. Musicians have their own language which outsiders probably wouldn't understand. One who played piano occasionally, didn't tell the band what tune he was going to play, but for Green Dolphin Street, he'd just shout out 'Sydney', because there was Sydney Greenstreet [the actor]. You had to know his own little code. Strutting At Some Barbecue, an old Louis Armstrong tune. He'd shout out, 'Barber's queue'. You had to be quick, the audience couldn't understand how the hell we would know what to play.

April 1965 - Modern Jazz Sessions at Enterprise Club, featuring McNeill-Herbert Quartet. *(Courtesy Neal Guppy)*

Paul explains why the bass player in a band is important:

You may think you could do without him but if the bass player stops, the bottom drops out of the whole thing. It sounds like a steam engine only going on two cylinders. The pianist is putting the chords down but you could get away without the piano player if you had a guitarist in. You could get away without a drummer if it was a quiet gig. But you'd have a job to get away without a bass player in a jazz club. Bass player's missing everybody else may as well go home. And you don't realise what it's doing until it's not there. One night I had my amplifier catch fire in the Spotted Cow and the band carried on playing in the best

The Wednesday Band from the Spotted Cow c1978 at the Folk Hall, New Earswick. L to R - John Terry, Ray Cooper, Reg Sollitt, Cassie Laycock, daughter of dance band bass player Keith Laycock, John Addy, Carol Addy, Mike Dann, Nigel Nicholson. *(Courtesy Mike Dann)*

Titanic tradition! There was smoke coming off it! The band carried on for a bit but you could tell there was something missing.

Pete Williams had lessons on alto saxophone when he was 16 from dance band musician Len Cundall, and played occasionally with Johnny Sutton and Derek Dunning. He also played tenor sax with the Tye Bruce Dance Band:

I ended up with a spontaneous pneumothorax, my lung collapsed, I couldn't play any more. I was thinking about taking up the guitar, but Derek Dunning turned up at the house one day with a double bass. He said to me, 'Here, learn to play this, there's a shortage of bass players in York, and with a pair of ears like you've got, you won't have a problem'. So I learnt to play the double bass, and before I knew where I was, after six months, I was doing all sorts of things. I was playing with Harold Midgeley's band, a bit like Jack Carr, and then David Horner and David Atkinson formed their own band, called the Dave-a-tones, and I played bass with them for a good 18 months about 1961.

I was also doing some jazz things in York with people like Bobby Hirst, Ray Phillips, Ken Kenyon. Ray got the residency at the Caribbean Club, and he came and asked if I would like to work with him there. It was a great opportunity, so I left David and went to work with him at the Caribbean from 1961 till about 1963. That was good, because they had some top line cabaret names.

In 1970 Geoff Laycock asked me to go and play with his big band, a ten-piece band, the Double Five. I went to work with Geoff, and we did some BBC broadcasts and a lot of work in Scarborough, but the band would play all over the place.

I spent a lot of time playing at the Society Club, in Bootham. The guy who owned that, Charles Sykes, was like a champion for my music, and he would have a solo piano, and musicians would drop in there to play. It was a watering hole, we'd finish somewhere about 11 or 12 and wander down to the Society Club.

Music's an international leveller. It supersedes everything else, and no matter where you come from or what language you speak, or what your background is, music can tug your heartstrings and churn your guts. And if you're working with people in a jazz environment, there are odd gigs that you remember, because everything was just perfect. We did a gig at the Brasserie in Harrogate with Graham Hearne on piano, Al Woods on alto, and quite a few musicians came in. It was just one of those nights when it was really good.

There's a wonderful American jazz pianist, Bill Evans, he's dead now but I was lucky enough to see him in Ronnie Scott's in 1964 and it was almost a religious experience. The place was full of people but you could have heard a pin drop.

It doesn't happen every time you hear something, but there are times when you hear certain things that can have a really profound effect on you. I think music is very special, because it transcends everything, it's truly universal.

CHAPTER TEN. THE MUSIC MAN:
Sound Effect Records, York

A new record shop opened in August 1970 in King's Square, being run by Nick Banks. The name was Sound Effect and it was advertised as the 'shop with London style'. Nick's aim was to fill the gap in the market and provide a wider range of popular records and cassettes, which were sorted into categories such as 'progressive' and 'soul'. Two years later the shop announced the addition of a 'gear boutique' called Take Five, which sold Wranglers, smocks, sweaters, loons and T-shirts. Nick recalls:

I started initially as a sales promotion rep for CBS records, covering York and Yorkshire, and that soon developed into joining Polydor Records which is part of the Deutsche Gramophone Group, covering the north west and north east. At the time I'd got a fairly good knowledge of what sort of music people were wanting, and I felt I could create a market that was lacking in York. There were very few record shops in the city. I think the gap was in the market for young people. I concentrated on Northern Soul, because that was very popular, with Wigan Casino being a highlight for everybody's weekend, and I even imported records from America, to follow the demand, before they were released in this country.

The first year was fairly hard, getting people to realise that there was somewhere else that they could go, and what was available, but very soon after we started to reap the benefit, and, we were employing quite a few people, within a few years. I wanted to have something that people could recognise, but at the same time have a jokey atmosphere, so we used the old gramophone logo from HMV, but instead of the little dog Nipper, we put a monkey listening to the gramophone. As a result we used the monkey on all the advertising, which drew people's attention, because most people are quite fond of monkeys.

Shortly after opening we were approached by the British Market Research Bureau to be one of the shops to help compile the charts. We were given a diary to record all the sales, and they collected this each week in a sealed envelope, which was then sent to London to help compile the Top Of The Pops Top 20 Chart each week. We played music all day, every day, and anybody could come and listen at any time to a record in its entirety without any obligation. That sometimes became a bit awkward when people wanted to listen to two or three full LPs, but generally we managed to cater for most requirements. I didn't like the idea of booths, so we went for headphones, which was also innovative. Listening booths to my mind were a bit sterile

(*Courtesy Nick Banks*)

Desmond Dekker and Nick Banks at Sound Effect August 1975.

Dave-a-Tones March 1966. L to R - Dave Horner, Cindy Mottram (former lead alto with Ivy Benson), Dave Atkinson, Wnedy Floyd, Tommy Henderson. *(Courtesy David Horner)*

Christine Hepton playing piano, 1985. *(Courtesy Christine Hepton)*

and it was nice to be with the people and listen through headphones or just listen to it played over the loud speakers.

I suppose because of the knowledge I'd gained having worked for two record companies, prior to opening up my own shop, and time spent researching and reading, because it was of great interest to me; I liked to pride myself in the early stages, when my memory still had some semblance of order to it, people would ask for something and I could immediately remember what record number it was. There weren't any other record shops in close proximity to York who specialised in soul at the time. We did get people from Yorkshire who would come through, and we also did quite a bit of mail order as well. John Steel and Alan Rhodes were two people who'd do some of the nights at the Heartbeat, and we'd supply quite a lot of the records for them. For a short time we had a Sound Effect Mobile Discotheque, a couple of my good customers, we'd subsidise their efforts and get a bit of publicity out of it. They'd get the records at a preferential rate, that was part of the arrangement.

I remember in the mid 1970s hearing a song by Don McLean which I really wanted to buy. I did not know its title so I went into Sound Effect and asked Nick. Before I had even finished explaining, he said, it's called Till Tomorrow and it's on the American Pie album'. And it was.

We could almost guarantee what day of the week it was by the customers, and on certain days certain people would come in, and disc jockeys who were doing their mobile discotheque, or working in a club at a weekend, we knew that they would come in on a Friday, ready for the new records for the weekend. We'd put a little pigeon hole with their name on, and put the records in. You could almost determine their music tastes from what they'd previously purchased.

Nick's shop was the first in York to have stars coming in to sign records:

There was Desmond Dekker, Judge Dread, Barry Biggs. We'd advertise the fact that they were coming, forewarn people such as the council and the police, hoping that this would engender its own promotion, which it did. On most occasions we did actually need the police to control the amount of people. We were fortunate because record companies were keen to promote artists, with Top Of The Pops being so successful and popular, and they would give away free pictures and autographs. I'm sure on many occasions there were lots of children who should have been at school, but they enjoyed the public appearances in Sound Effect at the time. Other record shops might have had records signed by an artiste, and bookshops had books that might have been

196

Angel Pavement 1968. L to R - Paul Smith, Dave Smith, Al Reeve, Graham Harris, Alfie Shepherd. *(Courtesy Graham Harris)*

autographed, but to have personal appearances by recording artistes, and Top Of The Pops number one artistes, was unheard of.

We were always keen to give publicity and promotion to any local band. Unfortunately there were very few who had records out but if they did have a record we were more than willing to sell it on their behalf, and give them mostly the full contribution back from the sale, because obviously we wanted to encourage local talent. Angel Pavement were a popular band at the time. There were very few bands who had any longevity to them. I spent some time driving Angel Pavement in their van round England to various gigs, and carrying equipment. I knew the band members and it was something I wanted to do and I did enjoy it.

I remember one particular weekend when they played up in some castle in Scotland. It was in the middle of nowhere but when they appeared that night it was as if all of Scotland had come to the castle to see them play. They were a good band. It was a pity that they split up because I think the potential was good.

The shop in King's Square was a difficult shop. It was on two levels, the ground floor was quite small, whereas the basement was large. And it was always very difficult to have some records upstairs and some downstairs. There were very few boutiques in the city, so we thought this was a good opportunity to use the ground floor as a boutique. It became Take Five because King's Square no. 5 was where we were located.

I first took the premises on in 1970 and the lease had rent reviews in it. At my second rent review, the landlords, having seen this derelict decrepit shop become very successful and popular, decided that they wanted to quadruple the rent. And there was no way, with negotiation, that they would reduce this rent level by anything other than about 50 or 60 per cent more than what I'd previously been paying. It didn't seem to me logical, or sensible, to continue with the lease, because it would have meant that for the next two years I would hardly be breaking even, and then I'd be faced with another rent review. So that was why we looked for alternative premises and relocated into another derelict property in Davygate Arcade, which I think a lot of the other shops in the arcade at the time were delighted about, because we brought a big influx of customers into the centre.

People were spending more and more time going to theatres and concerts but there was no ticket agency in York. And I always believe, when you're in business, that you can't stand still and you've got to progress with the time, and it's all very well saying, 'I've got a successful record shop', today, tomorrow it might not be. So you've got to look for something else to supplement, and we built up the theatre and concert ticket agency side. We had contracts with most of the promoters and as a result they would give us an opportunity, when there was an event on, to supply us with tickets.

In 1973 Roxy Music came and played in the Museum Gardens, and the sales promotion people for Island Records, who Roxy Music recorded for, I was quite friendly with, from my days with the record companies, and I actually introduced the bands that played in the Museum Gardens. I acted as compere and both me and my wife went on the Roxy Music tour coach. It seems quite strange now to think back, Bryan Ferry sat on the coach playing cards.

We did have to work hard a lot of the time in making sure that we had the stock, and that we were meeting the market, because, of course, when the records had been sold, you can't wait to replace them, because the demand's there. You've got to get them back in quickly, which meant a lot of midnight oil making sure you were ordering the stock. And during the period of the 1970s, there were events that occurred whereby the demand for music was immense.

The death of Elvis Presley I shall never forget and the demand for Elvis records of any description, of any age. I remember driving through to Leeds to a depot to pick up some more copies of the Arcade Forty Golden Greats of Elvis Presley because the demand was so great we couldn't wait for the deliveries to arrive two days' later. We had people who were paying deposits, to make sure they got hold of a copy of this record instantly.

There were various specialist magazines. I think one was Blues And Soul, that used to list American charts, and soul charts, rhythm and blues charts, and these records often were in the American charts, but would take a long period of time before they became available in the UK. And of course no discerning aficionado of music at that time wanted to wait, he wanted them then. I decided that we weren't going to wait for them to be released in this country, and we'd try and bring them in from America, so I was finding importers in London and Birmingham, who would bring me in records from America that I'd identified. But I'd also take a chance and speculate on some of the artistes, thinking that if I gave them enough publicity probably they would sell.

There were some artistes who had records in the charts, and who'd be there for some considerable period of time. In 1970 we had Simon And Garfunkel, the Bridge Over Troubled Water album, which I think was in the charts for a year, and there were also other artistes in the less mainstream charts that were moving almost monthly. They'd come in maybe about number 50, go up into the top ten, the following week they'd start to drop out, and the fourth week they were out of the chart. So it was a short period, and especially if you were having to import from America you had to be pretty smart. There were some singles that we would sell a thousand of, and a single that we might sell hundreds of in a day. There was one particular soul one, George Macrae, Rock Your Baby, which we just could not get enough of. We would buy them in boxes of 50, and we'd maybe sell three or four boxes in a day, and this would go on for three or four days in the week, so maybe over 1000 had gone. And then it would dry up, and you would go on to the next one. The quantities were amazing, and if it was being played at Wigan Casino, in the discos and the clubs, they wanted it, and it was staggering the amounts that were sold.

We even had Margaret Thatcher in the shop on one of her electioneering jaunts. She came to ask about private business, and my opinions and views,

199

and I told her that the Government never did enough for private business, so she didn't stay very long.

In the 1970s music became much more a market for people buying, rather than just listening to. Obviously the Beatles were in the 1960s, and people were buying those by the boxload, but in the 1970s more and more people were building record collections, and we had regular customers who had collections that ran into thousands.

I think I created something that wasn't just a record shop. I created a meeting place, and an ambience for young people. On a Saturday, 'Well I'll meet you at Sound Effect', didn't mean they were coming to buy a record, it meant they were coming to see people, to meet their friends. So as a result it was almost like a club. There was music being played, they'd have nothing else available for them other than the people who were there and the music, but it did become a meeting place, and I'm pleased I did that, it was something that York needed, and I wish it could have it today.

CHAPTER ELEVEN. ALL THE YOUNG DUDES:
The Early 1970s

As the 1960s, that incredible decade, drew to a close, things were already changing. The beat explosion was beginning to abate. New sounds, new singers, were appearing and another complete change (that of punk and new wave) was on the horizon though it would be much less memorable than the 1960s sounds.

Meanwhile, the working men's clubs were doing a roaring trade by the beginning of 1971 and some were so popular that they had to spend money on extensions and renovations. The New Promenade Club reopened in February 1971. Holgate Club celebrated its golden jubilee in October 1970, Acomb Club advertised its new premises in November 1970, Clarence Club had an extension built in May 1970 and Tang Hall Club extended its concert hall in April 1970.

The 1900th city celebrations in Spring 1971 gave the city's young people a lift with a number of pop concerts. The Tremeloes played at York University, though the hall was less than half full. A song called Ride Ride Dick Turpin was composed for the celebrations. It told the story of two historical characters connected with York, the highwayman Dick Turpin and Elizabeth Fry the prison reformer, with lyrics by George Reed, author of the pageant script for the celebrations, and music by Alfie Shepherd, a York musician from Angel Pavement. The project was backed by the Hypnotique nightclub and the Morgan Record Company. But then the idea was thrown out by the celebrations committee who refused to contribute £250 towards the cost, even though the rest of the finance was in place. Some of the committee, including a local man, Don Nicolson, claimed that they had not been informed of the situation and that they would have backed it but it had been blocked by other members of the committee. Mr Nicolson said that the idea had been 'wrapped up in a peculiar cloak of secrecy'.

From April 26, 1971 the dial-a-disc service, run by the Post Office, started in York, the number to ring being 16. A different pop song from the charts was available each evening after 6pm. The service was available in nearly 50 centres throughout the country and received more than 60 million calls a year.

In July 1971 Radio One Club made a live broadcast from the Theatre Royal which was the first time that the BBC had put on a show in a theatre. The 960 seats were sold out weeks before the event. The biggest concert prior to this

York group Sorce 1971. L to R - Dave Baxter, Pete Wilson, Steve Bilton, Phil Eastwood and Rich Hall.
(Courtesy Pete Wilson)

was Freddie And The Dreamers in 1967. Two live groups, Boston International and Shelley, performed and the show was run by Ed Stewart.

The following year, in October 1972, in a national competition judged by Yedudi Menuhin and Colin Davis, conductor of the London Symphony Orchestra, York was named one of the top music-making cities in the country, which was largely due to the 1900th celebrations where a great variety of music had been on offer, ranging from the large Celebrations Choir, a concert featuring 800 children and the youth festival to a military tattoo.

The York Festival of the Arts was held in June 1973, and jazz, folk and pop were on offer. On the opening night folk singer Frankie Armstrong appeared in the King's Manor cellars. Charlie Galbraith And His All Star Jazz Band also played mainstream jazz there the following week. Julie Felix was the big folk act at the University's Central Hall and Ken Colyer, one of Britain's leading jazzmen, appeared in two concerts. The last night was the scene of a pop festival in the Museum Gardens where the 2,200 seats for the Mystery Plays were to be used. At the last minute the council made the decision to remove the chairs so that more people could sit and watch. The 2,500 tickets on sale were snapped up well before the event and Roxy Music topped the bill. Despite its popularity, the festival still made a loss of £60,000.

Kenny Dell meets Jimmy Savile. Scarborough 1965.   *(Courtesy Ken Pickering)*

Live music continued. In February 1974 a nostalgia rock 'n' roll show featuring Billy Fury, Marty Wilde, Heinz and Tommy Bruce rose up a storm at York Theatre Royal. Billy was said to have traded 'sideburns and tight trousers' for 'pink flares and platform shoes'. The show was so popular that it returned in June 1974. In October 1976 a York branch of the Incorporated Society of Musicians was formed. The society had 7000 members, all engaged in music as a career, either performing, composing or teaching it. In November 1976 Stacey Brewer reported in the Yorkshire Evening Press that beat music in the pubs was back, when York group Midnight (Mick Clift on vocals and guitar, Pete Wilson on bass, Dave Powell on lead and Colin Carr on drums) started playing 1960s music in York pubs. Before this, Pete Wilson played for some years with the group Sorce, on the university circuit as well as playing at RAF bases, supporting such bands as the Equals, the Tremeloes and Ashton, Gardner And Dyke.

In April 1974 Mackenzies advertised that its new record and television shop, 'all under one roof' would open in Low Ousegate. The manager Rod Mackenzie had taken charge of the business when his father died in 1969. George Mackenzie opened the business in Colliergate in 1933 selling radios and bicycles. The company moved to Micklegate in 1949. In 1968 staff had to evacuate the cycle shop in Skeldergate near the TV shop, as it was to be demolished. In the new shop there were two listening booths and an individual headphone canopy.

More local groups went professional in this decade, like Random Destiny (Pete Wilson, John Hine, Mike Cundall, John Henry, Dave Todd and Howard Welsh) who toured Germany and Austria in 1970. Their line-up was not that of a conventional group, as it included trumpet and saxophone. Paul Smith, who was in Angel Pavement, managed York group Flight who made a record in 1976.

Kenny Dell started out as a musician in Selby before moving to sing with a dance band in Liverpool. Before long he came to York:

I answered an advert in the Musical Express, a band called the Richard King Set at the Cat's Whiskers were asking for a singer, and I applied and got it in 1969. I'd been with various bands on Top Rank dance hall circuits and became professional in the mid 1960s. Before that I'd just been gigging locally round Selby as a solo singer.

I was obsessed with music and always have been. I wanted to become a star like most young kids, so at the first opportunity, I joined a dance band and left Selby. I worked as a professional for about 20 years.

At the Cat's Whiskers, we worked five nights a week. It was very popular and very busy, especially on a weekend, the place was heaving. Coach parties from all over Yorkshire. We played eight o'clock until midnight and that was interspersed with the DJs, Tony Adams and Roy Hewson, they'd alternate. It was strictly for dancers, so that anything that was in the charts at the time we would try and duplicate as near as possible. We'd buy the records and slavishly copy them in the hope that people would dance to them. We had to be versatile 'cos we were covering so many different types of material, from ballads to rock, up tempo and slow stuff, and the whole mixture of anything that was in the charts.

But the down side of that was there was nothing original, we were just duplicating someone else's stuff. But all of the band were very good musicians. We played there until late 1971 when we moved down to Tiffany's in London. But by 1974 we were back. I was in that tiny world of sleeping late, getting up and doing the gigs on a night, it didn't really matter where it was. The Cat's Whiskers was much livelier, a much more happening scene than what I'd been doing before, the big band, strict tempo, older audience type thing. The crowd was young and enthusiastic, and we were into what we were doing.

We were constantly learning new material, keeping abreast of what was in the charts. It was always fresh so you never got bored with the material. It was not a typical big dance hall, it was smaller and more intimate, the actual area where the revolving stage was. More like a supper club with a circular dance floor and table seats arranged around it, it was a nice venue, not a great big cavernous place.

We were ambitious to be famous, and we started broadcasting on Radio 2, Terry Wogan's show, Jimmy Young's, those sort of programmes. Then we were approached for a recording deal, and there was a York connection 'cos Geoff Gill, who lived in York, signed us up. We had a couple of singles released in 1972. Both died a death, but it was exciting doing them.

We were strictly contracted to work in the Cat's, they wouldn't have approved of us doing moonlight gigs around York, so we didn't actually do anything outside. We were too tired anyway and it was nice to have some time off from music on our night off. I wasn't aware of it being hard work, as it was something that I was really into doing and I'd get a buzz out of it. I suppose it was a strain in retrospect, but I wasn't aware at the time. I felt that I could hold a tune so I thought I'd be snapped up by all the gorgeous women, and earn lots of money. It was all I wanted to do, it was something in my blood. And I did it for a while and had a good time.

The obvious psychological thing was that I was someone when I was up there, and when I was off stage I was just an ordinary Joe. I think I probably became a bit obnoxious. Basically I was shy, and didn't feel very successful as a person, and it was a way to express myself. But the underlying main reason was that I did love music.

In the 1950s I started buying records and I was knocked out when I first heard Elvis Presley and Tommy Steele and all the early rock 'n' rollers. That's what really excited me, and got me into being a performer. Elvis was my god. He was someone I emulated, just the excitement in his voice. He was a white man singing black music and he led me to discover black artists I subsequently got to love, Ray Charles, Joe Williams, a lot of rhythm and blues and jazz singers.

I don't remember there was any rivalry in the band. We had heated discussions about the way we should do certain numbers, I didn't want to sing anything that I wasn't really into doing, but that also worked in a good way because I pushed them into doing things that they might not have wanted to do. I introduced it occasionally, but most of the intros were done by the keyboard player, Bill Jessop.

Kenny Dell and Trevor King. 1970s.   *(Courtesy Trevor King)*

Of course, at the end of the evening it was romantic when we played the slow ones, cheek-to-cheek stuff, but mainly it was just dancing facing each other. I remember fights and it did get quite violent sometimes and we had to retreat. It was a revolving stage, it was pressable, and we would disappear and leave them to it.

Trevor King came up to York from Reading to work at the Cat's Whiskers before Kenny joined:

I turned pro with the Richard King Set, and we were asked by the BBC to do certain recordings for radio shows. Mecca heard us, and this coincided with them opening a club in York called the Cat's Whiskers, a new concept for them called a theatre restaurant, where they would put a live band on, a DJ and a cabaret act per week. We came up and stayed for a while, and won the Gold Cup for Best Small Band, and worked with a lot of good people.

The original band was myself on drums, Bill Jessop on keyboards, Tony Carter vocals, Tom Williams bass, and Dick Smith on guitar. Tony the singer left after a short while and was replaced by quite a few different singers, but then we had Kenny Dell, and he stayed with us for a long time. Without sounding big headed we were really good at our job. We were very professional and would try and recreate the sound of that particular single in the charts, down to the minutest detail.

We'd predict what was coming into the charts so that we could basically do the whole top ten, and I think there was only a couple of numbers we refused to play. One was Sugar, Sugar and the other was She's A Lady. One minute you might have Frank Sinatra and the other minute you might have Free or Marc Bolan. All the bands that worked for Top Rank and Mecca would be cover bands, there was no original material, because people wanted to go and dance to the stuff that they'd heard.

The club finished at two o'clock in the morning, so by the time you get changed, go down, have a drink, or then go off to a club that might stay open after hours for musicians, it would be five, six o'clock before you got to bed. It sounds horrendous, but then you'd get up at say two, then you're rehearsing, home, changed, shower and back. Your whole life was just the music, that was it. But we were all young, we all enjoyed it, and we were good.

The record we made was Would I Lie To You? written by Ken, and it was under the name of Tin Biscuit. Ken worked a long time on it, wrote some great songs, but everybody knows what the music industry is like, it's not always very straight. They want results straight away, what they call artistic development isn't something the British music industry takes too kindly to. Hence, you get Pop Idols, all quick turnover, and that hasn't really changed, unless you're very lucky.

I started out on jazz, I was brought up with jazz, my father was a drummer and a fanatical jazz fan, so I cannot remember a time when there was not jazz being played in our house. I never learnt nursery rhymes but I listened to Bessie Smith and Billie Holiday and Sarah Vaughan, Basie, Ellington, Woody Herman, and never got into pop music until later on. I remember saying to my dad when I was about seven, 'Can you teach me some bits?' And he bought me a pair of brushes and we'd sit down, and I'd play on the Radio Times with the brushes. That was all I wanted to do really, I never did much else.

The biggest influence on me were three guys, Ed Thigpen with Oscar Peterson, John Reller with Dave Brubeck, and Levon Helm with The Band who Ken introduced me to when I was about 20 and I was just blown away. If I had to model myself on anybody it would be Al Jackson who played with Booker T And The MGs.

You can play yourself out, six nights, three rehearsals, band calls and everything else. One of the big things was that when I packed it in, it was at the height of the disco scene, and sitting there all night playing 16s with a back beat, does your head in. Once you've learnt how to do it, and put your little frills in, that's all you do for that era of music.

207

On stage at Cat's Whiskers. L to R - Bill Jessop, Kenny Dell, Dick Smith, Tom Williams (bass), Trevor King (drums). *(Courtesy Trevor King)*

[At the Cat's Whiskers] you paid your money at the box office, and you went up this incredibly long passageway, everything crushed velvet and little lights and brass. You walked along this lovely carpet, up some steps, and you'd pass a display cabinet with everything from perfume to whatever, and the first thing on your left was called the Kiosk which sold cigarettes, cigars, sweets and chocolates.

We backed 52 cabaret acts a year, everything from Dorothy Squires, Josef Locke, Max Wall, Ruby Murray, Dougie Brown and the guy who used to hit his head with a tea tray who did Mule Train. We even had one act that performed on stilts which was just absurd. They come along at four o'clock, introduction, the music was nothing outstanding and I thought, 'Well, I hope they do something good, because the crowd can be a bit hostile'. So it came to cabaret time, 'Ladies and gentlemen, the Cat's Whiskers proudly present...' whatever the name was, and all you could hear from the side of the stage was bang, bang, bang. We play the introductory number, and they come out and they did the whole act on stilts, well it was a farce, everybody was creasing themselves. Then there's Keith and Orville the duck. We got mates with Keith, and the duck and the orangutang, but the strange thing is, you sit in the dressing room with Orville the duck, and you talk to it, and that's weird, because you actually start thinking it's real!

How can I describe playing? Well there's not another feeling like it. The joy you get from seeing people, if you're playing and they're all dancing, that's one feeling, if you're playing and they're all sat down and they applaud, that's another feeling, and you get this fantastic adrenalin rush. There's nothing like being on the stage and 2,000 people out in front of you. Not that you can see 'em, because you've got club lights in your eyes, but hearing 2,000 people stamp while you're playing Hi Ho Silver Lining, and then getting told at the end of the evening, 'You're barred from doing that song anymore because it's gonna cause structural damage', that's a great feeling,

Arnie Gomersall liked a different kind of music from some of his contemporaries. He preferred the heavier bands and played in a band which emulated them in the 1970s:

We started with Ebenezer, a threesome in the late 1960s doing Hendrix, and Cream. Songs that lasted 15 minutes each. Then you got bands like Thin Lizzy. We never really played Beatle-type things, 'cos I was into off the road stuff, like Pretty Things, Yardbirds, a bit bluesy, that was the line I'd gone down. Then we went a bit upmarket and changed our name, called ourselves Caliban, a character from the Tempest. I suppose we got work because we were a bit different.

I loved Ginger Baker. Charlie Watts was probably a better drummer than Ringo Starr with coming from a jazz background, but if you listen to the Rolling Stones, he's not that noticeable. So Ginger Baker, as far as I was concerned, was the man. Then Ian Pace out of Deep Purple, and I was a big fan of Simon Kirk out of Free. Not because he was a particularly technically excellent drummer, but the way he's like a fly wheel, just seems to be right for them. I try to play a lot like him to be honest, single beats on t'high hat, but I think the most spectacular drummer was Keith Moon. He was the business. If you got somebody who was a drum technician, they'd say he was doing everything wrong, but it was just right for them, and it was awesome. We know now they were high as kites, but the energy he had came out to the audience. It must have cost Premier a fortune replacing his kits, but he really lifted an audience.

I remember, when I was still at school, 'What do you want for Christmas?'. 'I want a record player'. And I got one of them little ones, Dansette, in a little suitcase. You just put one record on at a time, and I got a couple of records to start it off with, Helen Shapiro, and Frankie Vaughan, Tower Of Strength, obviously not my choice. Then I bought Not Fade Away, and Pretty Things, and the Animals, it was all like rhythm and blues.

The House, early 1970s. Clockwise L to R from bottom left - Mick Miller, Steve Rogers, Eric Wragg, Phil Goddard, Tony Lea. *(Courtesy Mick Miller)*

We finished up with an agent from Scarborough, we had a problem with him, he'd get you the gig, you'd go, but they didn't pay you, they paid him, and we struggled. We played at Corner Café, on t'North Bay, for him, still haven't got paid for that! We got this gig in Wetherby and when we gets there, it's a working men's club that we're booked at, and we're playing heavy rock. There was hardly anybody in, and a bloke reading Sporting Pink so we just treat it as a practice, and we never got paid for that. We played somewhere and they gave us the money and he rings up, 'Where's my money?' 'You're joking aren't you, this is only part of what you already owe us'. So we didn't pay him and he deliberately double-booked us on a New Year's Eve in Malton, and there was two bands turned up and he'd booked us both. They were a completely different type of band to us, I think they had a couple of girl singers, and in the end we said, 'We'll both do it, for t'same money and just split it', so they got two bands for t' price of one and had a right good night. There must be hundreds of people who've been ripped off. Agents and record companies taking all the money. It all blew up in the 1960s and nobody knew how to handle it. All they knew was playing music, they just wanted to be stars and a lot of 'em got ripped off. I just enjoyed it, it was a laugh and it's never got that serious where it was a job. It was a release from everyday work, going out for a blast on t' motorbike or playing in t'band, I loved it.

Mick Miller did become a professional musician with a band called the House in the 1960s. He recalls:

We did a lot of live radio on the Dave Lee Travis Show and we'd go to Italy, Germany and around Europe. In 1970 we signed up with Parlophone and did a cover version of Chirpy Chirpy Cheep Cheep, which was written by a

York lad called Larry Stott. Middle Of The Road got to number one on the continent so they said they weren't going to push it in this country, so based on that we did the cover version. It got into the lower end of the charts, and the story goes, they had breakfast one morning with Tony Blackburn. We had the Hour Play at that point, which was a quite prestigious thing on Radio One, they played our version every hour, and then they stopped playing ours, and played theirs, and theirs got to number one, so we were a bit unlucky there.

We got an agent, McLeods of Hull, and he started booking us out every night, sometimes twice a night. We went three years without a single day off. Quite often we'd play a lunch-time working men's club, then an evening appearance and then to a nightclub. We had a massive van, and just put mattresses on the gear, and usually slept there. When we got a bit more professional then it was hotels, but you could never make a fortune. We went with this agent from the south of England, for a three-month tour of Italy, and these people were quite underhand. You ended up not getting paid and the expenses were quite high, the van and the equipment and so on. We did it for the love of music. We had a lot of energy as a band and whenever we played in York, which was rare after we became professional, it was usually somewhere like the Assembly Rooms where they could hold a lot, and it was always packed out.

York audiences were very knowledgeable music-wise. Almost 30 per cent of the audiences were other pop bands. We had Eric Wragg, terrific guitarist, and the drummer, Steve Rogers, he was absolutely fantastic. When he left, we had Steve Roberts, who went on to play with UK Subs. [Steve is the son of York professional pianist George Roberts who died in 2002. Steve recently received two gold discs and a platinum one from his UK Subs period in the 1980s]. *So we had a fabulous backing band and I was a nut case on stage.*

Later on when we'd made our records, we were mainly support bands for people like Sweet, the Nice, Amen Corner, and Hot Chocolate. Some good days. I was influenced by a lot by people like Otis Redding in those days, although we didn't do any of his songs, but we did a lot of Leo Sayer later on and the Eagles. Your influences change as you go through ten years. I liked to do a lot more harmony, rather than just rock 'n' roll.

On stage Mick became a much more confident extravert person. This was not due to alcohol as he never drank, but it was something about the music which brought out a different side to his personality:

I'm quite shy really, but on stage I wasn't. At the Queen's Hall, Leeds, there must have been about 5000 in there, and it was never a question of nerves.

Something clicks when you go on stage. Even the voice changes. It's just more power, more energy.

At the end of l971 the House were approached by York Theatre Royal to write the music for A Midsummer Night's Dream, and the star was Kathleen Byron, a big star in the Thirties and Forties. She played Titania. We were in the box playing the music live for a month. After that they kept us on for the pantomime, which was Cinderella and we wrote all the music for that. Because I was the singer, there was nothing else for me to do, so I went on the stage and did dancing just to keep me interested.

Probably the best song that we ever did was called Rhythm Of A Big Bass Drum written by Tony McAuley, and there must have been some contractual problems. The day it was released, apparently it sold quite phenomenally, it would have easily made it. We'd organised the Hour Play again, the best spot on radio, but it had to be withdrawn from the shelves, and we never knew the reason for that.

The best band I ever was in, was the last one, Just Add Water, or JAWS, for short, and we did a lot of harmony like Eagles and West Coast music. And we had a fabulous following in York then. The keyboards player was Tom Hall, Eric Wragg on lead guitar still, Sid Locker on the drums. He was one of the best in his day was Sid.

Although the working men's clubs were now an important venue for groups, with perhaps a trio of piano, bass and drums playing in the interval, the star of the show was usually the bingo. The pop groups found it very hard to take it seriously as Pete Willow recalls:

They had a system of blowing ping pong balls with numbers on, up through a hole. I'd sometimes take cheese biscuits and pop a few inside the machine so it blew cheese puffs out. That made it a bit more interesting. Sometimes we bent the spring off the top so when they turned it on, all the balls would blow out all over the place. Or you took one ball out and it would make the game last all night!

Most musicians do their job because they love playing. But there are certain disadvantages. One of the down sides can be problems with transport. Musicians were usually no good at mending vehicles, just as mechanics probably don't play in bands. Pete Willow recalls touring Wales with a group called Tracey one Christmas:

We had the van with all the equipment out in the street and we got some locks to fasten on it. The bass player and I borrowed a drill and when we were drilling into the van, a lot of nylon material started coming out of the holes. The drummer's girlfriend came along on tour but didn't really enjoy it and kept complaining. Anyway, we found we had drilled into her umbrella. So we turned it round and left it but every time we'd go anywhere in the van, if we saw a few spots of rain, we'd look at each other, hoping that it would stop by the time we got to our destination in case she erected her umbrella and got really annoyed.

Every time we had a booking, the singer borrowed a car and it'd tow us up and down the street trying to start the van. He'd get annoyed 'cos kids around would think it was great. The van would start backfiring and they'd shout, 'Can you do it again, mister?' When he got out the van and tow rope, they'd all follow behind on their bikes waiting for the explosions. On New Year's Eve the van wouldn't start so we hired another one, which was more expense. We got to the booking and played but then that one wouldn't start either and we had to sleep in the club.

Another band I was in, the brakes went five times on the van. It had three bald tyres and no spare wheel, so when the brakes went, we'd pour more brake fluid in, put mole grips and a bit of rag on it, nip the brake pipe up, but when you hit the brakes hard, you would drift across the road sideways. We once drove it home with three bald tyres and no brakes, you put the hand brake on and nothing happened with the weight of all the gear, it was lethal. The roadie had to drive at three miles an hour.

By the late 1970s, competition from discos began to alarm those musicians who made a living out of their craft. In 1977 the Musicians' Union started a national campaign with posters and badges proclaiming 'Keep Music Live'. The secretary of the York branch, Alf Field, a trombone player with dance bands, stated that the union was 'against canned music' and were 'fighting for the continued identity of the musician and the provision of work for reasonable rates of pay'. Most York musicians were not professional and made their living from day jobs, but even part-timers who worked in the pit at the theatre and entertained at concerts felt they were entitled to a minimum rate.

CHAPTER 13. BOTH SIDES NOW:
We Can Swing <u>And</u> Rock

The period of 1930 to 1970 was one which saw a huge amount of musical talent in York. There was a vibrant scene and, for much of that time, there was a wealth of different strands of popular music on offer. The musicians of the 1930s and 1940s were horrified at what came after the war, with rock 'n' roll and beat music, and the musicians of the 1960s and 1970s wanted to get away from what they perceived as old-fashioned music. But there were a few individual musicians who made the transition from dance bands or jazz combos into skiffle or beat groups, and sometimes back again. Perhaps they had to do this in order to find an audience for their music, but nevertheless it took skill to do so.

One example is Dave Johnson who was heavily influenced in the 1950s by watching the international groups which Jack Prendergast brought to the Rialto:

He was getting people to York, that big cities like Sheffield and Leeds wasn't getting, all that wonderful music to watch. That's when I decided to play the drums. The big bands finished on drum solos and one of the first bands I saw was Frank Weir And His Orchestra, who had five soprano saxophones, and played all the Glenn Miller stuff. They had a drummer from Manchester called Arthur Morgan, and he was a wonderful drummer, and he finished on a drum solo. The Ken Mackintosh Band came, with Kenny Ollick on drums, and Jack Parnell's Band came with two drummers who used to do duets. One of the finest jazz drummers I've ever heard was Phil Seamen. I once saw him play with his arm in Plaster of Paris, he'd fallen down steps and played with this and he was brilliant.

Dave went on to play in Johnny Newcombe's skiffle group but soon Derek Dunning invited him to join his dance band:

It took me six months to get me tempos correct, because it was strict ballroom dancing, and I was helped by a wonderful bass player called Reg Peel, he was maybe 70 by then, and he'd been a professional musician for years. The two main dance bands in York were the Derek Dunning Orchestra at the Assembly Rooms every Saturday night, and Johnny Sutton's Band at the De Grey Rooms. Then you had smaller bands like Sid Watson's at the Albany, Ted Rowell's Band at the Drill Hall, then Tye Bruce, a wonderful trumpet player that played with the Squadronaires. He formed an off-shoot from the Derek Dunning Band, an eight-piece band playing at the Folk Hall, New Earswick.

The Dominoes c1963. L to R - Dave Johnson, Richard Monfort, Gerry Stannard, Johnny Newcombe, Dave Kendall. *(Courtesy Richard Monfort)*

After about three years with Derek, the big band scene faded, as rock 'n' roll and discos came in. One Christmas when I'd just left the Dunning band, a friend of mine, Paul Whattam, who had a band that played in the Coach and Horses in Nessgate, was unfortunately killed in a car crash. His brother Peter Whattam played the guitar and I joined that band and started playing rock 'n' roll. Then the guitarist left, and I got the old guitarist from the Dunning Orchestra, Dave Kendall, a singer called Gerry [Stannard] who sang like Roy Orbison, and changed the name of the band to the Hi-Fi's. We didn't take rock 'n' roll seriously, Dave and I, because we'd been taught proper music. We tended to clown about with it. A man who saw us at the Buckles worked for Jim Binn's bookies and they had a club in Leeds, the Windsor Social Club, and he asked us to play there. Whatever comedy we did, it was on the spur of the moment, and we just brought the house down. We seemed to go from one club to another and instead of being in pubs in York like a lot of the other rock bands, we became a comedy show band on clubland, the Dominoes.

I was at Thornwick Bay Holiday Camp for three summers, drummer compere, and for two years I did the circuit. Primrose Valley, Reighton Gap and Barmston Beach.

Bryan Pearson's first group, the Spartans, was formed at Tadcaster Grammar School in 1963 and subsequently the drummer, Ed Bicknell, went on to become manager of Dire Straits. The group became the Crawdaddies and played a lot in the Zarf Club in Stonegate. After this, Bryan joined two York bands, the Morvans then Adrian Kaye And The Impacts. Bryan had taken piano lessons with Herbert Macintosh, of Wighill, near Tadcaster, and did some dance band work with Mr Macintosh's band Mac And His Music. Bryan believes that Mr Mac was a great influence in his musical development:

He'd tell me about when he was a child, he had to pump the organ for the organist at Wighill church. He practised in the evenings when it was very dark and Mr Mac was obviously scared being alone in the vestry behind the organ. To amuse himself he would let the pressure in the bellows get very low and when the organist called out to complain, would pump the bellows hard so he could hear the organ groan. He also told me about the secret broadcasts he did from the Odeon cinema in Leeds during the Second World War. These were for overseas audiences and the location of the broadcast was kept secret. I remember having my piano lessons in an old building in Kirkgate in the evenings and sometimes Mr Mac would have to leave early because he had a 'gig'. He always wore a grey jacket with silver threads through it when he played in the band and as a young boy, I was extremely envious of the jacket. As well as being a teacher and performer, he was a piano tuner and repairer. Thanks to him I could read music well and had a good ear. Later I had to read to be able to interpret, and back singers. This meant that I could fit in well with the dance bands and I think most of the older musicians respected me. But I do remember Bob Halford, the sax player, telling me that I played too loud and it made his hearing-aid buzz.

Through Mr Mac, Bryan met dance band leader Charles Hutchinson with whom he played from 1968 to 1971:

The band had a minimum number of three musicians, Charles on piano, his brother on saxophone and John Burton on drums. I was asked to play as number seven which was the maximum configuration of the band, which grew to three saxophones, trumpet, piano, bass and drums. I probably got the call because the electric bass guitar in 1968 was seen as very modern and I also doubled on piano. When the band was booked from 8pm to 3am, the band played the whole time. This was effected by splitting the band and I would move from bass guitar to piano, Mick the trumpet player would move to drums and Charles's brother would stay on saxophone, to play as a trio when the other members of the band took a break. At 3am the band would play The Queen and we would pack up the instruments, partake of soup on departure, and drive home, often having to go to work next morning. I remember on more than one occasion, having to dig my minivan out of the snow and then having to breathe into the frozen door handle to get the key in. Once inside the van, I would have to keep wiping where my breath had frozen to the inside of the windscreen.

Bryan also played with the Steve Jackson Trio and in 1968 joined the Karl Wynter Quartet at the Clarence Street Working Men's Club:

Karl was the pianist and the band was resident at the club for many years three to four nights a week. The alto sax and clarinet player was a postman named Bill who had for many years been a bandsman in the army. He played an ancient saxophone, a 'new century' brand that was held together by rubber bands where the springs had broken, and he used some sort of cloth down the bell of the instrument to smooth the tone. The instrument was so unreliable that each time he took it out of the case he would turn to me and say in his broad cockney accent, 'Well Bryan will it go?' He used to play an ancient clarinet, the 'Albert' or simple system much favoured by military bands, rather than the Boehm system now universally used. He'd recall how he played second clarinet in the pit orchestra at the Empire. The drummer was Tommy Davis and the story goes that once, whilst playing in the pit, there were some hecklers in the audience, so Tommy stopped playing, jumped over the brass rail of the pit, punched some of the hecklers and then returned to the drums!

Bryan moved into playing with beat groups in the 1960s:

I played in a band called Clive And The Crestas, a really wild band with long dyed hair. They developed a club act where they came out dressed as cavemen and sang I'm A Hog For You Baby by Screamin' Lord Sutch. This act really impressed the teenagers at the dance and I have fond memories of being swamped by adoring fans at the Coach and Horses.

The last occasion Bryan played with the Hutchinson band was 1971 before he left England to become a professional musician. He now lives in Australia teaching music and feels that his work benefits from having performed it. He runs concert bands and jazz bands in schools and the school big band has been very successful, winning competitions and making a CD:

I never regret playing, my love of music drove me to teach. There are a lot of skills I can bring to the job as a musician. The way my school big band counts in, with the signal to start being two high taps then four taps to bring in the band, came from John Burton in the Charles Hutchinson Band. In the absence of a conductor, the drummer brings in the band, and the lead alto stands up and stops the band at the end, like the Count Basie band did.

Another musician who has played everything from skiffle to beat to dance bands, and is now a popular after-dinner speaker is David Kendall:

217

My first introduction to music was Dringhouses Church choir and then the Minster School. Sir Francis Jackson was the choirmaster there, and we learnt the theory of music, singing and either the violin or piano, so I chose piano. I absolutely loved every minute of it.

Then my voice broke and I got a scholarship to St. Peter's School. We formed a skiffle group in Slingsby Grove, Dringhouses, with a school mate Paul Smith on drums, meself on guitar, a lad called Malcolm Precious, Patrick Byrne, [who went on to be in the Gambling Men], *and Johnny Lund on washboard, and we'd record sessions in Tommy Sykes' garage in Slingsby Grove. Then a lad called Malcolm Staveley joined us as singer. We were the Slingsby Demons.*

At school we were meant to do prep every night between half past six and eight. Although we were day boys we elected to do it at school, and then the rest of the night was ours. One night we went to the Clifton Ballroom where there was a talent competition and we won it with the skiffle group. A chap called Len Daly, a big charity raiser in those days, said, 'You're a credit to the school', and when we got back, we decided we'd better tell our housemaster, Mr. Rose, that we'd jigged off prep to go, if anything got back. It was completely taboo and he gave us three whacks of the cane each but it was worth it.

Another thing I did was play guitar at the Society Club about 1959, with Bobby Hirst on piano and Valerie Mountain on accordion. A lot of French stuff, like Under The Bridges Of Paris. Then I played with Derek Dunning's Dance Band, every Saturday night for 32/- a night. In about 1961, we played at the Conservative Party Conference, at the Spa in Harrogate, and Harold Macmillan, the Prime Minister, came across to Derek and congratulated the gentlemen of the orchestra for a wonderful night. With the dance band drummers there was a lot of brush work, and Ray Phillips was the master footer brusher of 'em all. I can only remember one singer, Janet, and Derek Dunning married her.

They did a recording of It Might As Well Be Spring and I'd taken along an acoustic guitar that Len Cundall, a wonderful musician, lent me. An old Dobro with metal resonating plates. I took my electric guitar, an amplifier and acoustic guitar, to Teddy Foster at Butlin's. Derek said, 'Which one do you want him to play on the recordings?' and he answered, 'You can throw that electric thing into the swimming pool', because electric guitars were frowned upon by the old dance band lads.

David played in both dance bands and pop groups and he explains the difference:

Charles Hutchinson's Band at York University, c1968 - Bryan Pearson, bass, John Burton, drums.   *(Courtesy Bryan Pearson)*

Reunion of musicians at Old Orleans, August 2001. L to R - Colin Berriman, Dave Johnson, Dave Garlick, Johnny Newcombe, Ron Goodall.   *(Courtesy Mike Race)*

Derek Dunning's Band, by gum they could swing some of these Tommy Dorsey numbers. He would buy arrangements of some of the old stuff so that I could feature, I learnt to play mostly Shadows stuff, and the band could play the notes, but they couldn't rock.

You name any of the top ten hits in the late 1950s and they were three chords. The dance musicians would say, 'They don't know a crotchet from a bloody hatchet'. But you're talking a different thing when the Beatles came along. Lennon and McCartney are definitely up there with Irving Berlin, Rodgers and Hammerstein and Cole Porter, who just happens to be my favourite.

In a way I ran with the hare and the hounds. We went with the full dance band to Harrogate playing proper dance music, and then this group came on, very loud, but giving the youngsters what they wanted, and they got as much for three quarters of an hour, between four, as we did, 16 of us, playing for about two and a half hours. Hold on, if you're going to go out for a night wouldn't you rather just play three quarters of an hour, and pick up five times as much?

It's a different genre, you had to be a good musician otherwise you wouldn't get in a dance band, by the same token you had to have youth on your side and some modicum of talent, not particularly musical, to keep the youngsters of the day happy.

I got to know Robert Atkinson very well when he had the Black Swan at Peasholme Green, he had medieval banquets and John Coleman and Ken Atha were my minstrels, the folk singers at the time. I was the baron, and we had young ladies, and punters could buy kisses off 'em. We'd organise silly things like a yard of ale drinking competition, and they'd have medieval food.

Charlie Abel is a well known drummer in York. There was music in his family as his father was a Minster choirboy who played violin:

I started when I was 15 and I joined the REME cadets in Tower Street. They slung a drum on me and made me walk up and down. It taught me two things. How to keep time, and keep in step. My mother thought I was saving up to buy a bike, and off I went to Precious's in town. That was a toy shop, but Precious had been in a dance band and had this drum kit in, and I says, 'Right I'll have it'. So she says, 'Where's your bike then?' 'I've bought a drum kit!'

The first time I played, was with the Cavaliers Dance Band at a hotel on Boroughbridge Road. And I was that nervous me foot wouldn't keep still on the pedals. We played In The Mood which, with me being nervous, got faster and faster till he couldn't get a note in on his trumpet. He had to kick me foot off the pedal. Then we got a job in the Knavesmire Hotel, in the back room we'd get coach parties in and people coming up and singing. There was Derek Arness, he played an accordion, Ken Vipas on piano and Dickie Wade on trumpet. [See volume one]

In the early 1960s, Charlie along with Johnny Newcombe, Barrie Wood and Murray Addison were invited to go to Stamford Bridge village school to run a workshop for nine to 11-year-olds. Student teacher Mike Lockey had asked them to take part in the last of a series of lessons about the development of modern music. Each of the four musicians talked about his instrument and traced the path of popular music from the work songs of the cotton fields to the beat groups of the 1960s, and step by step showed how the instruments blended together, with a final performance from the whole group. The headmaster said that 'it put pop music into its proper perspective for the children. I think it is the first time in history that Form Two has stayed 20 minutes over time without grumbling'.

After this Charlie joined a beat group, Ian And The Diamonds, which became Ian And The Shifters:

We played at St. John's College where we met a bloke called Ian Lightbody, fantastic fella and he got us going. We started to wear white shirts and then dinner jackets. Ended up with these amazing jackets, red mohair, cost more than a guitar! We were doing gigs round Harrogate and Huddersfield. We did a gig at York University. That was quite good and the first time we'd seen anybody controlling the sound on fallback speakers. That was just coming in, balancing groups up.

Ian Lightbody knew people at the BBC and we went to Top of the Pops. Rolling Stones was on and Billy J Kramer, sat in a corner reading a book, and the Bachelors. Girl singers, Dusty Springfield, Lulu, that's the range of music in those days.

There's two things. You've got to get on with the people you're playing with. This is important. It's no good having a friction, which can arise because you're producing songs between people. But if there's friction, it'll work for so long but eventually it'll crack. You get bands who stay together a long time, get an understanding of what's going on, and a relationship. And also you've got to be fit. It's high energy. Music is geared up to the speed of life, everybody's running and everything's a lot quicker. We had a Bedford Dormobile, you put your foot down in that and you had to wait for it to do 40 or 50 miles an hour. You get in a car now and before you're at the end of

Hawaiian Swingtette on board P & O liner Chusan. Hawaiian night at Pago Pago in the Pacific. L to R - Bryan Pearson, David Plues, Dennis Weston, Tom Plues.

(Courtesy David Plues)

L to R - Noel Porter, drums, Richard Monfort, Dave Kendall. c1963.

(Courtesy Richard Monfort)

the street you're up to 60, so the brain of that person in it moves at that speed. He's got to do, or he'd run into something. So when they listen to music, instead of relaxing they need that pulse as well.

After the crash which killed group members Ian and Bob, the Shifters reformed but it was a sad time for everyone and eventually Charlie moved on to playing with jazz groups. He explains how music can affect a musician:

It's like being on a high. You can go and play, feeling awful and the music'll cheer you up. You can have headaches, aches and pains where you'd normally go to bed but you can go and play. When you're playing it's buzzing and if the whole band is 'cooking', everybody's relaxed. You're still working and have to have the energy even though you're playing quiet. And you come home, you can't switch off for a long time. You just don't want to stop playing. You're high but you're sober, it's music that's done it. It's the only thing that can move people like that. You get requests for tunes that they haven't heard for years and you play it, and you can see how it's affecting them or what memories it's bringing back. You can talk to somebody, 'Do you remember so-and-so?' but you play a tune he used to play and he comes up and buys you a drink because it's wonderful.

One very versatile musician is Terry Herbert, who made the transition from the skiffle group, the Gambling Men, when he was 14 in the late 1950s, through to playing saxophone in a dance band at the age of 16, and clarinet in a Territorial Army Band. Later he moved into beat groups, became resident drummer in the York Jazz Club and by the beginning of the 1970s played in Geoff Laycock's big band. Terry had to wear several hats at once and it did not always go down well with everybody:

The dance bands were a bit sniffy about it, I think they thought that people who played skiffle and rock 'n' roll were not your proper musicians. I started on washboard, not a very dignified instrument, but within a few years I learnt to play the drums.

The older musicians scoffed at rock 'n' roll, saying it was not really music:

They're wrong. It was music. It was very simple, direct music, but it affected people and they responded to it. It's just a different form of music. I started with Norman's skiffle group and it gradually became a slicker operation when Jack Prendergast took Norman under his wing and tried to make a recording star out of him. The skiffle era was very brief, we were schoolboys. Then I had a spell playing in a band called the Tycoons. Michael McNeill, who was one of Norman's best guitarists, he and I were both very keen on jazz, so we used to play a bit together. Bebop had given way to cool jazz by then but the only kind of jazz that you got an audience for were the traditional jazz bands like Chris Barber and Ken Colyer. That had a massive following in student circles, and people used to dance to it. Although I'd have loved to be a jazz player, it was extremely difficult to play good jazz, so I suppose I enjoyed most playing rock 'n'roll, a good bash and we were pretty happy.

1964 was the peak. The Beatles ruled the world, and Mersey bands of all sorts were very popular. It got to the stage where lads from Yorkshire would be ringing up clubs and putting on Mersey accents. Then Ginger Baker and Keith Moon, they stood the whole thing on its head really, they started doing it properly, making it into an art form.

Bands were mostly run by the singers and it was often a question of who the singer liked. Norman was really knocked out by Ray Charles, so he sang a lot of Ray Charles songs, whereas other singers would be big on Mick Jagger so they'd become Rolling Stones look-alikes. People developed their own thing, but the one thing the groups had to do was play a good selection of songs in the hit parade.

I worked with a superb piano player who was in York for a few years, Colin Dudman, doing dinner dances and cabaret music. It entirely depended on the quality of the piano player, you need a really smart piano player for that kind of work, because you've got to be able to accompany singers extremely well, play in any key, know an absolute library-ful of standards, and know how to work the crowd. You were measured by the extent to which you could give people a good time and the test for a dance band was if people danced. That was very skilled work. One musician, Ian Early, [who had been in the Gambling Men] *went professional as a guitarist and was for a long time in the Northern Dance Orchestra which was a big institution on the radio. He did lots of cabaret work and whenever she was in the north of England, Shirley Bassey would book him, she was very taken with his playing. And he did a lot of work on the big liners.*

I worked for a long time with Pete Williams and the York piano player George Roberts, it was Westfield Country Club in Hull and we were playing this complicated piece, piano, bass and drums. George was in total control of the situation and I was struggling a bit at the back and he turned round and said, 'What the... are you doing Terry?' 'I'm just playing, George'. 'Oh that's all right, I thought you were building a... shed'. This is in the days when cabaret was king. Every big name act did the cabaret circuit and you'd spend a day on band calls, there was so much music you could wallpaper the bloody walls, and it was terrifying. Four or five hours on a Sunday to go through it and then an hour off and then you were in at the deep end with 300 people there. Nothing fazed George, he could just read it. That's the whole thing. If you get a drummer playing dots, it's very hard to relax and play the music at the same time, it's very difficult. But that was a great experience 'cos Pete was good too.

Backing singers wasn't really my cup of tea. It was very difficult and that's why it was so liberating playing rock 'n' roll. That doesn't mean that some people wouldn't do it badly and some would do it well, but it was fundamentally easier. You didn't have to worry about the dots, you had a lot more freedom, people could do their own thing.

The Goodall family are well known in York musical circles. The guitarist Bob Goodall had four sons, Les, Ron, Norman and Dave, all musicians, and two daughters, Betty and Irene. Ron recalls that his mother had five brothers who were all musicians, and that his paternal grandfather was a clog dancer and sand dancer and his grandmother a pianist. They went round the music halls. His father, Bob, actually made his first guitar. In those days it was more for playing rhythm rather than the solo instrument we know today. When Ron was 17, the brothers played together in a skiffle group, the Linesiders, and Dave the youngest, had to stand on a chair to play string bass as he was only 13. At the end of the 1950s Ron had to do National Service, but two years later he was still keen on music:

To me it was like the awakening of the young person having his say. I formed the Rockafellas. Barrie Wood was on bass, we had a guitar and converted it into a bass, and we made our own speakers. We got a job three times a week at the Wild Man. We had no transport and we had to catch buses there. I'd always liked to have a woman singer 'cos of the glamour side, but it caused that many rows, it was more trouble than it's worth. They'd say, 'I saw you looking at her', which was a shame because there was one or two good girls in York who could sing. My sister sang a few times, things like Fever. She'd sing that at the Wild Man and the blokes would go crazy.

A lot of stuff we did, you'd buy the records and learn your part and come together on a Sunday morning, learn three numbers and play them at night. There was so much music being churned out, it was incredible. The Beatles, they sang the keys that nobody else could sing in, so you had to adapt to our singer's range.

Then our singer Geoff Atkinson had a very bad throat and had to leave. So we got Gerry Harrison in, Gerry B. We didn't get on very well and I left to join Johnny Newcombe's band, and then Dave Johnson's band the Dominoes.

Rockafellas c1963. L to R - Barrie Wood, Johnny Newcombe, Ron Goodall. Armley Baths, Leeds. *(Courtesy Ron Goodall)*

I was interested in jazz and I'd done a gig at the Windmill Hotel in Leeds, and I ran a band there for three years doing all dinner-dance work. We had some really good keyboard players, Bobby Hirst, Laurie Kleeton, George Roberts, Brian Thacker, Norman Hughes on sax, Colin Berriman on drums. We were called the Vince King Set.

It was a great era to live in for me, although I'd like to have lived through the 1930s and 1940s, because I'd have enjoyed playing with the big bands. I finished up actually doing some big band work, and a few cruises on the Canberra. It was a professional band, I was probably the only amateur on there. I was recommended by George Roberts as they needed a bass player.

Music's been important in York, probably more than a lot of other towns. There's still quite a bit of live music even now. When I played with that big band I was sat on a stand and there was the music in front of me, all the numbers that we were going to play, and then it was eyes down, concentration. You couldn't really appreciate the overall sound. But eventually when you got to know the dots you could relax a little bit and listen to the band play. And then you start really enjoying it again. You don't get really good on anything unless you keep doing it over and over again. The more times you do it the better you get. And although it may be boring to keep doing it over and over, it's worth it. When I'm on stage, I feel very

Gerry B and the Rockafellas at Wild Man 1963. L to R - Rob Illing, Barrie Wood, Johnny Newcombe, Ron Goodall, Gerry B.
(Courtesy Ron Goodall)

privileged. I remember as a young man, I looked at bands on stage and wished I was on that side. Sometimes you take it for granted, you get a bit blasé. But I'm always very grateful that I'm on that side. I feel sort of special, and when the music's right it's a great feeling.

York did not have many women musicians but Christine Hepton became a pianist in the city's pubs in the 1960s, after having basic training. As a child she recalls playing on bank holidays at the local working men's club. Her repertoire increased from a few tunes until now she can play several hundred songs, from Skye Boat Song to Hoagy Carmichael tunes, film scores, to Elvis Presley and the Beatles:

I've got to wind down when I come back, because my head's just so full of the music I've been playing. You see, you're playing one song, and part of your mind's on what you're playing, and the other part's on what you're going to play next. If you were part of a group you would have to know beforehand, unless it's modern jazz. There again a lot of it's improvisation anyway, but as a solo artiste you can more or less please yourself. It depends on the mood you're in. Sometimes I'll feel like having a mad five minutes, so I'll look over some marches, Sousa and things like that, play them a little bit faster than I should, but that's how I feel at that particular time. Plus you look round at your audience and see who you are playing to. When I was at the Royal York Hotel, if there was a lot of old people, I'd go back to the 1920s and 1930s, but if you've got younger people in, you'd play more up-to-date stuff.

I couldn't go anywhere for a drink if there was a piano there, because somebody would say, 'Oh, there's Christine, give us a tune'. And once you start, it's the loneliest job in the world, obviously, because you're sat there, you're concentrating on what you're doing, everybody's round you, talking and laughing, and you can't join in. And if you stop to say anything to somebody, they'll say, 'What have you stopped playing for?'

But I love it. I think that's why there wasn't so much trouble on the streets years ago, because people went out, and they had a drink, and a good sing-song and got rid of all their energy. You could hear people in pubs singing, if you walked past. Music must reach some part of you inside. I went occasionally to Claypenny Hospital. Somebody had donated them an organ, they had it in this big hall, and it was amazing how they reacted to the music, the children. They might just sway to it, or wave their arms in time, they couldn't sing, but it was like Simple Simon Says, the nurses would help them to do the actions. So if it reached them, that were emotionally disturbed, it must reach us inside somehow.

Hawaiian Swingtette 1962, Ainsty. L to R - Tom Plues, unknown, Betty on piano, Dave Plues, George Turvey on drums. *(Courtesy David Plues)*

David Plues began to perform in 1960 when he was only 12. His father Tom Plues played Hawaiian guitar and Dave also learnt the guitar and would go out with his father:

To the Oasis on Tadcaster Road on a Lambretta, with a guitar between us. That was my first ever playing gig, in a nightclub, which was really quite cool. In the 1960s we had to find somebody who was in the dance band era and they taught you a few chords, but they didn't understand anything but playing for dancing. They didn't understand the different rhythm techniques. I played at the Post Office Club, in Marygate, usually on holidays, and eventually I was taken into the band every Saturday night, and I got paid 50 pence.

When I was 13, 14, it was a bit uncool to be playing with a dance band in a working men's club, I didn't want to be playing for quicksteps and slow foxtrots, when all this excitement was happening, and girls. So I started playing with a chap called Dick Rushton from Haxby, Shadows' type material. A man named Ken Mason ran a band called The Corvettes, and they played at the Imperial, and were looking for a rhythm guitarist. So about 1963, I became a very young Corvette. It was all Shadows' covers but we then saw the need for a vocalist and enter Adrian Kaye. He was very well dressed, sleek haircut, slightly American influence, Elvis Presley-type singer, and he could sing in tune. So we took on Adrian, and that started a change of direction. He was a showman, as a 19-year-old he was just waiting to join a band. He needed something in his life and suddenly he found it.

He developed this stage act, based round Whole Lotta Shakin' which was the last song we did. It started as a five-minute affair and finished up taking about 20 minutes, which was built on Adrian shaking his body almost into fits. He was on the stage, he was acting, and it took over completely. And he did this wonderful impersonation of someone getting further and further into the music, getting more excited and the sweat would lash off him. Then he started to appear in very expensive silk pyjamas and from the first moment he did this it had to be in every night. He was a wild man before the wild man appeared later in the 1960s with the Who. He was before them, unique.

We merged with some members from this other band, Danny Adams And The Challengers, Ken Newbould and myself on guitar, Ian McClaren on bass, Norman Hughes on sax. We could do rhythm and blues properly, we'd got a sax player in the band, and we had a huge fan base that followed us about, and loved what we did. Norman Hughes was excellent. He was playing with loud amplifiers, and the natural thing to do was to get a Reslo microphone and stick it down the horn of the sax, put it into the AC30. Then his trick was, 'If the guitarist can use the Wem Copycat to pre-amp your sound and put a wee bit of echo on, that's for me too', and suddenly you've got this wonderful, absolutely storming sound of Peter Gunn with slight distortion, that just naturally fitted in with the guitar.

David left the beat groups and went back to playing with his father in the clubs, but a chance meeting with the Entertainments Manager for P & O, got them a chance to play on the liners. Bryan Pearson joined them on bass, and they became a Hawaiian act:

My father sounds a little bit like Django Reinhardt on a steel guitar, and I could do the rhythm part of it and there was a swing influence right through this music. P & O had 12 or 13 liners before the jumbo jets. They were very happy ships to be on. We had two trips, and were the last ship to go round South Africa, Mombasa, up to Bombay and down to Australia, two world cruises going round the long way, whilst Suez was closed. In the winter months you would cruise to Australia, and do cruises from Sydney, out into the Pacific, Pago Pago, Fiji and New Zealand.

Once you've had your heyday, if you don't progress, if you don't learn new things and become a better musician, if you don't keep experimenting all the way up to modern technology, then you hang up your guitar. If you had a reverb on your amplifier, you were moving ahead. It took off to the extent that we've got now with the computers.

When you look at the people that really made it, the Led Zeppelins, the Jeff Becks, they were always at the forefront of using a primitive fuzz box. If you didn't have a fuzz box, you doctored up your amplifier so that it did the same thing. But it was still using technology, using a lot of valves, and things moved on. The big bands would have been horrified at this, they didn't believe in these sort of things. We were playing with Vox AC30s, and you can link them together, and provide this beautiful wall of sound which was seen at the Queen's Golden Jubilee Celebrations, when Brian May was on top of Buckingham Palace. He was using a guitar which his dad made for him, out of the top of the fireplace, through a bank of Vox AC30s.

There is something quite special about the music of the 1960s. Today, in the 21st century, nearly 50 years afterwards, groups and solo singers copy the sound of the Sixties, shrewd marketing makes use of the upbeat and cheerful songs of the era in advertising, and nostalgia bands try to recreate it. There is the phenomenon of the tribute bands like the Bootleg Beatles and the Counterfeit Stones. There are countless appreciation societies for Elvis Presley, Little Richard, Buddy Holly and many others, where members meet to discuss the minutiae of their heroes' lives and play their records.

More than at any other time, there was a sense of excitement and delight in living, which is reflected in the music and it was a York jazz musician from an earlier era, Bobby Hirst, who recognised that feeling. He simply said,

There was something in the air.

GROUPS PLAYING IN YORK IN THE 1960s AND EARLY 1970s

Absolute Dirge
Adamil Bond
The Affluent Society
Angel Pavement
Ansermet Swing
The Astrals
Auntie's Dog
Badge
Baskerville Mood
Ray Charles And The Beat Boys (later Ray Charles And The Gaylords, then Ray Charles And The Ousebeats)
The Beat Sect
The Beautiful Delilahs
The Blackjacks
The Boneshakers
The Borderbeats
The Mike Brown Five
Bulky Jar (later Pharmacy)
Bunter
Butch
Cader-Idris (folk)
Cat, Toad And Goat
The Chariots
The Cheavours
The Chevrons
Circle B Combo
The Circle Four
The Clubmen
Cold Sweat
Tony And The Comancheros (country)
Adrian Kaye And The Corvettes (later Adrian Kaye And The Impacts)
The Counterpoints
Country Expression (country)
Country Style (country)
The Country Wranglers (country)
Gerry B And The Courtiers
The Crawdaddies
Clive And The Crestas

The Crimple Mountain Boys (folk)
The Crofters (folk)
Cucumber
The Cult (later Respect)
Cyrus Choke
The Czechers
The Davrolls (country)
Tony Adams And The Dawnbeats
Daze
The Demolition
The Deneagers
The Derwent Valley Rockers
The Dions
The District Line
The Dominoes
Ray Duval Trio
Brian And The Easybeats
Ebenezer (later Caliban)
The Eclipse
The Embers
Steve Cassidy and the Escorts (previously Sammy Browne And The Escorts, later
    Sylvia And The Escorts)
Eskimo
Eustacia Vye
The Everblues
The Exiles (folk)
Faintly Blowing
The Five By Five
The Fix
Flight
The Flintones
The Foresters (folk)
The Four By Four
Billy And The Four J's
The Four MPs
Four Of A Kind
Friction Level
The Gambling Men
Garden Gate (previously the Dimples)
Gideon's Few
The Ginger Group
The Grid

The Grit
Linda And The Group
Hedz
The Hi-Fis
Hijax
The Hornets (previously Gerry B And The Hornets)
The House (previously Matchbox)
The Inner Mind
The Innominates
Instant Summer
The Intruders
The Dave Jackson Rhythm Group (or The Dave Jackson Sound)
Jenny's Chance
Johnny Starr And The Jetsons
The Bryan Kenny Four
The Richard King Set (later Tin Biscuit, later Festival)
The Kossacks
The Pete Latta Band
Lazy Poker
Little Dedication
The Locomotion
The Lollipops
The Machine
Makin' Time
The Manhattan Folk-Rock Band
Metropolis
The Misfits
Mixed Company (later Midnight)
The Mood
The Moonrakers
K-Wallis-B And The Morvans (later just the Morvans)
The Motives
The Mousetrap
N'Chants (later Zebedee's People)
Obadiah
The Ousebeats
The Pakt
Patches
The Pathfinders
The Pentagons
The Pinewood Ramblers
Please (members of Flight and Cyrus Choke)

The Privileged
The Psalters (folk)
Random Destiny
Red Dirt (later Snake Eye)
The Roadrunners
Gerry B And The Rockafellas
The Roll Movement
The Roosters
Garry York And The Scorpions (later The Scorpions And Linda, later Four Shades
    Of Black, later Four Shades Of Blue)
Shelley
Ian And The Shifters (previously Ian And The Diamonds, later the New Shifters)
The Screen
The Silver Moon Band
The R G Simpson Band
The Slickerjacks
The Small Sound
Smokey's Balloon
Somebody Else
The Sons Of Witch
Sorce
Sounds Of Sight
The Spartans
Spring Fever
The Starliners (or Ray And The Starliners)
The Statesmen
Stavin' Chain
Strange Brew
The Strangers
The Stray
The Strollers
The Sunsets
Sweet Image
Barry Adams And The Swingalongs (later Danny Adams And The Challengers)
Syndicate 5 (from Driffield but looked after by Neal Guppy)
Syracuse
Three Plus One (from Driffield but looked after by Neal Guppy)
The Thunderbolts
Joey Young And The Tonicks
Tracey
Trident
The Trinkets

The Truetones
The Two Caballeros (country)
Mal Dyman And The Tycoons (previously The Stalkers, then Mal Dymans And The
Stalkers, then Mal Dyman And The Stalkers)
The Tykes
The Vampires
Ventura Highway
Tony Adams And The Viceroys (members became The Shots, then The Smoke)
Sammy King and the Voltaires
The Wabash Four (occasionally augmented to The Wabash Five, later Joni And
The Newcomers)
Washington Boulevard
Dave And The Wayfarers
Wellington's Boot
Wesley Hardin's Shotgun Package
The Western String Band (country)
The Wild Men
The Xenons
Roy And The Zeroes

Other titles by the same author

History Of A Community : Fulford Road
District Of York. (College Of Ripon And York St John) 1984.
Reprinted 1985.

Alexina : A Woman In Wartime York. 1995

Rich In All But Money : Hungate 1900-1938.
(Archaeological Resource Centre) 1996

Beyond The Postern Gate : A History Of Fishergate And Fulford Road.
(Archaeological Resource Centre) 1996

Humour, Heartache And Hope : Life In Walmgate. (Archaeological Resource
Centre and York Oral History Society) 1996

Number 26 : The History Of 26 St Saviourgate, York.
(Voyager Publications) 1999

York Voices. (Tempus Publishing Ltd) 1999

Voices Of St Paul's. (edited) 2001

Rhythm And Romance. An Oral History Of Popular Music Vol. 1.
(York Oral History Society) 2002

Other titles by the same publisher

York Memories. 1984

York Memories At Work. 1985

York Memories At Home. 1987

York Memories Of Stage And Screen. 1988

Open Minds. 1990

Through The Storm : York Memories Of The Second World War. 1992

Public Houses, Private Lives. (co-published with Voyager Publications) 1999